African Politics and British Policy
in the Gold Coast 1868-1900

LEGON HISTORY SERIES
General Editor A A Boahen PhD

African Politics and British Policy in the Gold Coast 1868–1900

A study in the forms and force of protest

Francis Agbodeka PhD
Department of History, University College of Cape Coast

Longman

Northwestern University Press

Longman Group Ltd
London

*Associated companies, branches and representatives
throughout the world*

Published in the United
States of America
by Northwestern University
Press, Evanston, Illinois

First published 1971

ISBN 0 582 64077 6 (L.G.)

ISBN 0-8101-0368-0 (N.U.P.)

Library of Congress Catalogue Card No. 73-175916

Made and printed in Great Britain by
William Clowes & Sons, Limited
London, Beccles and Colchester

Contents

MAPS

Acknowledgements

The author and publishers are indebted to the following for permission to reproduce copyright material:

The Controller of H.M. Stationery Office for extracts from Crown-copyright records, C.O. 96 series; the author for extracts from *Great Britain and Ghana: Documents of Ghana History 1807–1957* by G. E. Metcalfe.
The Mansell Collection for the illustrations between pages 38 and 39.

Abbreviations

Adm.	Administration
BZ	Buitenlandes Zaken (Archives of the Dutch Ministry of Foreign Affairs)
C.C.	Cape Coast
C.C.C.	Cape Coast Castle
C.O.	Colonial Office
D.C.	District Commissioner
D.S.	Downing Street
D.R.B.	District Record Book
F.O.	Foreign Office
G.C.	Gold Coast
G.N.A.	Ghana National Archives
I.A.S.	Institute of African Studies
K.V.G.	Nederlandsche Bezittingen der Kuste Van Guinea (Dutch Possessions on the Coast of Guinea)
M.V.K.	Ministerie Van Koophandel in Kolonien (Dutch Ministry of Trade and Colonies)
P.P.	Parliamentary Papers
P.R.O.	Public Record Office
S.L.	Sierra Leone
T.H.S.G.	*Transactions of the Historical Society of Ghana*
W.O.	War Office
B.B.P.	Bescherden Betr. de Buitenlandse Politick van Nederland 1849–1919 Vol. I (Documents relating to the Foreign Policy of the Netherlands)

Preface

Writers on British colonial policies have generally treated the subject as though British colonial policy in the nineteenth century was entirely formulated in Whitehall. There is no suggestion in the works of scholars such as Kerr, Hargreaves, Gallagher and Robinson of any major influences outside Britain. But while it is true that the policy-makers were influenced by British institutions and personalities, events in the colonies themselves also constituted important factors which had to be taken into account before final decisions were reached.

The influence of the early scholars was so great that even those who later embarked on regional studies of the colonies found it difficult to tear themselves away from the old theories. For instance, a number of scholars such as Claridge, Ward, Coombs and Wolfson wrote on the Gold Coast. But, although they described local events, they attached little importance to them, failing to recognise their influence on the formulation of colonial policies. Since these African activities affected British policy, these scholars also failed to see what that policy actually was on the Gold Coast.

Claridge, for instance, maintained that Britain did not have a policy of intervention in the Gold Coast (Ghana) until after 1890. Writing in 1915, he was able to say that a 'policy of non-interference . . . had been persistently followed' (Vol. 11, p. 351). His influence on later students of African history was so great that even a scholar like Kimble, who (in his *Political History of Ghana 1850–1928*) definitely attached greater importance to African politics, failed to see British policy in its true perspective. Nearly fifty years after Claridge, he wrote: 'It might be argued that the trouble was not, as Brandford Griffith thought, a policy that had been tried and found unavailing, but the lack of any clear British policy at all' (p. 285). Later in the same chapter he referred to a new policy: a firm attitude to Asante which he believed came into existence about 1894 as a result of European competitition.

It means therefore that (*a*) neither Claridge nor Kimble saw the activities of the states of the Gold Coast leading to an active British policy of intervention; (*b*) they denied the existence of a British policy of intervention in Asante before 1890 and attributed that policy after 1890 to European competition. In this way they failed to bring out clearly the full force of African politics, at the same time presenting a mistaken view of British policy in the Gold Coast.

Professor W. D. McIntyre in *The Imperial Frontier in the Tropics, 1865–75* has tried to correct this imbalance in the earlier accounts of colonial policies. He has maintained that the expansion of British influence in the tropics came as a response to particular crises there and not as part of preconceived plans made in Whitehall. He goes on to say that probably the most crucial element in this response was the attitude of the man on the spot. But in assessing this attitude, McIntyre has not been able, in a general work such as his, to consider the various aspects of the local events which shaped it. Thus the imbalance remains.

This book seeks to show that the formulation and execution of colonial policies did not depend entirely on the men in Whitehall. It explains that on the Gold Coast, African political activities affected both the formulation and execution of British policy.

To attain this objective, the nature of these activities is carefully defined. There were broadly two types. First, there was the protest movement directed against the local British Government. These protests occurred over national issues such as taxation, the Lands Bill, etc. and were therefore nationalistic in outlook. The entire population was united under its leaders in protesting against the British. We have examples of such protests in Anlo, Fante and Wassa, and we may describe them as protonationalist.

Secondly, in some states, such as Akyem, Krepi and Asante, (especially before 1890), local disputes, into which the British were sometimes drawn, frequently occurred. These disputes were nearly always spontaneous outbursts, with no such careful organisation as in the protest movement. British involvement meant that the activities of a section of the people concerned, though primarily directed against their local opponents, tended to be hostile to the Gold Coast Government officials. In some conflicts, the British were not involved in any way, the issues being wholly local; but even these affected British policy. In this work, all those activities which involved no direct confrontation with the British are also included in the wider term 'African politics or activities'.

Briefly, therefore, it may be said that African politics, of which protest was an aspect, affected British policy on the Gold Coast.

In considering the first type of activity, a brief comparison with modern nationalist movements in Ghana and elsewhere in Africa will be useful. This protonationalist type of political activity bears some resemblance to modern nationalist movements in their aims and objectives. Even though it is true that the protonationalists wanted internal self-government, while modern nationalism demanded full independence, the Fante agitators, the Wassa and Anlo activists, for instance, aimed at progress just as much as did modern political parties as the C.P.P. in Ghana and the R.D.A. in French West Africa in the 1950s. The main difference between the two movements lies in organisation, methods and techniques. Modern political parties in Africa are organised on the lines of Western political parties. Modern politicians use methods and techniques unknown to the Mankessim Constitution-makers and the petitioners of the Lands Bill days. The protests of Anlo between 1879 and 1889 were organised on traditional lines and lacked the modern features of present day mass protests against colonial regimes. The use of slogans, mass communication media, etc. has resulted in the rise of nationalist movements which cut across traditional boundaries. The protonationalist movements of the nineteenth century, lacking these modern techniques, tended to be confined to traditional areas. This is one of the chief differences between these incipient nationalist movements and modern African nationalism.

The main objective of this work is to show that the whole range of political activity, including protest, affected British policy either in its formulation or in its execution. The Fante Confederacy compelled the British to change their policy of non-intervention to one of intervention; hence the cession of Elmina (1872), and the establishment of the Protectorate and Colony (1874). In Wassa the opposition of the chiefs and people forced the British to abandon the policy of deciding dynastic succession. The protests against the successive Lands Bills also forced Britain to change her land policy several times until finally she abandoned altogether the attempt to control the country's lands.

The process of changing a policy followed this pattern. As protests mounted on the Coast, the man on the spot either acted in response to these protests and faced the Colonial Office with a *fait accompli,* or he reported the protests to the Secretary of State, who authorised a change in policy to meet the demands of the Africans.

The activities of the states of Anlo, Asante and Krepi also affected the execution of British policy on the Gold Coast. In Anlo British policy was executed by force and with unnecessary cruelty. In Asante mounting pressure first delayed and later hastened the execution of British policy. In Krepi the British resorted to force to overcome Taviefe opposition.

Such a thorough treatment of the subject aims to show the true nature of African political activity and its effects on British policy on the Gold Coast.

Sources used include manuscripts in the Public Records Office, London, Ghana National Archives, Private Papers, Dutch and German sources. Among the printed sources were confidential prints in the P.R.O. and command papers, as well as contemporary newspapers in the British Museum. Oral tradition was also found invaluable.

The C.O. 96 series in the P.R.O. have been used before, notably by Kimble, but not as exhaustively as here. The same applies to the C.O. 879 series, and the A.D.M. series in the G.N.A. But it must be pointed out that the use of these sources as well as the command papers and confidential prints is insufficient for a balanced view of events in the Gold Coast. These sources are not just English, they originated mainly from the officials of the Gold Coast Government, and naturally tended to give only the Government's point of view. To understand the motives of the African states, therefore, it is vital to check these sources against non-English sources such as those of Ghana, Holland and Germany, etc.

This has been one of the objects of this work. English sources present the Asante as a warlike and bloodthirsty people, but Dutch sources present the same activities as an attempt by Asante to maintain trade, the lifeblood of the nation. It is in this way that the *Nederlandsche Bezittingen de Kuste Van Guinea* and the *Buitenlandse Zaken* series, as well as the manuscript sources in the Furley Collections, helped to give a balanced view of events on the Coast. Again, without checking English sources on Asante activities in the north between 1890 and 1894 with those deriving from German travellers like Klose, who wrote *Togo unter Deutscher Flagge: Reisebilder und Betrachtugen,* and Krause, no student of Asante history can get a clear picture of what the Asantehene was up to at this time.

Equally important are private papers and oral traditions from various parts of the country. (A further discussion on the usefulness of oral tradition is to be found in the Bibliography.) All these sources have been utilised with the view to presenting the African political activity in its true perspective as has never been done before.

It would have been impossible to avail myself of this last source of private papers and oral traditions without the cooperation of a number of friends, including Mr S. Vroom, Dr J. W. C. de-Graft Johnson (Prospect Hill, Cape Coast), Mr E. Agyeman Duah, all of whom were very helpful either in introducing me to informants or in giving me information themselves. Mr K. Agyeman Duah, my friend and former student, also helped me with a great deal of interpretation during the collection of oral evidence in Asante. The Konor of Manya Krobo, Nene Azu Mate Kole and Nana Kwame Baffo III, Nkoranzahene, also gave me invaluable oral information, as did Nana Ankomako, Chief Fetish Priest of Nkoranza. To all these and other informants I express my thanks. I also wish to express my gratitude to the University College of Cape Coast for paying the cost of oral research carried out in the country.

My thanks also go to the management of a number of institutions who gave me access to their libraries. These include Mfantsipim School, The Methodist Book Depot, Cape Coast, Ghana National Archives, Public Record Office, London, the British Museum, London University Library, School of Oriental and African Studies, Balme Library and University College Library, Cape Coast.

I have also to thank Dr C. A. Ackah, former Principal, University College, Cape Coast, who granted me a term's overseas leave in July 1964 for the purpose of collecting material in London.

I received a great deal of encouragement from a number of friends including Messrs Robert Sprigge, Edmund Collins and Albert Van Danzig, whose collection of Dutch sources I found extremely useful. Mrs Marion Johnson, formerly Librarian of the Institute of African Studies, Legon, referred me, from time to time, to useful source material. I also found her collection of Salaga Papers most illuminating, and I must thank her for all this. I am also grateful to Professors Adu Boahen and Ivor Wilks who supervised my Ph.D. thesis on which this work is based.

F. AGBODEKA

Cape Coast,
January 1970

Introduction

This introduction gives a brief survey of the important states on the Gold Coast in the first half of the nineteenth century, including their government, political institutions and trade. It also discusses the main lines of British policy on the Gold Coast before 1865. It shows how the state of affairs on the Gold Coast in the first half of the nineteenth century was bound to lead to an outburst of political activity by the African states.

Asante and Fante

By 1820 Asante had established her influence on the greater part of what is now Ghana. The Asante Empire included Nkoranza, Banda, Gyaman, Wassa, Fante, Sefwi, Denkyira, Twifo, Aowin, Tekyiman, Akyem, Assin, Akwapem, Akwamu and Kwahu,[1] apart from the core of Asante with which Adansi must be numbered.

Of the states in the southern portion of the empire, Fante proved to be the greatest obstacle to Asante progress to the seacoast. Fante was able to obstruct Asante because, though disunited for most of the time, during crises the Fante states did form powerful military combinations with other states such as Wassa, Akyem, Denkyira and Twifo, for this purpose. On such occasions the various divisions in Fante were known to have formed themselves into a confederacy. This was what Meredith meant when, writing in 1812, he testified that the Fante frequently changed their forms of government to meet the specific requirements of the moment.[2]

Because of the stubborn resistance of Fante, Asante found it difficult to maintain a firm grasp on the southern portion of the empire. Thus by the third decade of the last century, their control, though still firm in the north, was already weakened in the south, and more or less came to an end with the battle of Dodowa in 1826. Asante tried to restore her control of the southern states but could not succeed until 1873.

Although Asante and Fante were such great antagonists, both of them, as well as the other states within the empire (those in present day northern Ghana), belonged to the Akan race. Their government, political and social institutions were much the same. At the head of the government was a paramount ruler, the king. But he did not have unlimited power since he had to take his decisions with

1 W. W. Claridge, *A History of the Gold Coast and Ashanti*, London 1915, 1964 ed., Vol. I, p. 228

2 H. Meredith, *Account of the Gold Coast of Africa*, London 1812

the consent of a council of chiefs and elders. The members of this council in their turn never took decisions without first consulting the interests of their people.

Generally, therefore, the pattern of politics in the Akan states was based on the monarchical system, but there were variations from place to place. In the early nineteenth century, for instance, Asante was still busy trying to strengthen the authority of the monarch, not only over the metropolitan states but also over the entire empire. The political service within the empire was radically modified as the hereditary position of the *okyeame* or linguists, who were the traditional ambassadors in charge of negotiations with other states, was changed into an appointive office. This was to increase the efficiency of supervision and consequently the power of the Asantehene.[1]

The states to the south of the Prah, such as Denkyira, Wassa and Fante, also enjoyed monarchical government. However, in these southern states, especially those bordering the sea, the exercise of political power was much less centralised than in Asante. This meant that the divisions in these states, like those in Fante, enjoyed autonomous existence. The supreme ruler of Fante, 'the Brafo of Fantyn' in the person of the King of Abora, for example, exercised supreme power over all Fanteland only in times of crisis.[2]

Other important institutions arose out of the ownership of land. In Akan tradition all land is held by the village community, and becomes attached to the stool of the head of the village. When a tribal community finally settles on a definite tract of land, the land begins to be the basis of society in place of kinship, and the chief with the village council has the control of such land.[3] Above the chief or the stoolholder is the Omanhene or king, such as King Aggrey of Cape Coast, who has control of the stoolholder and the land attached to his stool. The Omanhene often has under him several stoolholders and their peoples who together constitute the oman (the community), bound together not by kinship but by land. All these peoples have the duty of attending the annual festival of the Omanhene, where they refer various cases of the outgoing year to his tribunal for arbitration, his court being their final court of appeal. It is therefore the territorial rights of the Omanhene which give him judicial rights over the oman. By the nineteenth century some variations from the general rule occurred, mainly in the sea-board towns and especially in Cape Coast, where allegiance became largely personal instead of territorial. But even in Cape Coast, King Aggrey claimed, as we shall see in the next chapter,[4] that the exercise of judicial rights involved ownership of land.

The pattern of military formations was also common to all the Akan speaking peoples. At its most advanced stage we find the army divided into four columns as follows:

1. A central column (Adonten) consisting of: scouts, advance guard, main body, the Commander-in-Chief, carriers, camp followers, rearguard.
2. Rear column (Kyidom) operating in the rear of the central column.

1 I. Wilks, *Ashanti Government in the Nineteenth Century*, Legon 1964. See also A. A. Boahen, 'Asante, Fante and the British, 1800–1880', *A Thousand Years of West African History*, London 1965, p. 343

2 J. M. Sarbah, *Fanti National Constitution*, London 1906, p. 25

3 *Ibid.*, p. 7   4 See below p. 17

3. A left wing (Benkum). This column operated on the left of the central column.
4. A right wing (Nifa) also fought on the right of the central column.[1]

In Asante, each state within the confederacy was assigned a position in the fighting formation once and for all time. For instance, Bekwai belonged to the right wing and Nsutah the left wing. Besides, the command of wings was also a fixed appointment and the Ejisuhene and Asumagyahene were assigned the right and left wings respectively.[2] The appointment of the Commander-in-Chief also had its origin deep in Asante history. It is said that Okomfo Anokye advised Osei Tutu not to command the army himself and at once the Mamponhene, Boahen Anantuo, offered his services and was accepted.[3] He was thereafter the commander-in-chief of the Asante fighting forces. These carefully conceived arrangements of the fighting forces benefited Asante and were an important factor leading to the many victories of her armies.

In other inland states like Akyem, Wassa, Akwapim, etc. the arrangement of the army approximated to that of Asante. On the coast, however, in Fante in particular, the army organisation received less attention. Positions of the various wings were not permanently fixed, so that when faced by an opponent, as in the 1824 battle of Efutu, the Fante often carried on long disputes as to who should occupy which position.[4] Poor organisation also caused other difficulties in the Fante forces. Desertion was common. Retreat was often so badly carried out that it nearly always ended in a rout.[5] It is no wonder therefore that Fante forces were on the whole unable to withstand Asante invasions of the coastal states.

Financial administration was also very highly developed in Akan society. In Asante, where once again this aspect of Akan administration reached its most developed form in the early part of the nineteenth century, there was a special stool – the Gyaasewa Stool – which looked after financial affairs of the state.[6] In Asante and in the other Akan states, there were several avenues open to the traditional authorities for raising revenue. These included tributes, poll taxes, death duties and tolls. Tolls on trade were probably the most important and great care was taken to see that the toll posts worked efficiently. Toll posts were known to have existed at Kwisa in Adansi, in Manfe in Akwapem, and at Agyema-Nkwanta at the Asanta–Nkoranza border. Traditional authorities in Akyem and Akwamu were in the nineteenth century collecting tolls on trade at the Insuaim and Senche ferries[7] respectively, and the interest they took in these ferries indicates the importance they attached to them as sources of revenue.

We shall next consider the economic activities of Fante and Asante. Asante had earlier developed a prosperous trade with the Mande-speaking peoples of the Middle Niger and with the Hausa states. In the nineteenth century, this

1 R. S. Rattray, *Ashanti Law and Constitution*, Oxford 1929, pp. 121–2

2 Boahen, 'Asante, Fante and the British', p. 171

3 Sir F. C. Fuller, *A Vanished Dynasty: Ashanti*, London 1921, p. 17

4 Claridge, Vol. I, p. 370   5 Claridge, Vol. II, p. 26

6 Wilks, *Ashanti Government*

7 These toll posts had been established since the late seventeenth or early eighteenth century.

northern traffic was still useful but less so than in the past. These northern routes were:

1. Kumasi through Nkoranza to Bonduku to Djenne.[1]
2. Kumasi, Nkoranza, Kintampo, Salaga to Hausaland.
3. Kumasi, Atebubu to Salaga and Krachi.

There was also a southern traffic directed along the following routes:

1. Kumasi through Sefwi to Krinjabo, Asinee and Axim.
2. Kumasi, Bekwai, Prahsu, to Cape Coast, Elmina and Saltpond.
3. Kumasi, Juaben, Kwahu, Akyem, Akwapem directly to Accra, Ningo and Prampram or through Krobo and the Volta Basin.
4. Salaga, Kete-Krachi, Krepi to the sea coast.[2]

The commodities carried along these trade routes included Kola, which went from Kumasi to Salaga directly but later through Kintampo. European-manufactured goods from the coast also flowed along this same route into the northern towns where, like the kola, they were exchanged for leather goods, etc. from North Africa, brought down by Muslim merchants.[3] Among the European-manufactured goods traded north from various points along the sea coast were spirits and firearms, the two most important items. Less important items included cloth, knives, cutlasses and mirrors. The goods which reached the European trading posts from the interior were gold dust and forest products like palm oil and ivory.

Asante stationed tax officials at vantage points in the empire to collect tolls on trade. The proceeds of this tax were partly expended on clearing the paths and keeping them safe for traders.[4] To prevent outbreaks of disorder along the trade routes, Asante residents were stationed in the key towns along them. Their presence in a town, like that of Akyeampon in Elmina after 1824,[5] signified the acceptance by the population of Asante influence and organisation of trade. Another aspect of this was that all trade should pass through Kumasi. For example, when the Asantehene defeated Gyaman in about 1819, he stationed troops on the banks of the Assinie River and elsewhere on the frontiers of Gyaman to prevent their communicating directly with the coast. All other trade had to pass through Kumasi.[6] Contemporaries like James Bannerman and other Cape Coast merchants maintained that one of the aims of the Asante in the nineteenth century was to monopolise the position of middlemen for all trade between the countries to their north and the sea coast; and it is said the Asante built up the large market of Salaga in the north to promote this aim.[7]

1 Wilks, *The Northern Factor in Ashanti History*, I.A.S., Legon 1961

2 C.O. 96/120, G.C. no. 87, Freeling to Carnarvon, Accra, 28 March 1877

3 C.3386 encl. 2, Rowe to Kimberley, 10 May 1882; Further Correspondence London 1882, Vol. XLV, p. 1

4 Rattray, *Ashanti Law*, p. 110   5 Fuller, pp. 28–30

6 *Ibid.*, p. 65. Dupuis had to sign a supplementary treaty with the Asantehene in 1820 to have the troops removed. But since the Dupuis Mission failed, the Asantehene must have reverted to his original plans. See J. Dupuis, *Journal of a Residence in Ashantee*, London 1824, p. 229.

7 G. E. Metcalfe, *Great Britain and Ghana*, London 1964, p. 80

The Asante were not the only people who were anxious to organise the trade of the Gold Coast in their own interest. The Fante also sought to organise their trade so as to give them the benefits of middlemen between the sea-board and the interior. They established two huge inland markets at Foso and Manso, and insisted on Asante trading with them in these two markets. This was one of the factors leading to frequent conflicts between the two states.

Ga

Ga territory was originally the plain between the sea and the chain of hills some ten miles inland; some of these hills were Okakwei, Adzangote and Lanma. Ga land was then bounded on the west by the River Densu and on the east by the Tsemu Lagoon.[1]

The formation of Ga towns appears to have occurred on a piecemeal basis. Ga traditions of origin maintain that the ancestors of the Gas arrived in separate groups from the east and occupied the hills on the northern boundary of the plain. Then they moved, again at different times, to the seacoast and founded the towns of Accra (consisting of Ga and Kinka) Osu, Labadi, Teshi, Nungua, Tema and Kpong.[2]

As a result of this piecemeal development, Ga towns retained their independence of each other right into the nineteenth century. Each town had its own territory, quite distinct from that of its neighbours, and its own independent government. Even when a number of villages sprang up behind the coast towns, some as late as the early nineteenth century, each village belonged to a partticular town, thus emphasising the separate existence of Ga towns.[3]

The judicial system of Ga communities further strengthened this feature. Whenever disputes occurred, no matter how far from the town of the people concerned, they had to refer the case to the town authorities. In the town, the Chief *Wulomo*, or high priest, presided over a council of lesser priests to investigate the matter and to inflict a punishment on the guilty party. This council possessed the power of life and death but only over those who were strictly members, that is patrilineal descendants, of the town.

The government of a Ga town, as it still existed in the nineteenth century, was headed by the Chief Wulomo, the high priest. He was the priest of the oldest quarter of the town. There were in some towns about seven quarters, the oldest representing the founding members of the town. The later quarters represented the groups of new arrivals who were admitted into the membership of the town and given new sites to settle on by the founding members. Each group arrived with its own god and therefore with its own priest, who continued to exercise immediate control over it. The Chief Wulomo became the protector of all these groups against inland invaders, and in this way came to assume political and religious control over all the quarters of the town. Ga governments were thus originally absolute theocracies and the only rulers were the priests. This custom, which partially survived into the nineteenth century,[4] must have come into existence in the fifteenth century but later in the

1 M. J. Field, *Religion and Medicine of the Ga People*, London 1952, p. 1; C. C. Reindorf, *History of the Gold Coast and Asante*, Basel 1895, 1966 ed., p. 24

2 Field, *Religion and Medicine*, p. 1

3 *Ibid.*, p. 2   4 *Ibid.*, p. 3

seventeenth century some new features had been imposed on Ga society. These changes were brought about by problems of defence and the development of trade.[1]

First, as we have seen, the high priest was not only the religious leader of the town but also the protector of its inhabitants. In this capacity he had to perform some political duties, and these increased with the increasing problems of defence as inland peoples, especially the Akwamu, began, in the seventeenth century, to invade these coastal communities. The high priest therefore gradually delegated his political duties to two lesser priests, who were installed as chiefs in the Asante or Akwapem fashion. But this did not solve the problem and the need for a military confederation of all Ga towns was felt and gradually translated into action. When this happened, one of the chiefs of the most powerful state, Accra, became the supreme commander of the forces of the military confederation under the title of King of Accra. This was the post occupied by the Tackies in the nineteenth century.

The authority of the King of Accra extended even beyond the original boundaries of Ga, the chief contributing factor being trade. Along the Ga coast there was a series of lagoons, and these supported fishing and salt industries. Since the seventeenth century the Gas had developed the trade in fish and salt, taking their goods inland, especially to the Volta States. These traders needed protection as they traded inland and so the King of Accra extended his moral influence over some of these inland districts which needed the fish and especially the salt from the coast. Later they wanted European goods which again could only reach them through Accra or other Ga towns. For this reason they were willing to cooperate with the King of Accra whose orders, since the eighteenth century, were being obeyed as far north as Akwapem and Krobo. During this process of change the Ga country extended its influence to the Volta in the east, to Winneba in the west and to the Akwapem hills in the north. Ga–Adangbe towns too came within the Ga confederation as a result. They were Poni, Gbugbla or Prampram, Ningo, Ada, Shai, Krobo, Osudoku and Asutsuare.[2]

The most spectacular result of these changes therefore was that, even though Ga towns retained their independent character, cherishing their age-old customs, they could still achieve a military confederation to resist foreign aggression. It was these circumstances which made possible resistance movements among the Gas against European interference in the second half of the nineteenth century.

Ewe

Eweland occupies the area between the Rivers Mono and Volta. It has about eighty miles of seacoast and a depth of about the same distance. Here we are concerned only with western Eweland which is about a third of the total Ewe country and lies within the boundaries of modern Ghana.

The Ewe-speaking people have never formed a single political unit, but have remained as a loose collection of independent subdivisions.[3] The original sub-

1 *Ibid.*   2 Reindorf, p. 24

3 M. Manoukian, *The Ewe-speaking People of Togoland and the Gold Coast*, London 1952, p. 30

divisions may have been the groups in which the Ewes arrived into their present homes from Notsie about the middle of the seventeenth century. It has been suggested by Mr Amenumey[1] that the reason why these subdivisions have remained independent is their relative self-sufficiency and the consequent lack of large-scale trade among them. This does not mean, however, that some of the subdivisions had never tried to achieve larger political units.

First, during times of war, subdivisions like Anlo and Adaklu formed alliances which, however, ended with the war. Secondly, two subdivisions in particular, Anlo and Peki (Krepi), tried to extend their power beyond their original boundaries. Originally Anlo consisted of thirty-six towns, but by the middle of the eighteenth century the state had expanded and controlled the entire area between the Volta and Aflao, extending inland to Adaklu. In 1833 Peki, too, made great efforts to expand its territory and did establish some influence over Awudome and the Kyerepong towns of Anum and Boso; but this influence did not survive the Asante invasion of the Volta basin (1869–70). The majority of the subdivisions, however, did not even try to achieve larger political units. At the beginning of the nineteenth century, therefore, western Eweland consisted of a large number of independent subdivisions referred to in Ewe as *dukowo*. Some of these were Anlo, Peki, Adaklu, Ave, Tove, Ho, Kpando.[2]

A subdivision or *duko* consisted of patrilineal groups (*fome*) as in Anlo. A fome is a group whose members trace common patrilineal descent from a named ancestor while the members of a *hlo* claim, without being able to trace, common descent from a remote ancestor. In areas where fome is the smallest unit, each village or town is actually made up of a number of these, called *fomewo*. In Anlo the hlo cuts across the town or village and there are fifteen of these in the entire subdivision.[3]

Ever since the early days, the government of the subdivision or duko was vested in a hierarchy of chiefs and elders. Chieftaincy was quite an old institution among the Ewe, although in the eighteenth century they borrowed the embellishments of the system, such as state umbrellas, etc. from Akwamu. The clan heads or lineage heads who led the Ewes from Notsie to Eweland were in fact chiefs.

A lineage or clan head is the most senior member of the fome or the hlo. He administers the lineage or clan property and settles disputes among members of the group.[4] His jurisdiction cuts across towns and villages.

As well as the clan chiefs there were territorial chiefs whose duties were both civil and military. There was some Akwamu or Akan influence on the development of the system of territorial chiefs in most parts of Eweland, Akan terms being very often employed to describe the various institutions. There was the ward chief, for which the indigenous term was *tofia*, but the Ewe often refer to him as 'Asafohene'. He was responsible for the affairs of the ward and led the ward in times of war. Then came the village or town chief or *dufia*. He was the most senior ward chief or tofia, and his jurisdiction extended to the whole village or town.[5]

---

1 D. E. K. Amenumey, *The Ewe People and the coming of European rule, 1850–1914*, M.A. thesis, University of London, 1964, p. 28

2 *Ibid.*, pp. 38–47   3 Manoukian, pp. 22–3

4 *Ibid.*, p. 37   5 *Ibid.*, pp. 34–5

There were also three divisional chiefs. An Ewe subdivision or duko was territorially divided into three parts for military purposes.[1] There was the lashibi chief who was commander of the left wing of the army of the duko. He had also peacetime jurisdiction over a number of towns or *duwo* whose inhabitants belonged to the left wing of the army. Then there was the chief of the *dusi* or right wing who exercised similar power over the towns forming the right wing of the army. These two chiefs, sometimes referred to as lashibi safohenega and dusi safohenega respectively, were appointed to their posts at a general meeting of the duko, for their bravery in war. The chief of the centre, the *awadada*, on the other hand, held a hereditary post and together with the other two divisional chiefs was responsible for the day to day administration of the entire subdivision. The awadada was also the commander-in-chief of the entire army.

At the top of the hierarchy was the king or the paramount chief, called *Awamefia* in Anlo or *Fiaga* in other parts of Eweland. The post of the king was hereditary in two clans as in Anlo or in two or three lineages as in Peki, Ho, etc.[2]

Both the clan chiefs and the territorial chiefs were advised by councillors who were the senior members of the clan or ward. But important matters affecting the subdivision were often debated in public where the commoners were invited to express their views.

Apart from this hierarchy of chiefs and their councillors there was a commoners' association in each ward, called *sohe* (plural, *soheawo*), who chose their own leaders. These associations were devoted to social welfare and community development. Each member of the sohe could call on the group for free services on his farm, or for building a house, etc. Because they were so devoted to the interests of the commoners, the soheawo tended to form pressure groups within the community with the view to defending those interests in the general meetings of the subdivisions. Very often therefore they found themselves opposed to the chiefs and councillors.[3]

Although trade in western Eweland was for a long time on a small scale, since the eighteenth century economic activities had assumed some importance. The Anlo maintained an inland market at Adaklu where they disposed of smuggled goods. It was here they sold firearms and spirits to inland traders like the Asante. Some Anlo traders went further west to sell their goods in Krobo.[4] Peki at the beginning of the nineteenth century was mainly interested in the slave trade, and apart from this there was practically no other economic activity until about the mid-century when agricultural produce began to assume some importance. It was these increasing economic activities which, as we shall see,[5] were later in the nineteenth century to contribute to the resistance movement in Eweland against Europeans.

1 The Akan example was here imperfectly copied. For the Ewe army was divided into three columns instead of four as in the Akan system. There were the left, right and centre columns. The rearguard had no recognised status in Ewe warfare. Anlo tradition informant, Amega Dzefi, an elder of the Wifeme clan.

2 Amenumey, p. 25

3 Anlo tradition: informant Amega Dzefi, an elder of the Wifeme clan

4 C.O. 96/128, encl. in Ussher to Hicks Beach, G.C., 12 November 1879, Accra

5 See below pp. 65–6

Asante, Fante and British in the first half of the nineteenth century

In the nineteenth century, the trade and politics of the states of the Gold Coast caused conflicts among them, particularly between Asante and Fante.

In the eighteenth century the Fante had striven to reserve for themselves the rights of middlemen between the interior states and the European trading posts on the coast. It was about the middle of the eighteenth century that they set up the markets of Foso and Manso with the view to compelling interior traders to stop there. But this restriction of interior traders became a disorderly affair, for the Fante were themselves disunited, and conflicts, such as those between Cape Coast and Komenda, led to predatory activities.

In these circumstances the Fante Braffoes became a terror to all. They often closed the trading paths to the sea-board, to the dismay of Asante traders, who were sometimes insulted and attacked coming to and from the coast.

The result was that at the beginning of the nineteenth century Asante had no easy access to the central coast towns. Although their traders could reach Apollonia and Anlo with comparative ease, they still wanted an equally easy access to the central districts for trade, the lifeblood of their nation. Asante therefore found these interruptions in Fanteland most irritating.

It is further significant that Captain George Maclean, probably the most observant contemporary, in his careful study of the Asante–Fante dispute in 1830, concluded that the one important cause of the conflict was trade and that to restore peaceful conditions, this problem, like that of politics, must be tackled at the root. For this reason, when he arranged the 1831 treaty of peace, he included the clause:

> The paths shall be perfectly open, and free to all persons engaged in lawful traffic; and persons molesting them in any way whatsoever, or forcing them to purchase at any particular market, or influencing them by any unfair means whatever, shall be declared guilty of infringing this Treaty, and be liable to the severest punishment.[1]

Another reason for Asante invasions of the coast in the nineteenth century was the Asantehene's desire to re-exact allegiance from rebellious states. In 1853, for instance, he first tried to bring Assin back into the Asante fold by diplomacy. When this failed he sent an army across the Prah to do this by force. But when the British in Cape Coast appeared to be ready to fight if the Asante persisted in their designs, the Asantehene ordered the troops to recross the Prah, which they did without striking the British troops.[2] In 1872, however, the Asante army came as far south as Fanteland. To re-establish Asante rule over Fante was clearly one of the reasons for these conflicts.

The conflicts occurred in 1806, 1811, 1814, 1824 and 1826 in the first half of the nineteenth century. In 1853 and 1863 Asante forces again crossed the Prah but did not reach the coast. These wars had very important consequences on developments on the Coast. The effects on the British deserve close attention since it was these conflicts which compelled them to attempt to influence the trend of Coast politics.

1 Claridge, Vol. I, p. 410

2 W. E F. Ward, *A History of Ghana*, London 1961, p. 212

In the eighteenth century, Europeans did not exercise any significant influence on African politics. But in the nineteenth century, with the abolition of the slave trade in 1807 and the substitution of legitimate trade, peaceful conditions became absolutely vital. The Asante–Fante wars disturbed the peace and so the Europeans, the British in particular, considered it necessary to influence Coast affairs to restore peace for legitimate trade.

There were several reasons for the abolition of the slave trade, which in the eighteenth century had been the main link between Europe and West Africa, and its replacement with legitimate commerce. Humanitarian considerations drove people like Grenville Sharpe, William Wilberforce and Fowell Buxton to launch the abolition movement in the 1780s. But humanitarianism alone could not bring about total abolition and it was not until economic considerations came in that the 1807 Act outlawing the trade was passed in England.

The first economic consideration was the need to prevent the further glutting of the British sugar market in the closing years of the eighteenth century by regulating the import of sugar from the West Indies. This in turn necessitated the regulation of the export of slave labour to the West Indian sugar plantations. So most British sugar planters began actively campaigning for the abolition of the slave trade.

Secondly, British economy, which used to depend largely on the West Indies, was changing with the rise of the Industrial Revolution. What British industrialists needed now was no longer slaves but raw materials. So, by the early part of the nineteenth century, attention was already turning to trade in agricultural produce like palm oil, groundnuts, cotton, rubber, etc. For these reasons, Britain outlawed the slave trade in 1807 and thereafter strove to encourage legitimate commerce which the British, in the disturbed circumstances of the Asante–Fante dispute, had to protect on the Gold Coast in the first half of the nineteenth century.

To protect this legitimate trade on the Gold Coast, the British had to rely on their forts and settlements, established mainly in the eighteenth century on the sea-board. Cape Coast Castle was the chief of these and it was here that British local affairs were administered. There were other forts and settlements all along the seaboard from west to east in which British merchants or officials now had to influence the affairs of the Gold Coast states so as to protect the new trade.

Although European participation in African affairs had precedent, in the nineteenth century it turned out to be a difficult assignment for the British. From 1807 Colonel Torrane, President of the Council of Merchants in Cape Coast Castle, and his supporters decided that the best way to influence the course of the Asante–Fante dispute was to back Asante's claim of overlordship of the coastal states, including Fante. They hoped this would strengthen the Asantehene in his effort to establish an Asante peace south of the Prah. This tendency to favour an Asante control of the coast continued until 1821 when it was written into the Treaty which Dupuis, an agent of H.M. Government, signed with the Asantehene.

But Torrane's policy was not acceptable to all British traders on the Gold Coast. From about 1817, when Hope Smith became President of the Council of Merchants in Cape Coast Castle, the merchant authorities rejected Torrane's policy and supported the Fante against Asante. Hope Smith and his associates felt that the British could get what they wanted by playing the divided Fante states one against the other. If Asante was allowed to establish a centralised administration over Fante, this would weaken the merchants' chances of bargaining and Asante would dictate terms of trade to the British. Indeed with the Coast under Asante the British would become extremely vulnerable. These ideas spread and in 1817 Hope Smith sent a mission to Kumasi where the Bowdich Treaty of that year, which embodied them, was signed.

The central clause of this treaty was that Asante should regard the British as responsible for the conduct of the Fante. In other words, Hope Smith's mode of influence was to substitute British for Asante supervision of Fante conduct. But this proved difficult to implement at the start. In 1818, for instance, Hope Smith failed to check the Komendas from molesting Asante traders. And in 1824 MacCarthy's hasty campaign on behalf of the Fante proved disastrous, ending in his own death.

It is clear, therefore, that the British found establishing a sphere of influence difficult from the beginning. This can be seen in the frequent changes in their method of exercising influence and the continuation of the disastrous wars, which this influence was supposed to terminate, till 1826, the year of the Battle of Dodowa.

But from 1828 onwards, the early difficulties were over, and a definite method was at last found. In that year, Captain George Maclean was appointed President of the Committee of Merchants, and he accepted Hope Smith's policy of Britain being responsible for the conduct of the Fante. He set about the task of supervising Fante conduct very seriously. First, he arranged the 1831 Treaty with Asante and from that time onwards held a regular court in Cape Coast Castle where he prosecuted and punished, among others, those guilty of disturbing the public peace. He put two policemen in each important Fante town and carried out punitive expeditions against recalcitrant chiefs. Between 1828 and 1843, when he was in charge of affairs of the British settlements, there was no conflict between Asante and Fante and from about 1840 the volume of trade increased threefold.

Even after Maclean, his mode of influence – the exercise of certain judicial powers – was so well established that the Crown had to accept responsibility for the Fante. In 1844 Governor Hill arranged the signing of the famous Bond, in which British interference into certain areas of jurisdiction in Fante and adjacent states was acknowledged. The British were to try cases of murder, robbery, etc. By their behaviour the British also gave the impression that they would protect the maritime states. Thus an informal protectorate came into being.

The first and the most important result of the Asante–Fante wars was, therefore, the growth of British influence on the affairs of the states of the Gold Coast. After an uncertain start, the British eventually settled for a definite mode of influence, thanks to the hard work of Maclean. By 1850 British participation in the exercise of Coast judicial powers was clearly marked.

The second result of these wars was the acute financial difficulties which plagued British possessions on the Coast. In the first place, the exercise of influence on Coast affairs meant increased commitments. The British Government insisted on the cost of these commitments being met largely from local resources. During the entire period of Maclean's administration, for instance, H.M. Government expected the settlements to be largely self-supporting and so made available to the Committee of Merchants no more than a maximum annual subvention of £4000, the figure often being less. In these circumstances the Coast authorities needed a prosperous trade to be able to administer British possessions and protect British nationals effectively. But the Asante–Fante conflicts often interrupted or brought trade to a standstill. Consequently, the British were nearly always short of funds, always on the verge of total bankruptcy, except in the later part of Maclean's term of office.

In the late 1840s the Coast authorities tried to solve this financial problem, without success. They thought the best way of increasing their financial resources was to buy the Danish possessions so as to levy custom dues on trade on an extended coast line. But as soon as they bought out the Danes in 1850, their responsibilities were increased out of all proportion to the financial gains resulting from that purchase.

Outbreaks of disorder in Ningo, Ada, etc. forced them to send military expeditions. Earlier, in 1848, the British had been obliged to send a very expensive expedition into Apollonia to deal with the excesses of its king. Because of these expenses the Government could not make ends meet. Plantation economy was tried; the growing of cotton and coffee was begun, but labour difficulties caused the abandoning of this project. The Poll Tax Ordinance of 1852 was a further attempt to solve the financial impasse, but it proved unpopular and also had to be abandoned.

This acute shortage of funds in turn had important results on the British connection with the Gold Coast. As we have seen, the British had, since 1844, given the Fante to understand that they would protect them in the event of war with the interior peoples. But because of lack of funds the British failed to give adequate protection to the Fante and this led to unrest among them. As the threat of Asante invasions increased, the coastal states began to feel that since 1844 they had allowed certain of their ancient privileges to be encroached on by the British in return for protection against their enemies and the provision of modern amenities, neither of which was now forthcoming. The feeble military efforts of the British in 1853 and, especially, in 1863, on behalf of the coastal states showed the Fante in particular that they would not gain anything in return for their sacrifices. We find James Bannerman and Brodie Cruickshank on 22 August 1850 sounding a warning to the effect that an explosive situation had been created by the British not being able to meet adequately the increasing requests of the people.[1]

So although the Asante wars encouraged the growth of British influence on the Coast, at the same time they caused this influence to be confined to the relatively inexpensive field of judicial authority. The exercise of influence on inter-state conflicts was expensive and so strictly restricted. But this was exactly the area in which the coastal communities would have liked British support against their adversaries.

Another important effect of these wars on the British was the vacillating nature of their association with the Gold Coast. In 1807, when Asante forces reached Anomabu, it was the Company of Merchants which was looking after British interests on the Coast. In 1821, in face of considerable pressure from Asante to dominate the coastal states and the failure of merchant administration to cope with this, the British Government, hoping to restore better conditions for trade, abolished the Council of Merchants, and the forts on the Gold Coast came under direct Crown rule. And yet, after two more clashes between Asante forces and coastal levies under British officers in 1824 and 1826, H.M.

1 Metcalfe, p. 219

12

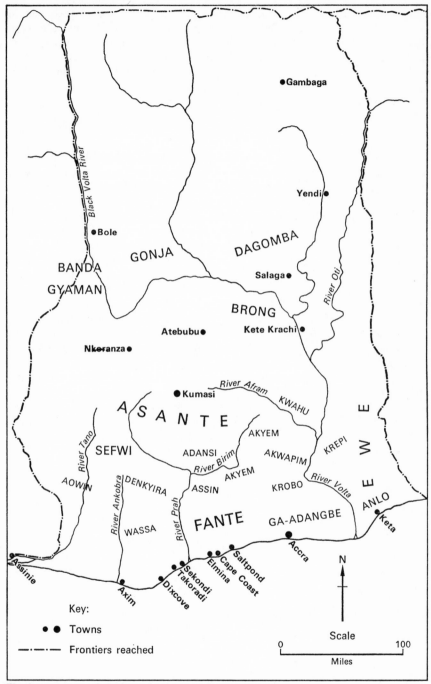

Gambaga

Black Volta River

Bole

Yendi

GONJA

DAGOMBA

BANDA

GYAMAN

Salaga

River Oti

BRONG

Atebubu

Kete Krachi

Nkoranza

River Afram

Kumasi

KWAHU

A S A N T E

E

AKYEM

River Tano

SEFWI

ADANSI

River Birim

AKWAPIM

KREPI

W

AOWIN

DENKYIRA

AKYEM

River Volta

E

ASSIN

KROBO

River Ankobra

WASSA

River Prah

FANTE

GA-ADANGBE

ANLO

Assinie

Accra

Keta

N

Saltpond

Elmina

Cape Coast

Sekondi

Takoradi

Axim

Dixcove

Key:

● ● Towns

—·—·— Frontiers reached

Scale

0   100

Miles

The States of the Gold Coast in the nineteenth century

Government, afraid of further expenditure, returned the Gold Coast to merchant control in 1828. Crown Government was reinstated in 1843, but in 1865, after general conflicts had narrowly been averted in 1853 and 1863, the Parliamentary Committee advocated abandonment of the Gold Coast once again, although this was never carried out.

The long-drawn-out conflict between the Asante and the Fante in the first half of the nineteenth century clearly had some important effects on the behaviour of the British on the coast.

Summary

After this brief survey of the states and the British position on the Gold Coast, it may be useful to indicate some of the factors in the Gold Coast situation which were likely to lead to important African–British interactions in the second half of the nineteenth century.

First of all, as we have seen, these states had well-organised military forces with which to back any decisions they chose to make. So it is reasonable to assume that the African states would not hesitate to protest against any obnoxious measures of the British. There were several occasions on which states like Asante or Anlo used the army to resist British demands.

Secondly, these African states possessed, by the beginning of the nineteenth century, a great many traditional institutions. It was natural that they should be proud of them, and their anxiety to preserve them affected their conduct towards the British. Consequently the activities of these states had to be taken into consideration by the British in the formulation and execution of their policies on the coast.

Finally, in the first half of the nineteenth century the British had to exercise influence on African affairs to restore conditions suitable for the new trade. But because of shortage of funds this influence was largely confined to judicial matters. Influence on the politics of the states was so restricted that British policy in the first half of the nineteenth century is aptly described as one of non-intervention.

CHAPTER ONE

The Fante Confederacy 1865–1871

The continuation of the African British interaction into the second half of the nineteenth century was fed by a number of political activities of the states of the Gold Coast. The earliest of these was the Fante Confederacy, a protest movement of great magnitude which therefore belongs to the first category of political activities of the Gold Coast states defined in the Preface. To find out exactly what the Confederacy was, we must analyse its origins, nature, achievements and finally how it came to an end.

Origins of the Fante Confederacy

The Fante and the rest of the 'Protectorate' were, in the 1860s, greatly concerned about their judicial rights. The Fante had conceded, through the Bond of 1844, some very limited judicial powers to the British.[1] It is important to stress that these concessions to the British were restricted not to judicial matters in general, but to the trying of murder and robbery cases only. In addition, the Bond implied that only by consent of the kings, chiefs, and peoples of the 'Protectorate' could the British acquire any further judicial rights. So, before 1874, the British had hardly any jurisdiction on the Gold Coast and, what is more, they could not assume any powers without the express consent of the people.

This assertion could be proved in various ways. First we find Cruickshank, a merchant and for a short while in 1853 an Acting Governor on the Gold Coast, writing in 1865 that Britain had no jurisdiction on the Gold Coast, that it was not acquired, purchased or ceded to them. More recently, the late Dr J. B. Danquah, in a paper on 'The historical significance of the Bond of 1844', has pointed out that British jurisdiction outside the settlements was clearly understood by Her Majesty's Government to be optional and made the subject of distinct agreement' with the African chiefs.[2] It is true that the chiefs on several occasions swore allegiance to the British Crown but, as Mensah Sarbah has explained, the chiefs were only rendering the military services of vassals to a superior; African laws and customs were never understood to have been abrogated or affected by it. Sarbah further pointed out that in their dealings with Europeans these African rulers thought of no 'allegiance', as that word

1 See above p. 11

2 *Transactions of the Historical Society of Ghana*, Vol. III, 1957, p. 4

was understood by the British.[1] It thus appears that before 1874 the people of the Gold Coast were theoretically in full control of their judicial rights.

In practice, however, things were different. Since 1844 the British had usurped a great deal of the judicial powers of the kings and chiefs. They were so successful in this that in the 1850s they even wanted to abolish African courts in favour of their own. They achieved this by paying regular stipends to the Fante caboceers (chiefs and dignitaries in towns and villages), who feared that they might lose these stipends if they objected to the encroachments of the British on their ancient rights and liberties.

In the 1860s British officials, on grounds of economy, were no longer able to pay these stipends regularly. The chiefs therefore decided to withhold from the British the privileges which they had so illegally acquired. The people began to assert that no criminal or civil case was beyond the jurisdiction of the Court of the Omanhene.[2] Most communities followed these assertions with action and refused pointblank to refer their cases, no matter how serious, to British authorities on the Coast.[3] In his *Political History of Ghana*, Kimble cites further examples of the people's concern about getting back their judicial powers from the British. He writes that as early as the 1850s both traditional authorities and the merchants of Cape Coast were challenging the Government's jurisdiction, that an African court was set up for the town, and that in 1854 the Acting Governor was involved in efforts to prevent the people becoming even more 'refractory and opposing to the Government'.[4]

Secondly, the origins of the Fante Confederacy could be traced to problems of defence and security of the 'Protectorate', which had also assumed great importance since the 1850s. To the peoples of the 'Protectorate' the problem of defending their firesides against the forces of the King of Asante was, of course, a perennial one; but in the decade before 1863 this problem became really serious. The events of 1853, when Asante thought of invading the Coast, left a deep impression on the Fante mind. When Dr James Africanus Horton reported that in this period Asante were successful in trade to the sea-board,[5] he was unwittingly confirming the fact of Fante uneasiness; for the Fante had always associated Asante success in coastal trade with Asante military supremacy and consequently with their own weak and helpless military position.

The Fante felt that they had to do something quickly about their problems of defence. The situation was so explosive that it took a common Asante refugee like Kwasi Gyani no effort to bribe some of the principal Fante chiefs to take up his cause (1862). They immediately seized and detained a large number of Asante in the Coast towns, an act which quickly drew Asante forces into the 'Protectorate', thus increasing the military problems of the Coast. These events gave birth to a desire among the educated Fante leaders of the Coast towns to build a united army for the defence of the land. Mr Hutchison, a wealthy local gentleman, therefore started in 1863 the Gold Coast Rifle Volunteer Corps.

1 J. M. Sarbah, *Fanti National Constitution*, London 1906, pp. 88–9

2 *Ibid.*, p. 92   3 J. M. Sarbah, *Fanti Law Report*, London 1906, p. 172

4 Kimble, *A Political History of Ghana*, pp. 196 and 197

5 Dr James A. Horton, Letter No. 4 to Granville, 12 November 1869, Cape Coast Castle

After the Asante War of that year, however, the British disbanded the corps.[1] This action did not kill the Fante desire to work for their own security, it merely drove the movement underground; and, as we shall see, it was this desire which contributed to the formation of the Confederacy.

By 1865 we find the Fante and the rest of the 'Protectorate' restless on account of judicial and military matters. This restlessness resulted in protests by the Fante which were eventually organised into the Confederacy. These early protests began in 1865, when the movement, driven underground by the British disbanding the Gold Coast Rifle Volunteer Corps, came into the open, led by John Aggrey, King of Cape Coast. Aggrey's two main concerns were the preservation of the traditional judicial rights and the military question, in connection with which he sought to establish a full-fledged army for the security of the state.

Closely related to the question of judicial rights was the question of ownership of land already discussed in the Introduction (see p. 2). King Aggrey based his protests on the arguments (a) that Britain, not having acquired the land of the Gold Coast, could not exercise any jurisdiction without the distinct consent of the chiefs and peoples, and (b) that because land could not be alienated the belated British claim to land around the castles had no legal basis.[2]

Before the year 1865 was out King Aggrey formally claimed land adjacent to the very walls of Cape Coast Castle. In this he enjoyed the unanimous support of his chiefs who, when required by the British Administrator to append their signatures to an instrument confirming territory around the castle as British property, replied in council that they had always known that all the land belonged to the Queen, but the signing of a piece of paper was doubtful to them.[3] They therefore refused to sign.

King Aggrey and his chiefs increased their opposition to the British authorities. On 6 September 1866 the King gave Edward Conran, Administrator of the Gold Coast, a copy of a petition of 5 September 1866 which he intended forwarding to the Governor-in-Chief of Her Majesty's West African Settlements in Sierra Leone. The petition was an objection to Conran's acts and his administration of government, pointing out that British law was 'an extraneous growth' and that the chiefs and peoples of Cape Coast preferred their own laws.[4] Conran forwarded a copy to Blackall, the Governor-in-Chief in Sierra Leone and there was clear evidence that the latter was disturbed by the news of increasing opposition on the Gold Coast.[5]

The King followed his first petition with a 'seditious communication' to Conran, who was terrified by Aggrey's threat of a repetition on the Gold Coast of the late Jamaican rebellion.[6] At this juncture it was becoming clear to the colonial authorities that Aggrey's final aim was self-government. When, after

1 J. B. Anaman, *Gold Coast Guide*, London 1902, p. 53

2 See Kimble, p. 218   3 *Ibid.*, p. 210

4 Adm. 1/687, no. 74, Conran to Blackall, 6 September 1866

5 Blackall had six months earlier expressed concern about the growing opposition on the Gold Coast to Her Majesty's officials there. See Adm. 1/461, Blackall to Cardwell, 19 April 1866.

6 Adm. 1/687, no. 109, Conran to Blackall, 7 December 1866

the second petition, Conran summoned the King to the castle, Aggrey indignantly refused to go, pointing out that he was the King of Cape Coast[1] but did not know who Colonel Conran was.[2]

These early protests in Cape Coast were already taking the form of a movement, and King Aggrey was supported by a number of influential people. Thomas Hughes, his 'prime minister', was the right-hand man of King Aggrey and helped to organise the protests against Conran. Martin and Carr, who had been the King's commissioners to the 1865 Select Committee, had given out upon their return that the inhabitants of the Coast were soon to govern themselves.[3] H.M. Government had set up the Select Committee because of the increasing financial commitments of the Coast administration. The committees had recommended retrenchment and withdrawal from the Gold Coast. It was this message which Aggrey's commissioners broadcast on the Coast. Partly through the influence of these men, enthusiasm for Aggrey's cause spread among the people and his moral influence on the chiefs of Cape Coast and elsewhere increased.

Apart from Cape Coast, Anomabu, another Fante state, began to protest against the British Government. It was Conran's interference in Anomabu affairs which caused these protests. Towards the end of 1866 the King of Anomabu imprisoned one of his subjects, Quasie Addo, found guilty of a civil offence in the King's Court. But Conran sent two magistrates, the Colonial Secretary, Ussher and Collins Brew, J.P., to Anomabu to review Quasie Addo's sentence. The magistrates got the prisoner released and fined the King for imprisoning him. At once the Anomabu chiefs rose up against Conran. They wrote him a letter pointing out that theirs was a sovereign and independent state and their king free to determine civil and criminal cases and imprison his subjects in accordance with the ancient laws of the land.[4] By their action 'they utterly denied the advantage of British over native law'.[5] To drive these points home, they urged their king, in spite of Conran's instructions to the contrary, to imprison a second person, Kofi Assainee, who had also been found guilty of a civil offence in the King's Court.[6]

This action incensed Conran. He marched to Anomabu in force to exact obedience. When, at a meeting of the chiefs and people at Anomabu, Conran asked for those who had signed the letter to be sent to him, all the chiefs owned up readily and boldly and Chief Appeah most insolently. Whereupon the Governor required Chief Appeah to come forward, 'but the old ringleader', as Conran called him, 'did not stir from his stool'. The entire meeting was prepared for a showdown with the British authorities once and for all. The chiefs refused to produce their king, arguing that he was out of town when in fact he was not far from where the Governor stood. Indeed it was only by a display of force that the Governor eventually got the chiefs and people of Anomabu to comply with his requests.[7]

1 King Aggrey normally styled himself 'King of Cape Coast and its Dependencies'.

2 Kimble, p. 218   3 Adm. 1/687, no. 112, Conran to Blackall, 31 December 1866

4 Adm. 1/461, no. 102, Conran to Blackall, 26 November 1866

5 Adm. 1/461, no. 61, Blackall to Carnarvon, 24 December 1866

6 Adm. 1/461, no. 102, Conran to Blackall, 26 November 1866   7 *Ibid.*

There was a third area in Fanteland where the people organised early protests. In Abura lived the Adontenhene, the king of the Central Fante State, military headquarters of all Fante. Immediately to the east lay Mankessim, the religious capital which gave Fante its kings.[1] This implied that Mankessim served as the headquarters of the Fante judiciary system, which role it played throughout the nineteenth century. In April 1867, King Otoo of Abura, described by European sources as a most powerful caboceer, made a most significant move. He established himself at Mankessim, 'capital of Fante',[2] and summoned before him King Hommah of Adjumako and Chief Mooquah of the same state.

King Otoo's irresistible desire to sit in judgment over Fante affairs was inspired by the outbreak of serious disturbances in Adjumako, following a heated dispute between Mooquah and Hommah. The intervention of Chief Ortabill of Gomoah, who had taken up Mooquah's quarrel and despatched 2000 men to drive Hommah out of Adjumako, increased the general disorder. This was why King Otoo summoned the two rulers to Mankessim for arbitration. Ussher, the administrator, ordered Otoo to retire from Mankessim, but the King refused until Ussher threatened to drive him out by force.[3]

In Agona, too, King Yaw Dodoo of Nsaba refused, in May 1867, to appear before the Governor for his alleged breach of the law in taking the cause of justice from the hands of Her Majesty's Government and hanging one of his own subjects who was found guilty of murder in the king's court.[4]

By 1867, therefore, it was clear to the British that there was a widespread movement in Fanteland to overthrow their authority,[5] widespread enough to inspire similar protests among the chiefs and people of the Eastern Districts. Accra and the rest of the Eastern Districts began to protest against British activities from about 1867, just as the Fante were doing. Eventually they formed the Accra Native Confederation, after the Fante had formed their Confederacy.

The first thing to note about these protests in the east is that they, too, were due to the concern of the Eastern Districts about the loss of their judicial powers to the British, and the increasing problems of defence. Secondly, although they started in Accra, they were not confined to this town but extended to the whole of the Eastern Districts. Because of these developments in the east a clear picture emerged of the entire country south of the Prah and between the Tano and the Volta being involved in the early protests. The reason why the protests spread over the entire Eastern Districts was because of the Ga military confederation and the growing influence of Accra and its king already discussed in the Introduction (see p. 6).

In the 1860s the three kings of Accra – Cudjoe of James Town, Dowoonah of Christiansborg and Tackie of Dutch Accra – were already expanding their influence to the various parts of the Eastern Districts.[6] We find Zimmermann,

1 Both Oguaa (Cape Coast) and Mankessim sources agree that Mankessim is the spiritual centre of Fanteland and that the Fante kings were consecrated there.

2 Adm. 1/687, no. 22, Ussher to Blackall, 29 April 1867

3 *Ibid.*   4 Adm. 1/687, no. 33, Ussher to Blackall, 6 May 1867

5 As early as November 1866, Conran had written that there were evidently emissaries at work throughout the whole of the protected territory, endeavouring to upset British authority. See no. 102, Conran to Blackall.

6 Horton, Letter no. 5 to Granville, 12 December 1869, Cape Coast Castle

a Basel missionary stationed in Akwapim, writing on 26 July 1867 to Freeman, the British Government's Commissioner for the Eastern Districts, to explain that King Cudjoe of Accra enjoyed the status of a military overlord in respect of Akyem. Similarly, the *African Times* of 22 September 1866 had given out that King Tackie of Accra was considered to be the king of the whole of the Eastern Districts,[1] his influence extending to Akyem, Akwapem, Krobo, Ada and Krepi, etc.

It was within this widening area of influence of the Ga chiefs, especially of Tackie, that the protests occurred. The Accra chiefs led the movement, and their people, the Asafo, followed. The chiefs flatly disobeyed British instructions and substituted their own. For instance, since 1866 the three kings of Accra, encamped at Ada, refused to move from there as ordered by the Governor through George Cleland, an Accra merchant. The kings, who were there for plunder, argued that they were guarding the place against the Anlo. In spite of Ussher's threats (January 1867) of sending the civil commandant to seize them,[2] the kings continued to reside in Ada. When eventually they left on their own accord, King Cudjoe proceeded to Ningo, thirty miles east of Accra, and, said Ussher, in face of the proclamation deposing and outlawing him, 'had the impertinence to request myself or the civil commandant of Accra to meet him and to confer with him'.[3] Ussher was now determined to arrest and transfer Cudjoe to Cape Coast.

The Asafo, the rank and file of Accra, also committed numerous acts of disobedience to British orders. The *African Times* in 1866 reported that the Accras were wont to look to King Tackie, not to the British, as their leader. In the (1866) invasion of Anlo, for instance, the Accras refused to take orders from Captain Humphrey, who consequently left the war leaving Lieutenant Herbert in his place. He, too, threatened to leave with the European officers and the guns and rockets if the men continued to look to King Tackie as their commander on the field of battle. But even this had no effect on the captains of the companies, who continued to behave exactly as if Herbert were not there.[4]

There was another example of hostile activity against the British. On the evening of 22 September 1867, when Governor Ussher was waiting with some local gentlemen at Mr Addo's hotel for the canoes to take them to the vessel to return to Cape Coast, he perceived about a thousand Gas celebrating customs which the Governor considered to be revolting. He decided to interfere, but the Gas would not allow this. They attacked with stones the three constables who were Governor's emissaries, then Bannerman and Addo. All these were compelled to return without stopping the celebrations. Ussher attributed this to an organised attempt at revolt on the part of the Accras.[5]

In Ningo, as in Accra, there were yet more protests against the British. Here the chiefs and people decided to claim back the power which they had lost to the British – the power of life and death. Accordingly, at their annual festival they

1 *African Times*, 22 September 1866, p. 28

2 Adm. 1/687, no. 41, Ussher to Blackall, 4 June 1867

3 Adm. 1/687, no. 54, Ussher to Young, 1 August 1867

4 *African Times*, 22 September 1866, p. 28

5 Adm. 1/687, no. 72, Ussher to Young, 24 September 1867

decided to execute all those condemned to death in the course of the year. Ussher, ignorant of the African judicial machinery, promptly branded this as human sacrifice and sent a strong force to Ningo to stop it. The same spirit of what Ussher called 'the outrage' of resisting British authority lay behind the refusal of the people of Pram-Pram in October 1867 to surrender two thieves who had disturbed the peace of this populous trading centre. The Pram-Prams claimed they were competent to deal with their judicial problems without the British Government's interference, and so they resisted the Governor's warrant.[1]

Apart from these protests there was evidence that the hinterland districts of the Ga Confederation such as Akyem, Krobo and Akwapem were organising protests at this time. Ussher's concern about these inland districts clearly demonstrates the nature of the difficulties that the British were facing there.[2]

The protests within the Ga Confederation gradually increased the desire of the Accras to form an Accra Native Confederation which could better organise Ga resistance to British authority. Africanus Horton recorded this movement and himself suggested, early in 1868, that the whole of the Gold Coast be given self-government and that an independent Fante Kingdom as well as an Accra Republic be set up, the latter to include Eastern Akyem, Winneba, Accra, Akwapem, Adangbe and Krobo.[3] The educated inhabitants of Accra, including the merchants Bannerman, Bruce and Hutton Mills, also expressed a growing interest in the establishment of such an organisation, which could help them to achieve their cherished aims.[4]

Early in 1869, therefore, they formed the Accra Native Confederation. Its aims included the organisation of the protest movement in the Ga Confederation, the preservation of their independence and the formation of 'a strong, compact native Government, which would command the obedience of all the native Kings and Chiefs'.[5]

It pursued its policy in conjunction with the Fante Confederation, and when the latter declined the Accra organisation also faded away. Its very formation, however, shows how widespread were the protests inspired by the Fante Confederacy, not only in the west but also in the east of the Gold Coast.

This description of the origins of the Fante Confederacy would not be complete without discussing opinions attributing the rise of the Confederacy to other causes. The first of these views, which scholars such as Kimble sometimes quoted,[6] was that the Confederacy was nothing more than the intrigues of disgruntled 'half-educated' mulattoes.[7] But this view cannot stand any critical examination.

In the first place, the British officials such as Conran, Ussher and others,[8] the

---

1 Adm. 1/687, no. 89, Ussher to Young, 30 October 1867

2 Adm. 1/687, no. 40, Ussher to Young, 1 July 1867

3 J. A. Horton, *West African Countries and Peoples*, London 1868, pp. 123–5

4 Bannerman to Horton, 21 September 1869, in Horton, Letter no. 3 to Cardwell, 12 October 1869

5 Horton, *West African Countries and Peoples*, pp. 123–5

6 Kimble, p. 222   7 Adm. 1/687, no. 88, Ussher to Young, 30 October 1867

8 *Ibid.;* also Adm. 1/461, no. 43, Blackall to Carnarvon, 17 October 1866

authors of this statement, could not be said to have been sincere when they made these charges against the educated Africans. The officials on the Coast were anxious to prevent the withdrawal of the British Government from the Gold Coast, as was suggested in the 1865 Report. So they were trying to convince Her Majesty's officials in London that if they returned the Government of the Coast to the Fante Confederacy they would merely be handing over power to the educated Africans, of whom, in order to show that this would be impolitic, they painted as black a picture as they possibly could.

The Coast officials reported to the Colonial Office that the élite on the Coast were dishonest and inefficient. The administrator of the Gold Coast in a dispatch of May 1868 gave out that he had met with only two or three honest and conscientious 'native Government Servants' during eleven years.[1] About the same time the Administrator reported to Kennedy that 'Cape Coast is afflicted with a number of mischievous, half-educated mulatto adventurers, whose livelihood mainly depends upon keeping alive dissension'.[2] In addition, British officials often directed their vilifications against specific individuals. On 12 November 1866 Conran hastened to pour ridicule on Thomas Hughes, who was supporting King Aggrey, and classified him with some other supporters of the King whom he referred to as 'ignorant men'.[3] Similarly, Ussher called Labrech Hesse, for protesting against acts of discrimination on the part of the Government of Accra, 'a black and illiterate person'.[4] Conran, in particular, thought so little of the élite that he wrote in 1866 that the educated Africans could not govern for a week in the absence of a white man.[5]

But these accusations were insincere. The treatment of Hughes, for instance, shows this insincerity, Although they persisted in calling him all sorts of names when he was supporting King Aggrey, as soon as Hughes changed sides and became a supporter of Her Majesty's Government, no doubt through Ussher's influence, these same officials loaded him with praise as much as they had ridiculed him in the past.[6] Ussher himself wrote of Hughes: 'Although he may have been indiscreet and disaffected in Aggrey's time, he was, I think, badly treated, and had to answer for many offences of which he was not guilty.'[7]

Similarly, Labrech Hesse's treatment by the British was insincere. Colonel Conran found this local gentleman quite competent and as a result appointed him a civil commandant of Accra. But when towards the end of 1868 Hesse resigned his office in protest against acts of discrimination on the part of the chief magistrate in Accra, the Administrator arrested and imprisoned him, implying, in his description of Hesse to the Governor-in-Chief in Sierra Leone, that he was incompetent.[8] Equally ridiculous was Conran's accusation of dishonesty among the élite. Commenting on this charge, Kennedy, Conran's superior and Governor-in-Chief of Her Majesty's West African Settlements, retorted that 'the result of the Administrator's experience, that he has met

1 Adm. 1/461, no. 35, Kennedy to the Duke of Buckingham and Chandos, 29 May 1868

2 *Ibid.*, no. 38   3 Adm. 1/461, no. 43, Blackall to Carnarvon, 17 October 1866

4 Adm. 1/461, no. 116, Kennedy to Buckingham, 22 December 1868

5 Kimble, p. 213   6 Adm. 1/687, no. 94, see Ussher to Young, 5 November 1867

7 Adm. 1/687, no. 17, Ussher to Kennedy, 6 February 1868

8 Adm. 1/461, no. 196, Kennedy to Buckingham, 22 December 1868

with only two or three honest and conscientious native Government Servants during eleven years is unfortunate. I have no difficulty in finding as many as are required, who are entirely trustworthy'.[1]

Clearly, then, the attitude of Gold Coast officials to the élite was hypocritical, and no reliance can be placed on their claim that the Fante Confederacy was nothing more than the intrigues of the educated Africans.

Similarly, the claim that the 1868 interchange of forts was the real cause of the Fante movement is not wholly true. It is, of course, true that the interchange served as the occasion for the meeting of the Fante Chiefs in Council at Mankessim, but in this case, interchange could only be regarded as having strengthened the chiefs in their resolutions and not to have led to the formulation of those resolutions.

The interchange, which involved the rearrangement of forts on the Coast so that the British had all their forts east of the River Kakum and the Dutch west of it, was originally suggested by the British in 1865 as an economic measure; they thought it would make it easier to collect custom dues on the Coast and probably lead to an increase in trade. But in 1868, when the interchange of forts came to be effected, the reasons behind this action were entirely different. By 1867 British officials who still supported interchange did so, not so much on financial grounds, but rather as a means of strengthening their hold on the difficult Fante and Eastern Districts. British officials thought it unreasonable, in face of growing protests in the country, to continue dissipating their efforts along the entire coast when there was the possibility of concentrating them more effectively on the eastern half of it. In their calculations, the attractions of the east – the growing trade on the Volta, for instance – contrasted very sharply with the disadvantages of the Western Districts, where Apollonia was rapidly becoming a centre of resistance to British rule. We find Conran writing as early as 1866 that interchange would be of great advantage to the British in that by it they could get rid of Apollonia, the inhabitants of which had become so refractory.[2]

Similarly, the Dutch were by 1867 meeting so much opposition in Accra from King Tackie and his supporters that they were anxious to be rid of their eastern possessions. The cession of Dutch Accra to the British in 1868 was a great relief for the Netherlands Government.[3] Clearly, therefore, the 1868 interchange of forts was carried out to combat the African Protest Movement. It was thus a *result* of this movement and not its *cause*. The causes of the movement were those very pre-interchange events which we have already discussed.

Aims, nature and achievements of the Fante Confederacy

The aims of the Fante Confederacy were to provide security and protection for the Fante against their enemies. At the same time the promoters of the Confederacy were anxious to achieve modern development in Fanteland, and, lastly, they wanted internal self-government. To achieve these aims, subsidiary planning became necessary; the formation of a closer union was necessary for

1 Adm. 1/461, no. 35, Kennedy to Buckingham, 29 May 1868

2 Adm. 1/687, no. 75, Conran to Blackall, 6 September 1866

3 Adm. 1/461, no. 14, Kennedy to Buckingham, 5 December 1868

security and development. An alliance with Elmina was also important to ward off the Asante danger more effectively.

As early as 1866, when the protests were going on in the Western Districts, the Fante began to think that the formation of a permanent association would be useful, because it would help them to overcome the Asante parties which had sprung up over the years in such towns as Elmina, Komenda, Shama, Sekondi, Bushua and Atuabo in Apollonia.[1] By 1868 there was already a loose bond of union between the Fante states and Wassa, Denkyira, Assin and others; and when the exchange of forts occurred in that year, this confederation, together with Akumfi, Anomabu and Winneba, set itself a new task of preventing the Dutch occupation of towns formerly under British protection.[2] Horton's report says that, in secret conclave, the Fante entered into a formal alliance, offensive and defensive with the Kings of Wassa and Denkyira to oppose Dutch rule and 'to form a confederation among themselves for mutual support'.

The Fante and others in the Western District knew that the Dutch were friendly with their enemies, the Asante, and they realised that if the former became firmly established in the West the latter would find it easier to attack the coastal districts. It was therefore their concern about security which caused the Fante to oppose the Dutch.

While it was the aim of the Fante Confederacy to exterminate Asante and Dutch influence in the West, it was even more important to them that this should be achieved at all costs in the Dutch headquarters, Elmina. The control of Elmina was vital to the acquisition of the whole of the Western Districts. The Fante decided that the best means of achieving control over Elmina was to enter an offensive-defensive alliance with the town. They felt that in the absence of such a formal alliance, the Asante party would continue to grow in Elmina, and the town would consequently continue to support Asante in time of war.[3] It was to this danger that the Fante chiefs were referring when they explained to Kennedy, on his arrival on the Coast in November 1868, that 'they would never consent to remain between two fires as at present'.[4] They never tired of telling British officials that their solution to this danger, a formal Fante–Elmina alliance, was one of the chief aims of their Confederacy.[5]

Another aim of the Fante Confederacy was to attain internal self-government and to assume some degree of responsibility for their own affairs. There were probably several factors behind this. In the first place, they were disappointed with the failure of the British to protect them effectively against Asante. Then there was the high-handed manner in which the two European powers on the Coast exchanged territories and peoples under their influence without consulting the African governments. It looked as though the Dutch and the British were, by this action, asserting their ownership of the territories on which their forts stood. The Fante therefore wanted to be rid of the Europeans so as to stop these annoyances and to reassert their prior rights to these territories. In

1 For a fuller discussion of these Asante parties see below, pp. 38-9

2 Horton, Letter no. 2 to Cardwell, 12 September 1869, Cape Coast

3 Horton to Granville, 13 January 1870, Cape Coast Castle

4 Adm. 1/461, no. 106, Kennedy to Buckingham, 17 November 1868

5 Adm. 1/687, no. 85, Ussher to Kennedy, 17 July 1868

the oft-quoted letter of King Otoo of Abura to Ussher we learn that the Fante saw no reason why Komenda should be forced to accept the Dutch flag and why, when they refused, their town should be bombarded. We are told that the Fante kings 'reminded the Administrator that the land on which the neglected British river fort of Commendah now stands is the property of the people, and that they received ground rent for it when the African Company governed this Coast'.[1] The desire for internal self-government was clearly a burning issue.

In order to realise their aims, the Fante very carefully worked out the chief features of the Confederacy. Towards the end of 1868 they adopted, at Mankessim, the traditional constitution, and under it they set up a machinery of government for what used to be the 'Protectorate' as well as some adjacent districts. The constitution provided for a King-President at the top, supported by councillors (kings, elders, etc.) and then by a National Assembly. This assembly was made up of representatives of the *oman* from the various territories, including the councillors and the King-President. This meant that all Fante and the adjacent districts now possessed a confederate government with a single head. There was, however, a second constitution, the Mankessim Constitution of 1871, and as soon as this was drawn up in October of that year, a new organ of government, an Executive Council, was added to those already created under the first constitution.

The judicial system depended very much on the King-President who was president of the Confederate Court, held in Mankessim. A number of cases were referred to the King-President, but it is not absolutely clear which cases went to Mankessim and which went to the regions. We know, however, that cases dealing with questions of property and immorality were sent to the Confederate Court in Mankessim.[2]

Financial matters also received great attention. A poll tax was instituted and to make its collection easier, the territories under the Confederacy's jurisdiction were divided into districts, the boundaries of which coincided with those of the different states. Poll tax commissioners were responsible for the collection of the tax in specified districts.[3]

A military force was another important instrument of government that the Confederacy established. The Confederate army was started in February 1868 by King Otoo of Abura, who was eventually appointed its chief commander in 1871. The early recruits were mainly volunteers, but later the organisation of recruitment and the training of troops were improved; by 1869 spectacular results had been achieved. The right wing of the army then consisted of troops from Sefwi, Denkyira, Anomabu, Ekumfi, Twifo, Komenda and Wassa. The left wing was composed of Abura, Adjumako, Ayan and Mankessim. By about April 1869, the total Fante force was some 15,000 strong.[4]

What did the Confederacy, employing these instruments and organs of government, achieve? Its first major achievement was the setting up of a strong and effective government. King Ghartey was elected as first King-President in

1 Otoo to Ussher, quoted in Horton, Letter no. 3 to Cardwell, 11 October 1869, Cape Coast Castle

2 Letter to Ghartey, 6 July 1869, Ghartey Papers

3 Dawson to Ghartey, 22 December 1869, Mankessim, Ghartey Papers

4 Horton to Cardwell, 12 October 1869, C.C.C.

December 1868. Residing in Mankessim, the traditional capital of all Fanteland, he enjoyed supreme power among the people, and kings, chiefs and elders throughout the Confederate territories paid homage to him. In 1871 the Kings of Abura and Mankessim were jointly elected King-Presidents. Later it was Edu of Mankessim alone who held the office of King-President and Otoo of Abura became 'General Field Marshal of the Fante nation'.[1] Thus for the first time in about a century, Fante possessed a strong central authority, strengthened by the institution of an Executive Council. J. E. Amissah, J. H. Brew, F. C. Grant and J. M. Abadoo were elected as members of the Council.[2]

With a strong centralised government it was not surprising that more achievements were registered. The most important was in the field of justice, which was one of the assignments of the King-President. As King-President, Ghartey acted as Fante magistrate, based at Mankessim, where we find cases being referred to his court; probably the earliest reference to this activity was made by Kofi Ackeney in a letter dated 15 January 1869.[3] On 1 and 5 July King Otoo of Abura referred a number of cases to Ghartey. One held that 'these men came to me that they came from Amanfu stating to me that someone seized[?] their property and they like to take[?] the case to me and being the cases of such sorts is not in my rule so am oblige(d) to direct them to come to you at Mankessim'.[4]

A case of corruption came up the same month. Mr Benson, who had been on official duties in Akyem, put in claims for travelling allowances on account of his hammock expenses, but it was subsequently alleged that he had already got £4 from the Confederate Government for his journey into Akyem.[5] On 9 July a case of a completely different nature was referred to Ghartey, who now assumed the title of Chief Magistrate[6]; on that date Joseph Eshun from Kormantine submitted a case of improper conduct towards a pregnant woman.[7] This was followed by a case involving a stolen towel, in connection with which a summons was served on the correspondent's aunt by an inhabitant of Saltpond.[8] We have no accounts of the nature of satisfaction the parties to these cases received. But one thing is clear, namely, that after what must have been a considerable break, all Fante, once again as of old, looked to their ancient capital for the deep satisfaction that no alien system could efficiently provide.

As for the financial arrangements, the Poll Tax Commissioners did achieve something. In a letter dated December 1869 to Ghartey, Joseph Dawson mentioned that King Otoo of Abura had been commissioned to enter Assin and prepare the people for the payment of a poll tax. The money collected from the regions was sent to Mankessim to the treasury of the Fante nation.[9]

1 Kimble, p. 258

2 F. Wolfson, *British Relations with the Gold Coast 1843–1880*, Ph.D. thesis, University of London, 1950, p. 226

3 Kofi Ackeney to Ghartey, 15 January 1869, Ghartey Papers

4 Otoo to Ghartey, 1 and 5 July 1869, Ghartey Papers

5 Letter to Ghartey, 6 July 1869, Ghartey Papers   6 *Ibid.*, 9 July 1869

7 Eshun to Ghartey, 9 July 1869, Kormantine, Ghartey Papers

8 Letter to Ghartey, 28 August 1869, Ghartey Papers

9 Dawson to Ghartey, 22 December 1869, Mankessim, Ghartey Papers

Further, the following documents are to be found among Ghartey's papers.[1]

6 July 1869 Colonial Government in Accounts with Fante Confederacy CR.

    26 June–1 July £19. 0. 0.
    26 June–1 July £11. 4. 0

Also:

1871 Fante Confederacy Dr. in accounts with Ghartey Bros £117. 18. 10.

Scanty though they are, these figures seem to confirm what we already know, namely, that the Confederacy had a good start in financial matters precisely because the people were ready to promote the cause of the Confederate Government by paying their taxes promptly. The proceeds of the taxes paid by the districts were expended on various items ranging from hammock fees to salaries for Government officials. By 1871 the taxes must have declined with the general enthusiasm for the cause of the Confederacy, and so the wealthy Ghartey brothers had to finance almost entirely the day-to-day administration of the Government. Financial success was therefore only moderate.

The Fante plan to control Elmina has always been considered a failure from the start. But this is incorrect. The Fante cause in Elmina was in fact gaining the upper hand before 1870 when, suddenly, the tide changed and Asante influence replaced that of the Fante.

First of all, the Fante tried to build a party in Elmina to promote Fante interests against those of Asante and the Dutch. The initiative for building a pro-Fante party was taken by the educated Africans in the early part of 1868, when they first wrote to the people of Elmina. The following year, we find George Blankson of Anomabu continuing this exchange of communications with J. J. Molenaan and G. E. Emissang of Elmina.

Molenaan and Emissang expressed regret in their letter to Blankson that because of 'native custom', the head people of Elmina had not as yet given their opinion about the proposed armistice. Their attitude was exactly like that of Blankson himself, who on 7 August 1869 replied to his correspondents, asking to be informed as to 'the cases on which the peoples of Elmina are willing to come to terms with the Fante' and promising that he would do all in his power 'to effect so desirable an object'.[2] These communications reveal a growing desire and indeed a practical increase in Fante–Elmina cooperation. No wonder when Kennedy went there on 27 October 1868 and formally laid the Fante proposals before the town, we are told that 'the educated and intelligent portion of the Elminas' unanimously concurred.

Significantly enough, it was not just the educated Africans but also the *asafo* who were won over to the Fante side in Elmina. This was clearly illustrated by the general behaviour of the *asafo*. For instance, when the Fante besieged Elmina in the early part of 1868, it is said that the people of the town would not act except in self-defence. They regarded resistance as a 'white man's palaver' and expressed a disinclination to act or to involve themselves in a war with the Fante. Ussher further reported that the few volunteers from Elmina who went to fight the Fante in Komenda returned after a few days, having given

1 *Ibid.*   2 Molenaan and Emissang to Blankson, August 1869, Ghartey Papers

their arms back into store and declined to fight any more.[1] There is a clear evidence, therefore, that even among the *asafo* the Fante cause was gaining the upper hand.

But a final achievement of a Fante–Elmina alliance was thwarted by subsequent events. First, the Dutch in Elmina led by Colonel Boers, probably in collaboration with Asante agents, were determined to prevent it on the grounds that such an alliance would isolate Asante, where they were at this time recruiting labourers and soldiers for their settlements (Java) in the East Indies.[2] The second event was the despatch, by the Asantehene, of Akyeampon as envoy from Kumasi with full powers to reorganise the Asante party in Elmina.[3] In face of this renewed Asante activity, the Fante cause suffered a severe decline. This was why the Fante Confederacy was unable to achieve an alliance with Elmina, but it had come very near to it.

In 1868, therefore, the Fante were doing well and there was every hope of success. The Confederacy was so sure of final success that as early as March 1868 the Fante began to think of declaring self-government. Their wishes could be understood from the numerous acts of disobedience in which they indulged at this time. In Cape Coast, right under the guns of the Castle, the people, led by their chief, Quassie Atta, ignored Ussher's orders not to join the Confederate army. One by one they slipped away into the bush to fight against the Netherlands Government.[4] Ussher wrote that in May and June 1868 disturbances reached formidable proportions[5] because of the unflagging secret agitation of the Cape Coast people, who 'are in a most disaffected state and are giving me infinite trouble' and who 'literally defy the law'.[6] Ussher received nothing but disrespect from the Fante; they were defiant in their tone towards him and offensive in their actions; his police were insulted and his proclamations derided.[7]

By June 1868 the Council at Mankessim was reported to have reached resolutions to support and protect themselves, regardless of British interests or protection. From then on educated Africans were known to have discussed the question of self-government publicly. It was this which caused Ussher to complain 'that the Fantees appear from their present tone towards me inclined to throw off British allegiance; they are aided and abetted in their conduct by self-interested mulattoes, who doubtless aspire eventually to the reins of Government should Great Britain abandon her possession'.[8] A month later he made a similar complaint that it was the educated Africans who were giving out 'that the time has come to govern themselves, and to throw off our rule; retaining us here as advisers only'.[9]

There was now clearly a widespread feeling that the entire coast would soon come under the Confederate Government. This was partly shown by the fact

1 Adm. 1/687, no. 21, Ussher to Kennedy, 6 March 1868

2 Adm. 1/461, no. 1, Kennedy to Granville, 11 January 1869

3 See p. 39   4 Adm. 1/687, no. 24, Ussher to Kennedy, 19 March 1868

5 *Ibid.*, no. 52, 18 May 1868   6 *Ibid.*, no. 60, 7 June 1868

7 *Ibid.*, no. 24, 19 March 1868

8 *Ibid.* Ussher was of course exaggerating about the 'self-interested mulattoes'.

9 Adm. 1/687, no. 32, Ussher to Kennedy, 6 April 1868

that the hitherto 'loyal mulattoes' were now afraid to support the Government openly.[1] In August it happened. The Fante, Ussher wrote, 'are bold enough to reject and deny our right of interference in peace and war, in other words they throw off our allegiance'. In the same despatch he said: 'Our relations with the interior, for the present at least have ceased – and there remains now only the supervision of our trading posts along the sea-board.'[2] Obviously the Fante felt that the Confederate Government was strong enough to take over responsibility for Fante affairs.

In military matters, too, the Fante displayed great energy. The manner in which the Confederate army was employed was carefully thought out. There were official representatives of the Confederate Government in the various districts. These officials were responsible, among other things, for assessing the military needs of the districts they represented. Among these representatives were H. J. Clement in Armantin, for Eastern Wassa,[3] Davison, Kodjo Kwenin and Abraham Simmon in Dadiaso for Sefwi and the north-western districts, and J. Johnson and others representing Mampon district. It was these officials who, as well as the kings of the various divisions, were authorised to make out requests for military assistance for the districts.[4]

The representatives worked with utmost zeal. In August 1869, for instance, Davison and the other officials in Dadiaso (extreme west of southern Ghana) wrote to King Attah of Anomabu urging him to help in the supply of troops to the Sefwi region. 'Our object', they continued, 'is to beg your Majesty to put your head together with King Anfoo Otoo . . . and you send us about 500 armed men each of you'; this aid they sought so that their labours in the past two years would not be in vain.[5] Towards the end of 1869 and early in 1870 similar urgent requests were made from the town of Armantin in Eastern Wassa by H. J. Clement, the Confederacy official, and from Duamina Enemil, the King of Wassa himself.[6]

These requests for military assistance were met with equal zeal. The Fante kings, chiefs and officials met at Mankessim and decided that Boribori Ammanfoo and Nkusukum, Gomoah, Akyem, Assin, Abura, Akumfi and Anomabu should provide 500 troops each, to be despatched to Wassa. Even though recruitment did not go well, mainly due to other engagements of these states, they all strove hard to fulfil the mission, which the King of Wassa described as very sacred, and to promote the interest which 'is a general one like ours which does not belong to one tribe'.[7]

The Fante plan of war was carefully drawn up: as far as possible they would

1 *Ibid.*, no. 24, 19 March 1868   2 *Ibid.*, no. 93, 7 August 1868

3 Clement to Ghartey, 3 February 1870, Armantin, Eastern Wassa, Ghartey Papers

4 Davison, Kodjo Kwenin and Abraham Simmon to King Attah, 19 August 1869, Ghartey Papers. It appears the Confederate Council, apart from its own direct appointments, encouraged local men to act in a semi-official capacity. D. Amissah, for instance, seems to be an inhabitant of Wassa, and a semi-official correspondent of the Confederacy (Amissah to Ghartey, 1 February 1870, Ghartey Papers). Apart from the three correspondents from Dadiaso, Isaac Gibbs, Joseph Johnson, John Quashe (lawyers) were stationed by the Confederacy in the Mampon district. (Letter dated Mampon, 23 December 1869) Joe Dawson was apparently a travelling Commissioner. He sent reports from Kissi, Birasi, Daribuassi, etc. between May and December 1869.

5 *Ibid.*   6 Duamina Enemil to Fante Kings, 25 January 1870, Armantin, Ghartey Papers

7 *Ibid.*, 27 January 1870

employ the Confederate army to take Komenda and Elmina from the Dutch and establish Fante control along the entire coast of the Western Districts. Simultaneously the interior districts, especially those bordering Asante, were to be encouraged to organise their own defences without military support from the Confederacy, except in real crises, such as fears of an impending Asante invasion.[1] As soon as the Confederacy mastered the sea-board towns, the greater portion of the national army was to be sent to strengthen the defence measures of the outlying districts, particularly in Sefwi,[2] which Asante invading forces often used on occasions such as this. The making of this plan was a great achievement and had there not been obstacles in its operation the Confederate army would have achieved total victory.

Total victory was, in fact, expected from a national army that fought so valiantly. On 24 February 1868 King Otoo of Abura, at the head of the Fante army, hastened to bring military help to the people of Komenda, who were trying to prevent the Dutch occupation of their town. This help gave the Komendas a great advantage. Their geographical position provided other advantages. They had a convenient retreat in Komenda Bush, where Kissi Krom,[3] at the top of a slight incline some twelve miles inland, served as an ideal stronghold against enemy fire. Here in Komenda Bush they were sure of safety for their women and children in times of crisis. Thanks to these advantages, especially the assistance given by Otoo's forces, Komenda was able to put up a gallant resistance; the aggressive Dutch were held at bay and their sea power was rendered ineffective. Before the end of March the Fante forced Colonel Boers and the Dutch to abandon Komenda unconditionally. The Confederate army then completely surrounded the Dutch.[4] Meanwhile local troops of the north-western districts, especially those in Wassa, organised their own defences as best they could.[5] On the whole, therefore, we may conclude that the Fante allies did their best and were as close to military victory as possible, during the early wars of the Fante Confederacy.

But soon the tide began to turn. Towards the end of 1868 Colonel Boers, after abandoning Komenda, decided to concentrate his energy on the defence of Elmina. Fort Coenraadsburg on St Jago Hill and the defence works and redoubts[6] were hurriedly built or rebuilt to safeguard the headquarters. In addition, the Dutch managed at this time to get the Shamas to swell the ranks of their troops in Elmina.[7] Thus when the Fante forces launched an attack on Elmina at the close of 1868, they could not make much headway. The war degenerated into skirmishes, which frequently occurred in the Fante villages near Elmina.[8]

1 Clement to Ghartey, 3 February 1870, Armantin, Eastern Wassa, Ghartey Papers

2 Davison, Kodjo Kwenin and Abraham Simmon to King Attah, 19 August 1869, Ghartey Papers

3 Kissi Krom is now simply Kissi and has a very difficult approach, although the old Cape Coast–Takoradi road passed through it.

4 Adm. 1/687, no. 32, Ussher to Kennedy, 6 April 1868, C.C.

5 Clement to Ghartey, 3 February 1870, Armantin, Eastern Wassa, Ghartey Papers

6 These include Fort Nagtglas. The Dutch watchtower was also improved and put to use. Several of the outforts around Coenraadsburg were rebuilt to protect the town.

7 Dawson to Ghartey, 13 November 1869, Kissi, Ghartey Papers

8 These villages were Mamna and Abna (not entirely Fante).

The failure to take Elmina made the full implementation of the Fante war plan impossible. Troops could not be sent to distant parts of the country while the national army was still trying to take Elmina by storm. The war effort consequently began to tail off, but the Fante army kept at it till the close of 1872, when it ceased all operations, having failed to achieve its main objective, the occupation of Elmina.

The nature of the reaction of Asante and the British to the Fante Confederacy indicates clearly that it was a movement to be reckoned with. In Asante there was considerable concern over Fante affairs.[1] The Asante court came to the conclusion that if the Fante Confederate Government really intended to take over Elmina, as was then being rumoured by Asante traders from the coast, then it was time for them to act. First, the Asantehene sent messengers, early in 1868, to collect information about the coast. The Fante chiefs informed these messengers that there was 'no Governor now, and Fantes ruled the Coast'.[2] The Asantehene took fright at this, for if the Fante came to control the coast, then Asante would have a great deal of trouble from the coastal states. This was why Asante was hostile to the Confederacy and we shall see in the next chapter how they tried to counteract the movement.

The British, too, were positively hostile and decided to reassert their influence over the 'Protectorate'. The traditional means of self-assertion at their disposal consisted mainly of subverting traditional authority. A favourite technique of doing this was to give active support to one king against another. In Apollonia the British supported King Amacki against Chief Affoo; in Adjumako they supported King Hommah against Chief Mooquah (1868).[3] It was because they wanted to increase their own influence over the people in place of that of the Fante Confederacy that the British abolished, in 1867, the position of king in Cape Coast. Thus in April of that year Governor Blackall himself came all the way from Sierra Leone and supervised the installation of Quassie Attah as successor to Aggrey, insisting that he should be regarded only as headman, not king, of Cape Coast. He also took great pains to explain to the people that the duties of the new ruler were to be confined to passing on information from the Colonial Government to the people. The people did not accept this, and continued to treat Attah as king, but the British, too, were insistent that he should never enjoy the powers of Aggrey.[4]

When these methods of destroying the influence of the Fante Confederacy were found to be ineffective, Kennedy began, in May 1868, to make a series of suggestions which involved the use of more subtle methods. These methods included paying subsidies to the kings and chiefs to soften them,[5] directing their patriotic feelings[6] and exploiting their differences.

In May 1869 Governor Simpson went to Mankessim to carry out Kennedy's suggestions. He humoured the chiefs and played on their differences, planting

1 Adm. 1/687, no. 24, Ussher to Kennedy, 19 March 1868

2 *Ibid.*, no. 52, 18 May 1868

3 Adm. 1/687, no. 22, Ussher to Blackall, 29 April 1867

4 Adm. 1/461, no. 20, Blackall to Buckingham, 5 April 1867

5 Adm. 1/461, no. 24, Kennedy to Granville, 25 January 1869

6 Adm. 1/461, no. 38, Kennedy to Buckingham, 29 May 1868

seeds of discord among them. He told them that the Fante were right and the local Government wrong about Elmina,[1] that the Government was also wrong in carrying out the interchange without consulting the people. It was all right for the chiefs to have a council of war, but a council to regulate the internal affairs of the Fante state was a different matter. What powers, he asked, would the kings resign in favour of such a council? What were the rules or articles of union? Also implied in his address was the question, 'Who was to be the head of the entire Fante nation?' Simpson made sure that he fanned the dormant petty jealousies among the chiefs into life, and this went a long way to destroy the Confederacy.[2] In June Simpson was still pursuing his techniques of breaking up the Fante Confederacy.[3]

After these minor reactions the British planned extensive changes in response to the Fante protests. These changes involved a change in policy, from non-intervention to extension. The Fante Confederacy thus affected the formulation of British policy on the Gold Coast. This is discussed in the next chapter.

Although Fante protests had this important effect on British policy, the Confederacy came to an end in 1873. There were several reasons for its collapse. First of all, the failure of the military forces to take Elmina adversely affected the Sefwi and the Western Districts, through which Akyeampong led his Asante followers into Elmina in the middle of 1869.

Another important failure of the Confederacy was financial. In wartime the districts within the jurisdiction of the Confederate Government could not pursue peaceful trade, and so found it difficult to pay the poll taxes levied on them. Thus the Fante Government became short of money. An attempt was made in 1871 to revive the financial position and the Fante planned to levy tolls on trade passing through Mankessim to the coast,[4] and before the end of 1871 it was reported that the King of Mankessim was in fact already levying such taxes.[5] But again this failed because of British hostility. The British realised that the control of trade by the Fante would check British efforts to push trade into the interior. So Salmon, determined as he was to destroy the 1871 plans of the Confederacy, arrested and imprisoned all the members of the Executive Council except Grant, together with nine other prominent Africans.[6] The new financial plans of the Fante thus collapsed, even though the members arrested were soon released.

This doomed the Confederacy to failure. In 1872, its leaders made fresh plans for the better administration of the districts under its government, but the Fante still needed money to carry out their plans.[7] They appealed to the Cape Coast authorities for financial assistance in vain. In 1873 when the Asante

---

1 Simpson meant that the Fante desire to have an alliance with Elmina was the result of the British warning in 1864, that they should prepare to defend themselves against future attacks from Asante. Without Elmina their defence would be weak. It is also possible that he was hoping that if the British succeeded in getting Elmina to enter the proposed alliance, then the Fante could feel grateful to them and change their attitude towards the local British Government.

2 Adm. 1/687, no. 43, encl. in Simpson to Kennedy, 5 May 1869

3 Adm. 1/687, no. 53, Simpson to Kennedy, 7 June 1869

4 Adm. 1/462, no. 128, Kennedy to Kimberley, 6 December 1871   5 Kimble, p. 251

6 Wolfson, p. 228   7 Metcalfe, p. 342

invasion threatened the coast, the Confederacy once again asked for a loan to maintain their troops in camp, but R. W. Harley, the Administrator, ignored this request.[1] Unable to solve their financial problems in the face of British and Asante hostility, the Fante rulers found it impossible to continue their efforts towards a united Fanteland. They reverted to separatism, and by June 1873, the Confederacy came to an end.

Although the Fante Confederacy was short-lived, while it lasted, it was a movement to be reckoned with. The whole of the Fante nation was combined under one government, whose status carried great weight and influence amongst the people of the interior. 'It is', said Horton, 'the pivot of national unity; headed by intelligent men, to whom a great deal of the powers of the Kings and Chiefs are delegated. . . . The Fante [he concluded], could now boast of a National Assembly in which have congregated not only various kings and chiefs in scattered provinces, far and wide, but also the intellgence of Fanteland.'[2]

The Confederacy was a protonationalist movement, which sought to achieve internal self-government, security and progress for the Gold Coast. It was a carefully planned and organised movement. In this respect, even though it lacked modern techniques, the Fante Confederacy was a forerunner of modern Ghanaian nationalism. No wonder it caused the British to change their policy on the Gold Coast. The next chapter is devoted to a discussion of the influence of this incipient Gold Coast nationalism on British policy.

1 Kimble, p. 261   2 Horton to Granville, 2 May 1870, C.C.C.

CHAPTER TWO

Britain, Asante and the Protectorate

The change of heart

The Fante Confederacy was the first major protest movement to affect the formulation of British policy on the Gold Coast. In fact, the important decisions of that policy taken during the period 1868–74, such as the acquisition of Elmina and the establishment of the Colony and Protectorate (1874), were to a large extent the result of the Confederacy.

Before the Fante uprising British policy towards the Gold Coast was conservative. Local British authorities were anxious not to involve themselves too deeply in tribal conflicts; and in 1865 they actually warned the Fante that in future they would have to fight Asante without British support. Government officials in London, too, were against extension of territory on the Coast. There was clearly an anti-imperialist movement in Britain led by such important members of Government and Parliament as C. B. Adderley, Lord Stanley, Sir John Hay and Arthur Mills. These influenced Government as well as Parliament with the result that in the early 1860s there was general support for the policy of non-extension on the West Coast.[1]

But then came the Fante Confederacy. In the first place, the Confederacy threatened the economic position of the British traders on the Gold Coast. The Fante plans of 1871 to streamline their financial arrangements, as we have seen,[2] threatened to check British efforts to penetrate the interior for trade. Had the trade of the Gold Coast still been in decline, as in the 1850s, British authorities would probably not have been concerned about the economic activities of the Fante. But during the period 1867–74, trade was brisk and prosperous. The settlement was in 1870 not only self-supporting, but had a surplus of about £13,000,[3] the revenue and expenditure returns for the quarter ended 31 March 1870 having shown a credit balance of £12,421.[4] By April £3956 10s 9d in gold dust was forwarded to the Agents General to be placed at the credit of the settlement.[5] By July the Gold Coast had a credit balance of £17,000.[6] The following year, 1871, the total receipts for custom dues alone and the credit balance of the Colony were expected to reach the £26,000 and

---

1 J. D. Hargreaves, *Prelude to the Partition of West Africa*, London 1963, pp. 65–9

2 See p. 32   3 Adm. 1/462, no. 31, Kennedy to Granville, 23 March 1870

4 *Ibid.*, no. 56, 28 April 1870   5 *Ibid.*, no. 54, 27 April 1870

6 Adm. 1/687, no. 86, Financial, Ussher to Kennedy, 7 July 1870

the £20,000 mark respectively.[1] This increase in net revenue seems to have continued into 1873, when the total revenue of £65,706 18s 4¾d was collected, in spite of disturbances resulting from the Asante invasion of that year, and a net income of £21,641 12s 1¼d realised.[2]

This growing prosperity had spectacular results on British relations in the settlement. British officials like Ussher, the Administrator, and Kennedy, his superior in Sierra Leone, were delighted about this turn of affairs on the Coast, and compiled glowing reports of its prosperous condition for the Colonial Office.[3] In this way the British developed a very strong attachment for the Gold Coast and therefore took economic threats of the Fante Confederacy very seriously.

The Fante Confederacy also showed up the weakness of British political control on the Gold Coast. The lack of legal basis for such control[4] constituted a serious weakness in their position, and they knew it. When, therefore, the Fante suddenly decided to take over the exercise of political control in the 'Protectorate', this weakness was again forcefully in evidence. British concern was expressed by Kennedy when he wrote about the 1871 Confederacy: 'Our peculiar position in regard to territorial rights at the Gold Coast is of course well known to the promoters of this foolish and mischievous project and renders it difficult to deal with them legally.'[5]

The British were therefore very much worried about the political and economic implications of the Fante Confederacy. British officials consequently decided to change their policy of non-extension to an active policy of intervention in the politics of the Coast and to undertake the extension of British influence into the interior.

We have several illustrations of this change in policy. The first was the aggressive manner in which the British attacked the educated Africans on the Gold Coast, the destruction of whose power was, they argued, a necessary step towards increasing their control of the Coast. Kennedy advocated stringent measures against the educated Africans,[6] amounting to destroying their public image.

The Administrator on the Gold Coast, too, consulted Blankson in the hope of discovering the best means of weakening the power of the educated Africans. 'The important matters' on which he sought advice are indicated in a letter to Blankson: 'I am much annoyed about all the palavers re confederation.'[7] The British continued to study the problem of the 'educated natives' as a necessary step to increasing their own power.[8]

---

1 *Ibid.*, no. 127, 16 September 1870

2 Enclosure in C.921 of March 1874, Wolseley to Kimberley, 3 March 1874, C.C.C. Further correspondence respecting the Ashanti Invasion (London March 1874)

3 Adm. 1/462, no. 31, Kennedy to Granville, 23 March 1870   4 See p. 2

5 Adm. 1/462, no. 14, Kennedy to Kimberley, 9 January 1871

6 *Ibid.*, no. 104, October 1870 and no. 74, 25 July 1870

7 G.N.A., Blankson Papers, SC 1/13

8 Private papers reveal that at this time, the Administrator was very carefully studying the movement. This can be seen in his anxiously requesting the attendance of the Fante chiefs at Cape Coast on or before Saturday 5 January 1872, 'to sit with the judge in order that the views you entertain with respect to the new Confederation may be heard at the trial'. G.N.A., Blankson Papers, SC 1/13

A second illustration of the change in British policy was their desire to open up the country, which stood in clear contrast to their earlier policy of retrenchment. As early as 1870 Kennedy initiated efforts towards opening up the country by roads as suggested by Fitzgerald of *The African Times*. There were problems of porterage, sanitation, etc. which Kennedy tried to solve. He introduced wheelbarrows, and he tamed cattle as beasts of burden to solve the problem of porterage. He also forbade intramural burial so as to raise the standard of sanitation which was so important if Europeans were to be encouraged to reside inland. Although he failed to solve these problems, it was certainly not for want of trying.[1]

A third sign of the British change of policy was the way they cajoled the Fante. As early as 1869 Simpson went to Mankessim to begin what he called the policy of reconciliation. After Simpson, the British decided that the best way to increase their power in the country was to support, and then take over completely, the Fante Confederacy programme of activities against Asante. This was because the Fante programme was designed to give anyone who carried it out considerable power over the 'Protectorate'; and rather than wait to see themselves ousted by the increase in Fante power, the British decided to increase their own power, employing the Fante method. This Fante programme consisted of measures for terminating Asante commercial and political influence, which was increasing in the 'Protectorate' at this time. The British tried to increase their power by interfering in the dispute at every turn with the intention gradually to take over entirely the Fante side of the dispute.

For instance, early in the Confederacy period, Asante tried hard to maintain a trade route through Wassa. Both Wassa and Denkyira asked the Dutch for help against Asante. Shoemaker in his *Lastste Bladzijde onzer Nederlandsch West-Afrikaansche Historie* asserts that when they failed to get this help they rejected Dutch protection, thus paving the way for Anglo-Fante cooperation. The British did give them the help they wanted, for the King of Wassa later explained that he preferred the British connection to that of the Dutch, because of the support that the British had given him against Asante.[2]

Early in 1870 Governor Nagtglas of Elmina reported that in 1868 the Fante had committed an outrageous attack on one hundred Elminas accompanied by some Asante on the banks of the Prah, on their way back from the funeral of the King of Asante. The Elminas were driven back and robbed of 200 ounces of gold. The King of Asante had to send them back escorted by 150 Asante through Krinjabo.[3] The Fante were believed to be the aggressors, not only in this incident, but also in other parts of the 'Protectorate'; the result was, as Elmina Castle authorities maintained: 'Asante traders haven't been at Cape Coast since (1868), and bought their needs mostly at Grand Bassam and Assinie.'[4]

1 Adm. 1/462, no. 113, Kennedy to Kimberley, 2 November 1870

2 K.V.G. 727, Report Res. Adj. Le Jeune to Gov. Boers (Mission to Wassa) Amantsin, 19 February 1868

3 K.V.G. 728, Memo Nagtglas to Kennedy, 7 March 1870. See also Afst. IV, BZ/B79, 20 May 1871. Land P.L., Conference of Dutch Govt., Negro Govt. and Ashanti Deputation

4 B.B.P., Nagtglas to Min. of Colonies, 26 March 1871, p. 46

The British supported the Fante in this aggression. Shoemaker, for instance, was definite that the outburst of Fante activities in this period gave England 'a good opportunity to give more air to the fire of war, through lies and clever use of general nervosity'.[1] When the Asantehene attempted in 1871 to get the central trade route, which was so effectively blockaded by the Fante, opened, the English Administrator at Cape Coast did no more than request the Asante messengers to inform the King that the territory between the Prah and the sea would hence forward be unsafe for the King and his subjects, because, he added quite unnecessarily, its inhabitants had already captured many Asante.[2]

Apart from the central trade route, Asante traders had often in the past resorted to the western route which took them through Krinjabo to Grand Bassam, Assinie and also to the western ports in the Gold Coast, the most important of which was Elmina itself. The Fante plan was to win over the inhabitants of these ports to the Confederacy. This involved persistent persecution, not only of Asante traders in the Western Districts, but also of pro-Asante inhabitants residing in the ports. The Fante did not stop short of any means which could weaken the Asante partisans throughout the 'Dutch' possessions.

Early in 1869, for instance, the Fante states took a drastic step to weaken the morale of Asante partisans. Since the development of Elmina into the Dutch headquarters, with its consequent increase in population, the town had always depended on the importation of corn from Apollonia, to supplement the yield from the Elmina countryside. A brisk coastwise trade thus grew between the port of Elmina and the westernmost towns of 'Dutch' Guinea, very much like the early twentieth-century developments in the eastern part of the Gold Coast. This trade often went by sea, as the land route along the shore presented difficulties. To demoralise Asante traders, who in spite of the difficulties of the road found their way into Elmina from time to time, seventy-seven Fante chiefs from such places as Watjekrom and Annamaboe decided to disrupt the coastwise trade with a view to causing famine in Elmina and its satellite communities. They sent thirty-three messengers to the peoples of Wassa to apprise them of this new technique of mitigating Asante influence. Two of these messengers proceeded to Affoo, the King of Atuabo, with letters detailing instructions to the effect that no corn should be exported from Apollonia to Elmina. The letters also warned that Affoo and his followers should not permit Asante to pass along their beach road to Elmina. Affoo must fight against those supporting the Dutch and Asante. As proof of his loyalty to the Fante cause he must cut off the heads of the 'enemy'.

The British in Cape Coast encouraged these developments. King Affoo, in consequence, rejected the Dutch flag, saying that the territory from Ewinnoe to near Axim all belonged to the British. A Dutch merchant at Beyin, Reintjes van Veersen, who witnessed this flouting of Dutch authority, reported how King Affoo 'gives me 24 hours time to leave, with my goods, under safe conduct'.[3] Further attempts, which the British most certainly supported, to disrupt Asante trade along the sea coast were the conspiracy which the Dixcoveans

1 J. P. Shoemaker, *Lastste Bladzijde onzer Nederlandsch West-Afrikaansche Historie*, Hertogenbosch, 1900

2 BZ/B79, Afst. IV, 20 May 1871

3 K.V.G. 727, Ass. st. Apollonia – distr. Reintjes van Veerssen, Fort Willem III, Behien, to Gov. Boers, 23 March 1869

entered into with the Wassas (professing English alliance) to step up destructive activities on the western sea-board. They chased Elminese canoes, they blocked the road to Accodah, hoisted the English flag and imprisoned three Bousuah people.[1] So serious was the situation that the Dutch Commandant at Dixcove had to control the passage of people from the surrounding villages into 'Bossuah'.[2]

Naturally, British traders in Cape Coast were involved in this dispute, and it would appear that their sympathies were on the side of British colonial authorities who were busily supporting the Fante effort against Asante and the Dutch. A Cape Coast merchant, William Cleaver, for instance, had as his representative stationed in Dixcove none other than Mensah, who was an unflinching champion of the cause of Wassas, Komendas and Fante. In a letter to Cleaver, W. E. Sam of Dixcove explained that Mensah, 'being a Fantee man here to represent you, and you not having good feelings towards the Elmina people', was suspected by the Dixcoveans of selling gunpowder to the Wassa people.[3]

In the past, when such outbreaks of disorder occurred on the trade routes, Asante resorted first to diplomacy and negotiation to get round the states involved in these outbreaks. Only when the peaceful methods of negotiation failed did the Asantehene resort to arms. Thus the first phase of Asante's attempts to solve the questions raised by Anglo–Fante conduct in relation to the trade routes was peaceful, and consisted mainly of the creation of Asante 'parties' in the Protectorate. Reports available in Dutch records indicate that small bands of Asante messengers, passing up and down along the coastal routes under Dutch protection, were to be seen in the coast towns. It would seem that these were busy creating Asante parties. In particular, the Elmina canoemen were now hand in glove with Asante. Since the land communication between Apollonia and Elmina was strewn with Fante activists, it was perhaps necessary for Asante traders and messengers to travel by sea to Elmina, and these canoemen would be invaluable in this exercise. The cooperation which these canoemen received from the Dutch Commandant of Apollonia further encouraged them. When Cleaver of F. & A. Swanzy visited the area early in 1870, no doubt to inspect his firm's establishments there in these disturbed times, the canoemen actually threatened him with death, demanding a ransom,[4] for what, it is not clear. But the documents leave us in no doubt that both the Fante and the Asante sides, the one supported by the English and the other by the Dutch, were trying to outdo each other in diplomacy, which because of the grimness of the situation, appears to have involved both sides in some underhand activities – treachery, secret arrests, even murders. We know of the case of King Edoo's relation, who was guilty of murdering an Asante in one of the western ports.[5] Early in 1870 one of these Asante messengers was captured by Fante spies and handed over to Administrator Simpson in Cape Coast, who forced information out of him.[6] And now we learn that the Elmina men had

1 K.V.G. 727, Memo by Alvarez, 27 June 1869

2 K.V.G. 727, Report Res. Adj. Le Jeune to Gov. Boers (Mission to Wassa) Amantsin, 19 February 1868

3 K.V.G. 727 (n.d.)   4 K.V.G. 728, Simpson to Nagtglas, 10 January 1870

5 *Ibid.*, 25 October 1869   6 *Ibid.*, 13 January 1870

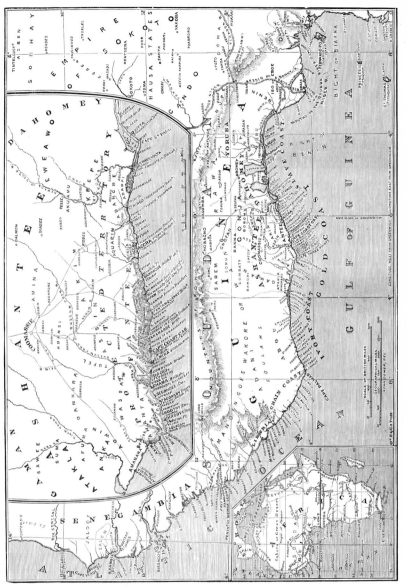

1 Maps of Africa, Guinea and the Gold Coast c. 1873

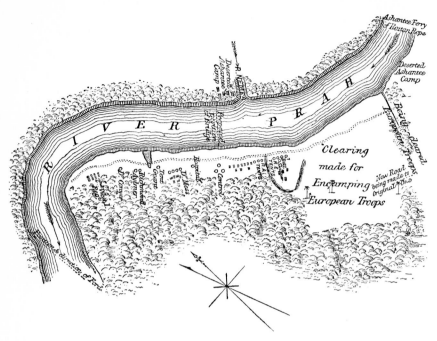

2 a) Sketch map of the British camp on the River Prah during the war of 1873-4
  b) The bombardment of the town of Elmina 1873

3 Stations on the road to Kumasi: (l to r) Accroful, Assin, Sutah and Bereku

4 a) Attah, King of Akyem, greets the British Commissioners, 1873
b) Reading the Queen's letter at the palaver of kings, Accra 1873. General view of the meeting: 1 kings' umbrellas 2 umbrella tent of Special Commissioner and staff 3 kings' drums 4 retinue of armed men 5 table in front of Special Commissioner on which Queen's letter is laid 6 guard of 200 Hausas 7 Fort James 8 lighthouse

cause to threaten Cleaver's life. In circumstances where the western ports were swarming with Fante activists and spies, it cannot be expected that the Asante envoys sent to create parties in these ports could avoid the use of similar methods. This must not blind us to the fact that it was diplomacy that they were expected to use.

Presently, to coordinate the activities of these envoys, Akyeampon was appointed to the post of chief envoy and sent down to Elmina, which was thus raised to the status of an Asante diplomatic headquarters in the 'Protectorate' instead of the traditional Abura,[1] now out of bounds to the Asante, and the messengers were expected to report to him. This was why the Elmina canoe-men, who also shipped corn from Apollonia to Elmina, were so important for the Asante scheme; for these envoys could only communicate with Akyeampon in Elmina by boat. Akyeampon began his career as chief envoy by trying to clear the road between Apollonia and Elmina, a step which had led to much misunderstanding, no doubt, due to the exaggeration of the English records on which writers like Claridge so much depended. Claridge in his *Gold Coast and Ashanti*[2] records that Akyeampon killed innocent Fante in cold blood all along his route of march to Elmina.

But the picture in the Dutch records is quite different. These clearly demonstrate that Akyeampon was sent on a mission of peaceful negotiation. As chief envoy, he was to direct the energies of the smaller messengers in the western ports. These messengers, as we have said, found themselves in circumstances where underhand dealings became absolutely necessary, if they were to perform their task of creating or strengthening Asante parties in these towns. Akyeampon saw for himself what the situation was. As chief envoy his life was in even greater danger than his subordinates. It was in these circumstances that he killed Enkookoo, a Fanteman in Apollonia. It was again these circumstances which compelled him to order the maltreatment of Fante under the Dutch forts, where he lodged.[3] Akyeampon probably killed more Fante, but if he did he was no more guilty than the Fante themselves, whose activities in these parts told a tale of horror. It was therefore inaccurate for Claridge and others to paint Akyeampon as a criminal guilty of murdering innocent Fante in cold blood, his sharp practices on his journey towards Elmina were meant to forestall people who would certainly have got rid of him had they struck first.

Akyeampon's activities in Elmina were similarly misunderstood. British accounts failed to present him as the permanent Asante envoy that he was. Indeed he was represented as a mere adventurer, even though he himself made it absolutely clear that he was expected to remain in Elmina during the pleasure of the Asantehene. Nagtglas, too, wrote that 'Atjempoe Jouw tells that he cannot leave without the orders of the King'.[4] Furthermore, when in June 1871 the Asantehene sent down a deputation to the coast and Nagtglas asked some of its members if Akyeampon could leave with them to Kumasi, they declared

1 See Wilks, *Ashanti Government*. Abora became the headquarters after the Asante defeat of Fante in 1814.

2 Claridge, *A History of the Gold Coast and Ashanti*, Vol. I, pp. 590–2

3 K.V.G. 729, Simpson to Nagtglas, report of complaints of Messrs Cleaver, Dale and Fynn, 10 January 1870

4 K.V.G. 729 (n.d.), Nagtglas, 'General reflections on the year 1869'.

that Akyeampon and their chief had been charged with different missions and therefore they could not leave together for 'Coomassie'.[1] Nagtglas informed the deputation that he had advised the King of Asante several times to recall Akyeampon (no doubt because of pressure from the Fante) but that he had received no answer. This shows clearly that Akyeampon's mission in Elmina was of a more permanent nature than that of the 1871 deputation.

British administrators like Ussher and Kennedy did not understand the nature of Akyeampon's mission, or if they did, they were not prepared to own it. Kennedy reported to the Colonial Office late in 1870 that all Akyeampon was doing in Elmina was instigating the people into disturbances,[2] and subsequent reports both from the Administrator in Cape Coast and from Sierra Leone continued to describe him as fomenting trouble in the neighbourhood of Elmina. One of the reports stated that Akyeampon's people were actually attacking Fante villages adjacent to Elmina. It was on these reports that Claridge and Ward relied so heavily for their description of the role of Akyeampon in the Elmina–Fante dispute.

Yet nothing could be further from the truth. Asante in Elmina were under strict orders, and their task was no less than to provide protection for the Elminas in order to consolidate an Asante party there so that this important port could remain under their influence or at least permit them to trade. The Asante party in Elmina under Akyeampon being charged with specific duties could not misbehave without incurring the anger of the Asantehene. Governor Nagtglas, who had better opportunity than the English of watching the activities of the Asante squad in Elmina, wrote that: 'Although these people [the Asante] behaved well, I must try to make them return to their country, as they form a serious stumbling-block for the peace.' There was therefore no question of their having misbehaved, as the English reports alleged. Nagtglas said exactly what they were doing: 'They protect women, who take water and fruits from the forest, but this gives a continuous cause to disturbances, because the forest people although narrowly related to the Elminas have gone over to the Fantees, out of lack of food.'[3] In this way, at least six to eight thousand people from Elmina bush were compelled by 1871 to join the Fante.[4]

Thus the Fante siege of Elmina, which was seriously disrupting its food supplies, was bound in the long run to lead to the surrender of the Elminas if they received no outside assistance. It was to prevent this that the Asantehene had charged Akyeampon not merely to attend to the diplomatic side of the Elmina–Fante question but also to utilise the small force at his disposal to maintain law and order in Elmina and its neighbourhood, to reorganise the system of food supplies to the town and afford protection to its inhabitants against the Fante. It was this activity that the British officers in Cape Coast from ulterior motives referred to as attacks on Fante villages. Whether the report that Akyeampon

---

1 BZ/B79, Afst. IV, Nagtglas M.v.k. (report) 1 June 1871

2 Adm. 1/461, no. 128, Kennedy to Kimberley, 12 December 1870

3 K.V.G. 729, Nagtglas, 'General Reflections on the year 1869', (no date). In 1869 famine arose because of the Fante blockade and also because supply of food by sea was hampered by the Komendas.

4 K.V.G. 728, (Draft) Nagtglas to Ussher, 20 May 1871

and his Asante were actually robbing the 'Agoonah people's plantation',[1] as Ussher complained to Nagtglas, is true or not, we cannot now know for certain. But in the circumstances of the famished Elminas, such conduct would not be surprising. Certain it is that one of Akyeampon's duties was to help to replenish the town's food supplies.

By the end of 1870 King Kofi Karikari began to sense failure in Elmina and he therefore decided to change his tactics slightly. He had heard that Elmina was to be transferred to the British, and he now laid definite claim to the forts, arguing that the town belonged to him by right.[2] His Excellency Governor Nagtglas spoke of a letter he got from Kumasi in which the King claimed that since time immemorial the fort at Elmina had paid contribution to Asante, that the Dutch had surrendered Elmina to Karikari's ancestor, Osei Tutu I, in exchange of a debt of £9000, and that Elmina was the legal property of the King.[3]

Akyeampon's efforts, coupled with the King's claim, caused the British to take over the Fante programme entirely and they determined to have Elmina ceded to them by the Dutch. In other words the British were now seeking to expand their territories on the Gold Coast.[4] Their action stands in sharp contrast to the pre-Confederacy policy of retrenchment[5] and therefore clearly illustrated how the Confederacy affected the formulation of British policy.

From November 1870 Kennedy began to make a series of urgent requests to Colonel Nagtglas, insisting on the removal of Akyeampon and his followers from Elmina,[6] so as to make transfer feasible. It was not until March 1872, however, that Akyeampon was finally expelled, but throughout this whole period, Kennedy kept on pressing Nagtglas to remove him. Between January and October 1871 he wrote no less than five despatches on the subject, blaming Nagtglas for not expelling Akyeampon earlier.[7] There were other obstacles to the cession, one of them the Asante claim to Elmina, made before the close of 1870. Kennedy strove hard, on the instructions of the Colonial Office, to get this claim quashed by the Dutch and his main concern was to get Colonel Nagtglas to state that 'the King of Ashanti has no recognised claim upon the territory or people of Elmina'.[8]

Similarly Ussher, the Administrator in Cape Coast, also made great efforts to get the Dutch authorities in Elmina to prepare the townsmen for the extension of British protection over them.[9] In marked contrast to the ideas of retrenchment expressed by the British in 1865, when they warned the Fante that they would have to defend themselves against Asante, Ussher, in the spirit of

1 K.V.G. 728, Ussher to Nagtglas, 17 January 1871

2 Coombs, 'The place of the "Certificate of Apologie" in Ghanaian History', *T.H.S.G.* Vol. III, part 3, 1958

3 BZ/B79, Afst. IV, Nagtglas to Karikari, 21 May 1871. See p. 46

4 Furley Collections   5 See p. 34

6 Adm. 1/462, no. 126, Kennedy to Kimberley, 28 November 1870

7 Adm. 1/462, no. 2, Kennedy to Kimberley, 2 January 1871 and no. 12, 11 January 1871

8 *Ibid.*, no. 6, 2 January 1871

9 Adm. 1/462, no. 116, Ussher to Kennedy, 4 December 1870

the new British policy, boldly addressed a meeting of kings, chiefs and people of Elmina (4 December 1870): 'You will receive complete protection against all and any enemies who may attack and molest you, no matter who they be.'[1]

Other events showed that British West Coast authorities were leaving no stones unturned to get Elmina and the Western Districts. Dutch sources maintain that the British officials in Cape Coast in 1870 were actually urging the Fante to capture Elmina and the fort.[2] British authorities on the Coast devoted their attention to removing all obstacles in their way of getting Elmina. The people of Elmina themselves were opposed to the transfer, for the Fante party there had dwindled, giving place to the Asante party built up by Akyeampon. Because of this opposition, Nagtglas wrote to Ussher: 'If the transfer may occur, I suppose, I should advise to have a convoy of men of war at your disposal.'[3] Bartels, a 'highly intelligent native gentleman of Elmina', gives us accounts which suggest that local opposition to cession must be gathering fast. He reported that there was dissent at meetings held in Elmina over the question of transfer.[4] What is more the King and elders of Elmina sent a petition to the Minister of Colonies in Holland, protesting against transfer.[5] Clearly, therefore, there was considerable resistance on the Coast to cession; the British nevertheless continued to press for it. This shows clearly that the change to an active policy of intervention on the Coast was really radical.

It was not only events on the Coast which illustrate the change in British policy. There is a clear evidence that H.M. Government in Britain had also changed its mind about the Gold Coast. In the pre-Confederacy period, colonial officials in London had conducted a conservative policy towards the Gold Coast. They had definitely opposed extension of territory. They had been afraid of heavy financial commitments. They had been afraid of involvement in Asante wars. Officials in London formulated the same caution towards other countries in Africa. But the Fante uprising on the Gold Coast clearly caused them to have a change of heart as the anxiety of the Colonial Office, for instance, to effect the cession of Elmina and to increase their territorial commitments on the Gold Coast shows.

As early as 1869 the British Colonial Office became convinced that the best way to deal with the explosive situation on the Gold Coast, created by the Fante Confederacy and the growth of Asante influence in the Western Districts, was to take over the Dutch possessions and establish British political power firmly over the entire Coast. In November 1869, therefore, the Colonial Office made a formal request to the Netherlands Government for the cession of Elmina to Britain. British officials pressed the Netherlands Minister for the Colonies so much so that he agreed to direct the Governor of Elmina to use 'toute son influence persuasive pour fair partir le chef Ashantee Atjiempon'.[6]

1 Adm. 1/462, no. 128, Kennedy to Kimberley, 12 December 1870

2 BZ/3002, Nagtglas to Min. of Col., 8 August 1870

3 K.V.G. 728, Nagtglas (private) to Ussher, 4 August 1870

4 Adm. 1/462, no. 6, Kennedy to Kimberley, 2 January 1871

5 BZ/3002, 8 August 1870. This 'Negro Petition' was signed by the King of Elmina, X Kobbena Edgen (Groot-Vaandrig), X Kobbena Emesang Bye-ssoefoe, X Eccra Kwakoe Terregant, and X Kwakoe Bontje in the presence of P. Alvarez (Resident), P. Hamed (Asst. Teacher), Le Jeune (Sec.), and Seen Nagtglas.

6 Adm. 1/462, no. 18, Kennedy to Kimberley, 25 January 1871

The British were so anxious to effect cession that they found the negotiations too slow. The Colonial Office therefore sought help from the Foreign Office, and Granville, the Foreign Minister, requested Harris, the British ambassador at the Hague, to pursue the matter diligently. Harris did so, and sent regular reports concerning these negotiations to the Foreign Office. He explained that powerful forces were against transfer, and that when the time came, the States General would probably reject the cession Bill. At once British politicians devised a strategy for overcoming this obstacle. They promised Holland concessions in the East Indies in exchange for territory on the West Coast. The cession Bill passed the First Chamber mainly because of this link between it and the Sumatra Convention.[1]

At the same time as the Colonial Office was trying to wring a concession out of the Netherlands Government, it was also concerned about obstacles to cession on the Gold Coast itself. The Colonial Secretary, Kimberley, was impatient. It was he who pressed Coast officials early in 1871 to get the Asante claim to Elmina quashed. But even before Plange brought back from Asante the denunciation in the form of the 'Certificate of Apologie' in September, Kimberley on 11 March had already declared himself satisfied with the evidence presented to him of the Dutch title to Elmina,[2] based entirely on statements made in Elmina by Colonel Nagtglas. Indeed Kimberley was so anxious that not even questions of money, which in the past caused delays in such negotiations, appeared to have been an obstacle to him. In September 1870 Kimberley, informing Kennedy of the payment to be made for the stores and fixtures to be left by the Netherlands before a convention could be finally determined in respect of the proposed cession, showed no surprise at the rather high value of £80,000 put upon these stores.[3] His only concern was that Kennedy should report to him 'as to the best mode of charging this sum on the Revenue of that settlement, which will be an indispensable condition of the proposed cession'.[4] When in November, Colonel Nagtglas produced on-the-spot estimates of the military stores, furniture, building materials, tools and provisions amounting to the much lower sum of £25,000, both Kimberley and Kennedy were highly delighted.[5]

At last, on 12 March 1872, copies of the ratified Convention for the transfer to Great Britain of the Dutch possessions on the Coast of Guinea reached Pope-Hennessy, Kennedy's successor, in Sierra Leone. He hastened to pass on the information to the Governor of Elmina and the Administrator of the Gold Coast. He held himself in readiness, he said, to leave Sierra Leone for the Coast on hearing that preparations of the Netherlands authorities for the transfer were complete. He then quickly entered into correspondence with Ussher on various matters concerning the transfer.[6] Colonel Ferguson, the new Governor of the Netherlands Guinea, had also written on 5 March to Sierra Leone, a letter which must have crossed Pope-Hennessy's to say that everything was in

1 Coombs, *The Gold Coast, Britain and the Netherlands 1850–74*, London 1963, pp. 92–4

2 Coombs, 'The place of "Certificate of Apologie" in Ghanaian History'

3 C.O. 402/12, Kimberley to Kennedy, 20 September 1870

4 *Ibid.*   5 Adm. 1/462, no. 120, Kennedy to Kimberley, 3 November 1870

6 Adm. 1/462, no. 31, Pope-Hennessy to Kimberley, 16 March 1872

order for the transfer,[1] and so by the end of the month Pope-Hennessy was already in Elmina.[2] He wasted no time but immediately held a long conference with the representatives of the nine districts of Elmina, with the Free Burgers, with the King of Shama and with the chief men of the other parts of the Dutch Protectorate. He managed to obtain the cooperation of Marman Smith, the Burgomaster of Elmina, and G. E. Emissang, who took a prominent part in the discussions. To prove to the Colonial Office that the town readily accepted the transfer, Pope-Hennessy pointed out that he was well received by the leading inhabitants, including David Mills Graves, who had been sent by the people of Elmina at the close of 1871 to protest against cession in the States General at the Hague.[3]

During an impressive ceremony in the 'palaver hall' of the Castle, Ferguson handed to Pope-Hennessy the ancient gold and ivory baton of Admiral de Ruyter which for 235 years had been the symbol of sovereignty over the Dutch possessions on the Coast. The British Flag was hoisted under a salute of 101 guns from H.M.S. *Rattlesnake* and 101 guns from the Castle itself.[4] The detachments Pope-Hennessy sent to Axim, Dixcove and Sekondi took possession of those places and the Dutch troops embarked on board the H.N.M. *Loo*. The British occupation of the territory ceded by the Netherlands was thus completed.[5]

The Asante War of 1873–74

With the 1873 invasion of the coast, Britain faced a new set of activities from Asante. Historians like Ward and Claridge,[6] resting on the authority of the captive missionaries and other contemporaries such as Captains Brackenbury and Huyshe, put forward several causes for the Asante war of 1873–74. These included outstanding questions like those of Kwesi Gyani, the captive missionaries, as well as the 'secret desire' of every Asante chief 'to measure themselves for once with the white man'.[7]

On the whole, the first major cause postulated by these historians is that Asante was trying to reclaim the coast. The Asantehene is reported to have said that his sole object in sending his army of invasion in February 1873 was to recover his provinces of Akyem, Assin, Denkyira – all his by right of conquest long ago, and tributary to him until they rebelled.[8] The second was that the Asantehene declared war to recover Elmina, which legally belonged to him. This view was first popularised by Claridge,[9] and was later supported by Hargreaves who, while discussing the subject of the transfer, stated that 'the one possible risk attached to the transactions seemed that of conflict with Ashante over her claims to suzerain rights at Elmina'.[10] Dr Coombs oscillated

1 *Ibid.*, no. 36, 18 March 1872   2 *Ibid.*, no. 38, 4 April 1872

3 F.O. 37/700, Harris to Granville, the Hague, 15 January 1872

4 Adm. 1/462, no. 38, Hennessy to Kimberley, 4 April 1872

5 *Ibid.*, no. 41, April 1872   6 Claridge, Vol. II, p. 3

7 F. Ramseyer and Kuhne, *Four Years in Ashantee*, London 1875, p. 205

8 Brackenbury, *The Ashanti War*, p. 131   9 Claridge, Vol. II, p. 4

10 Hargreaves, *Prelude to the Partition of West Africa*, p. 167

between the two ideas, of cession being both an occasion for and a cause of the Asante invasion.[1]

Now it is true that the Asantehene did want to recover Akyem, Assin, etc. and that he was much concerned about Elmina affairs. But the advocates of these two views imputed them solely to Asante political motives, and it is on this account that their views cannot be wholly accepted.

First, it must be noted that Asante decided to recover these provinces as a means of restoring order along the trade routes which the British, through their support for Fante, had helped to make unsafe for Asante traders. General concern about trade routes could further be seen in the Asantehene's action of dispatching Adu Boffo to the Lower Volta in 1869 to help Asante allies restore peace on this important trade route.[2]

Secondly, it is true that the King referred to Elmina as his but this does not prove his ownership. K. A. Daaku has recently shown that there is no documentary support for the Asantehene's claim.[3] Elmina tradition corroborates this view, maintaining that Asante had, from time immemorial, treated Elmina as a sovereign state.[4] So, although the King's claim was the immediate cause of the war, there is no evidence to support it.[5]

The Elmina affair led to the Asante War in the following sequence of events. Asante realised that if Elmina came under Fante and British control the port would be closed to her traders. To prevent this, Akyeampon was sent as ambassador to the town. But in spite of his strenuous efforts to encourage Asante parties in the Western Districts and to keep an uninterrupted trade route for Asante to Elmina, it became clear as the British plunged into the Dutch negotiations that Asante's aims could not be achieved. There were strong pro-Asante parties in the West, and particularly in Elmina, where since 1871 King Kobina Edgan had been waiting for the opportune moment to rise up against the Anglo–Fante alliance. But the persistent efforts of the British to effect the transfer of Elmina was undermining Akyeampon's work.

The Dutch Governor was compelled through his relations with Cape Coast Castle to detain Akyeampon for a brief period. Kofi Karikari, the King, in an

---

1 Coombs, *The Gold Coast*, p. 124

2 Asante seems to have controlled the Lower Volta trade route through its allies, Anlo, Akwamu and Kwawu Dukoman. By 1869 all three states were in trouble with their neighbours – Anlo was being attacked by Adas, Gas, Akwapems; Akwamu's Krepi subjects and Kwawu Kukoman's Buem subjects were in revolt against their respective overlords – and this disrupted trade on the Volta trade route. Asante sent military aid to its allies to help them reassert their authority over the rebels as a means of restoring peaceful trade on the Volta. See H. Debrunner, *A Church Between Colonial Powers*, London 1961, p. 216.

3 History Dept. Seminar delivered in Institute of African Studies, Legon (15 November 1966). Dr Daaku explained that the 'Elmina Note' and the liability of £9000 allegedly inherited from Denkyira also had no foundation.

4 Elmina tradition: informant Mr S. Vroom. About a mile west of the Dutch Tower and slightly more to the north of Bantama, the Asante headquarters in Elmina, there is a tall silk cotton tree under which, says tradition, the approaching band of Asante waited for permission to enter the town. This was one of the important ways in which one African state showed respect for the sovereign rights of the other.

5 Scholars like Ellis, Claridge and Coombs were under the impression that it was the ownership of Elmina which worried the Asantehene and so they devoted considerable space to discussing the validity or otherwise of the 'Certificate of Apologie'. See Claridge, Vol. I, pp. 609–12 and Coombs, 'The place of the "Certificate of Apologie"'.

attempt to avert the approaching catastrophe, laid claim to Elmina, merely to give himself time to carry out negotiations for a peaceful settlement, which involved Asante's commercial rights in Elmina. In pursuit of this he sent down to Cape Coast in 1871, a high-powered mission led by Affrifah, a chief of great experience at the Asante Court.

Affrifah's mission left no stone unturned to reach a peaceful settlement of the outstanding issues. In a matter like this the main issues at stake nearly always included securing rights of passage, which must be preceded by safeguarding those people who had been captured and detained as a result of the blockade. Since 1868 a considerable number of Asante traders, messengers, etc. had fallen into the hands of the Fante, Akyem, etc. and the head of the Asante mission now requested the Administrator to use his good offices to secure the release of such persons. But Salmon, the Administrator, would not do anything of the sort. On the question of opening up the trade routes and guaranteeing the safe conduct of Asante traders through Fante territory, Salmon's reply merely took the form of trying to impress on the Affrifah mission the effectiveness of the Fante blockade. Affrifah was forced to point out just what we should expect in such circumstances: that if the Gold Coast Government would not agree to a peaceful settlement of outstanding disputes between them and the Asante Government, the King would be compelled to resort to the use of force in restoring law and order and securing the release of the Asante captives himself. This warning came after Salmon had declined to do anything about releasing even those Asante still in captivity in Akyem.[1]

The mission led by Affrifah was thus a failure. Coming after the Asante envoy, Akyeampon, had been maltreated, this meant war. Kobina Edgan, King of Elmina, confirmed Affrifah's assertions that the imprisonment of Akyeampon, even for only a short time, would lead to trouble, as Asante never permitted such insults to be perpetrated on her ambassadors with impunity. Indeed, after a short meeting at which King Edgan, Affrifah and Akyeampon were present, the head of the Asante mission, who appeared not to be Akyeampon's superior, found it necessary to issue a fresh warning of impending hostilities and to intercede with Colonel Nagtglas to give Akyeampon adequate protection in an attempt to avert trouble. But Nagtglas continued to insist on the removal of Akyeampon,[2] and Affrifah had to leave with matters still unsettled.

This state of affairs persisted till the early part of 1872, when negotiations for the Dutch transfer were completed. All this happened without Asante having solved the disputes she was having with the coast. Even at this late hour the Asantehene was anxious to avert trouble and sent down the 'Certificate of Apologie' in the hope that it might keep the door for negotiations still open. But it had the opposite effect, for the British, who were anxiously looking for such a document, were now in a position to put pressure upon the Dutch to hasten the transfer, which was executed in April 1872.

Since the return of the unsuccessful Affrifah mission to Kumasi, Asante realised that they had to prepare for war.[3] When Elmina was ceded to the

---

1 BZ/B79, Afst. IV, 20 May 1871   2 *Ibid.*

3 BZ/300s, 2 August 1872. Reports from Plange. During Plange's second visit to Kumasi, Kofi Karikari, according to Dutch sources, asked the messenger's opinion about the strength of the combined Fante and English force which might be brought against him if he invaded the coast.

British, Asante definitely decided on war, but they had not by then acquired all the necessary munitions of war. Earlier, they had opened diplomatic negotiations with the Coast for the return of Asante captives in the Protectorate and also for the ransoming of the German missionaries to give them the chance to build up their war supplies secretly. Towards the end of 1872 the Asante completed their preparations, and an army 48,000 strong crossed the Prah into the 'Protectorate'.

When the Asante fury broke on the Coast, there was an obvious plan of campaign to follow. The King sent a wing of his army to eliminate Assin and crush the Akyem; another was to march down the main Kumasi–Cape Coast trade route, its destination being, of course, Cape Coast itself. A third was to devastate Denkyira and teach Kwaku Fram, the King, a lesson. A general conflagration was then expected in the West, and during this a systematic conquest of the coast would be launched. Kobina Edgan of Elmina, as we have seen, was to give the signal of Asante approach and to request the chiefs of the Western Districts to rise up against British rule.[1] He did so, and the rising took place.

To strengthen the resistance of the Western Districts, the Asante made a two-fold plan. First, Kofi Karikari decided to send Akyeampon with 3000 Sefwis to help Amaki against Blay in Apollonia.[2] Secondly, it was decided that the Asante army, after the disposal of Assin, Denkyira, etc. should capture Elmina, which they could then defend against the British. This would encourage the Western Districts and might prove to be the best way to keep the English at bay. Oral traditions of Elmina itself agree on this point.[3]

The preliminary campaign presented no great difficulties to Asante. The Fante, who disclaimed responsibilities for this fresh provocation of Asante, had to be prevailed upon with difficulty by Lieutenant Hopkins of the 2nd West India Regiment acting on orders from Cape Coast Castle, before they reluctantly gathered at Manso and Dunkwa. They then drifted to Fante Yankumasi and were there easily outwitted by the main Asante force. Both Denkyira and Assin retreated. In March a new camp at Dunkwa gradually grew to 25,000 strong, reinforced moreover by 100 men of the West India Regiment with an officer from Sierra Leone. Even then the allies hesitated to attack Asante, thus giving Adu Boffo, who had just humiliated Wassa[4] in a capital victory, time to join Amankwa Tia, the Asante General.

A series of engagements followed. In the last of these the whole of the allied forces was routed just behind Cape Coast.[5] Twice already in this brief campaign the Asante army came within striking distance of Cape Coast Castle itself. Panic seized the inhabitants. By mid-May the Asante left Dunkwa for Jukwa the Denkyira Capital. The allies at Abakrampa made a feeble move towards Jukwa when on 4 June Asante launched a heavy attack on them. The Denkyirahene, Kwaku Fram, fled, the whole army was crushed and finally routed.[6]

1 Claridge, Vol. II, p. 291

2 A. B. Ellis, *The Tshi-Speaking People of the Gold Coast*, London 1887, p. 291

3 Elmina tradition: informant, Mr S. Vroom

4 Ellis, *The Tshi-Speaking People*, p. 291

5 Claridge, Vol. II, pp. 20–5   6 Ellis, *The Tshi-Speaking People*, p. 295

People were fleeing from the neighbouring villages into Cape Coast, the way to which was now open to the Asante army. The Western towns led by Elminas, Shamas, etc. were already preparing to effect a junction with the Asante. At this point it may be profitable to examine the resistance of the Western Districts.

Akyeampon's work in the Western Districts had been to promote and organise the establishment of Asante parties in the various towns along the sea-board. He was fairly successful in this, even though he was ultimately removed from Elmina. He left behind pro-Asante parties in each of the important sea ports between Elmina and Assinie. The structure of Akyeampon's organisation was carefully planned. In each town there was created a nucleus of Asante supporters to whom more and more converts were added as time went on. At the centre of the organisation was the King of Elmina and the various pro-Asante parties had to take orders from him. Once the energies of these parties, scattered all along the coast, were directed from one point it would be possible for them all to give a coordinated assistance to Asante when the time came.

One of the places where Asante influence had been firmly planted was Sekondi. The chief of the Asante quarter was Andries, who was reported to be in frequent communication with the King of Elmina. He had been forced to receive an English flag at the time of the transfer, but he had never hoisted it. There had been a long boundary dispute between him and the second quarter of the town and this was now seized upon as a means of increasing support for the pro-Asante adherents. Very serious riots broke out and the popularity of the Asante cause was clearly demonstrated. During the riots which took place in the middle of January 1873 the chief of Takoradi sent messengers offering Andries assistance. Of the 300 armed men who marched in to help Andries most came from Takoradi. The rest were Shamas, who were also demonstrating their loyalty to the Asante–Dutch cause as opposed to the Fante–British cause. At the same time the Butris tried to join Andries and his supporters, but were just narrowly prevented by the Commandant of Dixcove.[1]

Butri was another place where Asante affiliations left the population very restless. The action of Hughes, Civil Commandant of Dixcove, in preventing them from joining the Sekondis had excited them all the more. The Butris, even more than the Sekondis, appeared to have been giving implicit obedience to the King of Elmina. The chief had to report important matters to Elmina for final decision. In accordance with this policy it became necessary for the chief to order a Butri man to pay a fine to the King of Elmina. Hughes was naturally opposed to this as it was consolidating Asante influence over the Ahantas. He stopped proceedings at the chief's court when the case of the fine was in progress. At once the people turned out, marching through the streets with guns, carrying a Dutch flag. They clashed with constables of the Government sent by the Commandant.[2]

Akyeampon's sons and other Asante (the greater portion of the original 300 who had come to Elmina with him) were still resident in Elmina. The King, supported by a considerable section of Elminas, continued steadily to oppose the British. With the departure of Akyeampon, Kobina Edgan, the King, assumed all responsibilities for the organisation of the Western Districts in the Asante interest. Just before the cession of Elmina he had been requested to swear an oath of allegiance to the British Government, but had refused. He

1 Claridge, Vol. I, p. 161; Vol. II, pp. 15–17   2 Claridge, Vol. II, p. 17

later sent his own brother to Kumasi to report to the King the proceedings on the Coast. Although Kobina Edgan was arrested and deported in March 1873 Elmina retained the leadership of the pro-Asante parties in the West.

Thus when the Asante army drew near to the coast, the Asante party in Elmina did not fail to give the signal for a general uprising of the Western Districts and to lead the rebellion. Kobina Edgan's party, even in his absence, began actively to prepare for resistance. The Government decided to disarm them, but they refused to deliver their arms at the Castle gate as ordered. Their quarter of the town was therefore destroyed, but not before they had fled into the bush, whence they soon joined the approaching Asante army which later advanced in full force to capture Elmina.[1] The Asante army which launched this heavy attack was fully prepared with scaling ladders to take the forts. Determined to dislodge the British, they fought like men who knew that everything in this war depended on this one assault.

The Elmina example served as the signal for rebellion. Throughout the Western Districts Asante parties rose up. In Axim, Sekondi and Shama fighting ensued, as the pro-Asante parties launched determined attacks on those who would not join them.

At the same time Adu Boffo was preparing to march into these towns to wipe out the opposition to the Asante cause that still existed. Adu Boffo was in charge of the central army, while Akyeampon was in the west with another force. A detachment of Adu Boffo's army at Mampon and Efutu was seriously threatening the British position in the western ports. Then came a rumour that Amankwa Tia himself decided to cross the Prah and join Adu Boffo. An attempt by Commodore Commerell to prevent this failed dismally, as the Shamas launched a heavy attack on the boats of the British party going up the Prah. The Commodore and others were severely wounded and it was with great difficulty that the seamen could find their way out of the river. The Shamas continued their offensive against more constables who were brought to be stationed in the fort there. Akyeampon and the forces in Apollonia were also helping Amaki and together they destroyed Blay's towns one after the other.

In spite of the strenuous efforts of the Asante, the resistance of the Western Districts was put down. The determination of their army might have been expected to carry the day when they launched an attack on Elmina, but they came up against a stumbling block – the natural defences of the town.

The observer from the Dutch Watch Tower has a clear view of nature's defence works in Elmina. To the south lies the Atlantic, into which flows the River Benya, describing a semicircle in the western part of the town and extending about two miles into the marches of the north. In the north-western direction lie the hills which lead on to Eguafo, with slopes gentle enough to permit an easy march to within half a mile of the town. But here, about a mile in width, can be seen one of West Africa's most obstructive marshes. The origin of the marsh is the River Benya itself which at high tide often floods the whole of this northern approach. Even at low tide the marsh is dangerous. Now this was the only approach which an advancing force could use, for the north-east was heavily guarded by Fort Nagtglas and smaller redoubts built by the Dutch. The Fante in 1868 had come up against this very problem of having to cross the marshes before taking the town and they had failed. Now the Asante army

1 *Ibid.*, pp. 29–31

came in full force, hoping to force a quick march through the muddy ground and rush the town. But the marshes delayed them and the British had time to work the huge guns of Fort St Jago, the Castle and the redoubts. Amankwa Tia's men, thus held at bay, began to sink into the mud and many were killed by fire from the guns. It was a terrible experience; despondency seized the remainder of the troops and they had to retire.

The rising among the Western Districts was also put down by the British. They had the advantage of the use of the forts which commanded the key towns. About July 1873 they increased the personnel of these forts with reinforcements from the U.K. and the West Indies. In Komenda the English fort, with its strong bastions overlooking the sea and the town, could comfortably defend itself against any local uprising. From the imposing Fort St Sebastian at Shama, with its thick triangular walls purposely designed for defence, the British could destroy the whole town with fire in a matter of hours. The forts at Sekondi and Dixcove would serve the same end admirably and although Fort St Antonio did not command the whole of Axim town, the hearts of any people advancing to take it would sink in despair at the sight of it. Built by the Dutch in 1642 this majestic fort, standing on huge boulders and rocks with strong bastions, was fitted with powerful cannon. St Antonio even today strikes awe into the tourist who realises that this ancient monument, though not as old as the waves, has for more than three centuries silently resisted their ceaseless beating against its bastions.[1] With such defences no wonder the British quickly put down the western rising and forced the local populations into submission. The heavy fire from the forts coupled with naval action won the day. After the bombardment of Elmina[2] the squadron visited all the western ports and its action was planned to strengthen the fire from the huge cannons of the forts. The Western Districts could not but submit.

In these circumstances the Asante army, already in trouble because of disease, decided to withdraw, and a masterly retreat by Amankwa Tia brought the war virtually to an end, when the troops recrossed the Prah into their own country.

For the British, however, the war had hardly begun. The decision to invade Asante initiated an imperial war.[3] That contemporaries considered this invasion of 1874 as an imperial war is demonstrated by three considerations. First the Fante said so. The King of Mankessim stated that Fante would have placed a strict embargo on the exportation of arms across the Prah into Asante if the Confederacy had not been 'deprived of their legitimate exercise and functions, by the action of Her Majesty's officials'.[4] Secondly, because they believed that the British should accept responsibility for the war the Fante were extremely reluctant to fight. Kwesi Edu's men, for instance, were, on the morning of 10 March 1873, more concerned with preparing and eating their breakfast than watching out for the Asante army, and when they were surprised by the

1 In the early part of 1964 I paid visits to the forts at the Central and Western Region in the company of my friend Albert Van Danzig, from whose knowledge of the background of the Dutch forts I benefited immensely.

2 Claridge, Vol. II, pp. 29–32

3 Wolfson, *British Relations with the Gold Coast*, p. 254

4 Hay, *Ashanti and the Gold Coast*, London 1874, p. 25

enemy, they promptly fled and returned to their homes.[1] Watching for an opportunity to leave the field, the rest of the allies no sooner heard that George Blankson of Anomabu was selling powder to the enemy than they faked anger, returning to their homes with the argument that they would not fight with so much treachery in their midst.[2] Again, when the Asante army marched on Jukwa, The Kings of Abora and Anomabu simply refused to come to the defence of the town.[3] Almost at the same time the Fante scouts sent out by the Cape Coast authorities to find out the position of the Asante army simply hid in bushes on the outskirts of Cape Coast, and when their food supplies ran out they came back for their pay, drawing on their imagination as to the position of the enemy.

Such was the apathy of the Fante in the war. When Sir Garnet Wolseley arrived on the Coast he must have been put clearly into the picture about their attitude. He called a meeting of their chiefs on 4 October, to enquire into the affair. Two days later they came back with a firm answer, hardly surprising, that they were not keen on the war.[4]

The third reason why contemporaries considered the war as an imperial one was the vigorous manner in which it was prosecuted. It was Sir Garnet who urged the British Government to send European troops for the invasion of Asante. It is suggested that he did so because he saw that this would be an excellent opportunity for discrediting the proud Fante, whom the British could dominate if they could lay claims to having defended them against Asante. Furthermore, observers maintained that the 1874 campaign marked the beginning of certain changes in British attitude to the Coast and that the war seemed to be less unpopular with the British public than previous ones.[5] We must conclude that both Her Majesty's Government and the British public had fallen in with Wolseley's suggestions that there could be no better opportunity than 1874 for raising England's national prestige on the Coast. H. M. Stanley wrote that 'England's honour demands that her army shall enter Kumasi and go through the form of taking possession'.[6] It was realised that not only military honour but the very survival of imperial and commercial interests on the Coast were at stake.[7] In his instructions to Wolseley, Carnarvon emphasised the point that 'if . . . you shall have succeeded after all in obtaining from the King of Ashantee a satisfactory recognition of Her Majesty's power and authority . . . your mission will have been attended with the fullest measure of success'.[8] Sir Garnet had written angrily to the Asantehene: 'You have even attacked Her Majesty's forts'; and *The Gold Coast Aborigines* suggested that for the real causes of the war we must look to Wolseley's anxiety to wipe off the dishonour to the British name attendant on Karikari's conduct.[9] Examined further, Sir Garnet's views on the war would seem to dispel all doubts as to why he invaded Kumasi. He had hoped, he said, when the invasion was

1 Ellis, *The Tshi-Speaking People*, p. 288   2 *Ibid.*

3 *Ibid.*, p. 292   4 *Ibid.*, p. 301   5 Hargreaves, p. 169

6 H. M. Stanley, *Coomassie and Magdala*, London 1875, p. 152; Stanley also suggests (p. 25) that the Asante war was not thrust upon the Government, but that they fought in order to conquer a rich neighbour.

7 Kimble, p. 272   8 C.922, Carnarvon to Wolseley, 13 March 1874

9 *The Gold Coast Aborigines*, 4 March 1899

over, that the territories of the Gold Coast would no longer be troubled by the warlike ambitions of 'this restless Power'.[1] But this was a by-product of the war, the chief result of which, according to Sir Garnet, was that 'the Flag of England from this moment will be received throughout Western Africa with respectful awe'.[2]

So, it was in order to have Britain recognised and respected as the power on the Coast that Kimberley decided to fight Asante, and to make the war an imperial concern.[3] The Imperial Government was prepared to finance the expedition,[4] while the local Government displayed firmness throughout the war.[5] In 1874 there was a general feeling among Coast officials that 'this is no time for feeble effort and winding orations about "humanity"'.[6] Her Majesty's Government did not think either that this was the time to spare European troops, in spite of alarming reports that by December 1873 there were already 146 cases on the sick list.[7] Even the Admiralty consented to the landing of seamen and marines in unusual numbers from the squadron,[8] and in fact displayed great energy in the matter. Early in December there was such a heavy concentration of the squadron on the Coast that the whole sea-board was effectively blockaded, regardless of the fact that only areas adjacent to St George d'Elmina, Komenda, Shama, Sekondi, Takoradi and Bushua needed to be blockaded.[9]

Wolseley, too, spared no efforts to solve the problems of the campaign, the chief of which was the question of transport. So grave was the situation that all ingenuity had to be called into play. Wolseley was at some point even thinking of utilising cattle from Madeira and St Vincent. Even more strange to relate, Britain paid runners in nearly every port west of the Gold Coast to race inland and catch Jolloffs, Mandingoes, Kroomen, Sereses, Marabouts, Apollonians, etc. for the transport service from Cape Coast to Asante.[10]

1 C.921, Wolseley to Kimberley, 28 November 1873   2 Ibid.

3 Wolfson, p. 254   4 Kimble, p. 272

5 C.892, Wolseley to Kimberley, 28 November 1873   6 Stanley, p. 103

7 C.893, encl. in Admiralty to C.O., 14 December 1873. There was a long correspondence between the War Office and Colonial Office about the choice of a suitable place for sending fever cases. A letter of 1 January 1874 from the Coast reported that 100 invalids had been sent to Ascension Is. An earlier communication of 15 December 1873 indicated that 102 men and three officers were then on their way to Ascension, weak, feeble and infirm because of the climate. Of these, forty men and two officers were invalided, malaria and dysentery being the chief cause of trouble.

8 C.893, encl. in Admiralty to C.O., 14 December 1873. So great was the number of marines and seamen landed that Commodore Hewelt felt compelled to order 'all the seamen and marines so landed to return to their ships forthwith, leaving on shore only the detachment of Marines, 105 in number, sent out in the Simoom for that purpose'. Normally, the Admiralty showed great reluctance in landing seamen and marines.

9 C.893, encls. 1 and 2 in Wolseley to Kimberley, 16 December 1873

10 C.922, encls. 1, 2 and 3 of 13 March and 10 January 1874 in Admiralty to C.O. In encl. 1 we find the following abstract of the numbers of Africans brought to Cape Coast in H.M.'s ships to act as carriers:
Apart from 167 King Blay's men and Dixcove men
780 ,, ,, ,, ,, Fantees
187 ,, ,, ,,
1009 Apollonians and the Groomooah(?) tribe.

The story of the Asante campaign has often been vividly told, with emphasis on the British victory in Kumasi. A close examination of the details of the campaign, however, reveals that the traditional view of this victory is misleading. British success was not unqualified and the real factors leading to this military achievement have not been appreciated.

In the first place the Asante plan of campaign was not entirely without merits. Asante was sure that in a land of forests the enemy would easily be defeated. All that they had to do, therefore, was to draw the enemy right into Asante so that, defeated, they could not recover their property in their flight back.[1] This plan would certainly have worked had not the Asante resistance at Amoafu failed. Asamoa Nkwanta was then in supreme command and he chose a ridge below which was a hollow filled with deep mud and a sluggish stream. The Asante had a great advantage in this position and as their assailants approached through the muddy ravine they opened a terrific fire. The Black Watch, 'one of the finest regiments in the British Army', could make very little headway against them. As they tried to climb the slope the British troops fell one after the other. The Asante were hidden in the forest and therefore had a great advantage over the white troops who were exposed on the slopes as they tried to climb up. Indeed, if the guns had not been brought up to pour a heavy fire into the forest on the ridge, Asante fire would have completely wiped out the Black Watch.

Even when they were eventually driven back because of the superior ammunition of the enemy, the Asante hoped that all was not lost. When they saw that the British had occupied Amoafu, they immediately organised flank attacks on them. In Asante military tradition such a manœuvre nearly always meant victory for the aggressor on the flanks. And indeed the detachments of Asante troops engaged on these flank attacks harassed the British troops near the village of Kwaman so much so that it took them a long time even with a seven-pounder gun to make a further advance. Another important fact was that the Asante plan of drawing the British troops as near to Kumasi as possible would eventually have succeeded if Juaben had moved, as arranged, to destroy the bridge on the Prah and had thus cut off the retreat of the enemy.[2] We shall soon discuss this episode in detail.

Furthermore, the Asante plan would have enjoyed a greater measure of success if confusion over the supreme command of the army had not occurred. When the army crossed the Prah in 1872 Asamoa Nkwanta, the experienced commander-in-chief, was having personal differences with King Kofi Karikari, and he refused to assume command of the fighting forces. Amankwa Tia, Chief of Bantama, was therefore appointed to the post. But when the enemy drew nearer and nearer to Kumasi, Asamoa Nkwanta was compelled to leave his

---

There were also 32 Kroomen from Sierra Leone and Grande Bassac and Cape Palmas. 60 Sereses, Jolloffs, Mandingoes, Marabouts and Kroomen from Bathurst and River Gambia 49 Grable and Sesstown Kroomen from Cape Palmas Poor River Namakros, Picaninny Seakos; 178 Kroomen and Grebo tribe from Monrovia and Cape Palmas. Total 2462 men.

Encl. 2 discloses that the Kroomen were to receive 15 to 20 dollars each while embarked. They would receive seaman's rations, and when landed an additional $1s$ a day for carrying together with the army ration of the natives, viz. 1 lb of rice, $\frac{1}{4}$ lb of salted meat, and $9d$ a day.

Encl. 3 describes the sending out of runners from the ports to enlist men as carriers.

1 Claridge, Vol. II, p. 138   2 Ward, *History of Ghana*, p. 282

retirement and to take over the supreme command at this late hour. This affected the smooth conduct of the war. The left wing, to which Amankwa Tia was demoted, began to fare so badly that complete disaster set in; the ex-general, shot in the back, fell and his side was routed.[1]

British strategy, on the other hand, though ultimately successful, contained elements of great danger which could have led to total disaster. Out of three auxiliary columns two failed. Captain Dalrymple, who had been detailed to recruit men from among the Wassas, Eguafo and Komenda, failed miserably.[2] Captain Butler, in charge of a column of Akyem, had an even more trying experience. When with great difficulty he managed to get the Akyem across the Prah, he discovered that their acts of disobedience increased with their progress towards Kumasi till on the night of 30 January 1874 the entire Akyem force deserted.[3] Captain Glover, who led the third auxiliary column, had similar difficulties with the Akyem.[4]

Captains Dalrymple and Glover both thought that the conduct of the Akyem was due to cowardice. But this was not so. They could only have got the clue in the communication which passed between Akyem and Juaben, but the contents of this were withheld from them.[5] However, the reluctance of both Juaben and Akyem to fight is unmistakably clear, and it is not difficult to see that they were anxious to avoid collision. Indeed, as soon as the King of Juaben sighted Glover and his Akyem levies, he sent in his submission.[6]

A recent survey of Akyem–Juaben relations is available in Dr Boahen's paper on Juaben–Kumasi relations in the nineteenth century.[7] Dr Boahen believes in the existence, before the Asante War, of a non-aggression pact between Akyem and Juaben, and he explains Juaben's decision to remain neutral in the war as entirely due to this pact. This would imply that the communications between Akyem and Juaben referred to by both Dalrymple and Glover were merely affirmations of an earlier agreement not to fight each other. The desertion of the Akyem thus becomes intelligible as their further progress might lead to a collision with their friends the Juabens. Similarly, the submission of Juaben was necessary for the observance of the friendship pact.

In the light of these facts we need to re-examine the nature of British success in the war. In the first place it is not unlikely that the news of a possible defection of Juaben[8] contributed to the final collapse of Asante resistance. Certainly the King's scouts must have reported the fact that Juaben forces were not moving according to plan and it must have occurred to the King that Juaben would disobey his orders. But even after this the King did not feel that all was lost. Sir Garnet destroyed Kumasi but he did not guard the city to prevent the Kumasis leaving with their arms to join their monarch at the village of Breman where he had repaired. This, coupled with the news of the sudden retreat from Kumasi of Sir Garnet's forces, must have helped the King to regain his confidence.[9]

The King could still resist; the success of British arms might turn out to be temporary and the bush might prove stronger than the cannon after all. But if the King entertained any such hopes, he quickly lost them again on hearing the

1 Claridge, Vol. II, pp. 114–25   2 *Ibid.*   3 Stanley, p. 215

4 *Ibid.*, p. 252   5 *Ibid.*, p. 183   6 *Ibid.*, p. 251

7 I.A.S., Legon 1965   8 Stanley, p. 257   9 *Ibid.*, p. 258

news of the arrival of Captain Glover and his force between Juaben and Kumasi. The failure of Juaben to contain the enemy 'at the line of the Anum River' had finally unnerved the King. Sir Garnet's forces began their retreat on 6 February; soon after the King's scouts must have reported the approach of both Captain Sartorius with twenty men and Captain Glover with 4600 local allies towards Kumasi. The King therefore had to send his peace envoys after Sir Garnet on the 9th before Captains Sartorius and Glover with their auxiliaries could reach his capital about the 11th and 12th. These must be the facts indeed which forced Stanley to the conclusion that it was Captain Glover who won the Asante War.[1]

The proclamation of the Protectorate 1874

By 1873 British policy, under local pressure, was already undergoing some change. In 1874, partly as a reaction to these Asante activities, the policy-makers had to sanction an even faster rate of territorial expansion than in the 1868–72 period. Proclamation of the Protectorate in 1874, following the Asante invasion of 1873 and the Asante War thus illustrates, more than anything else, Britain's new policy. Just as events in the 1872–74 period were connected with the Fante Confederacy, so was the declaration of the Protectorate. Furthermore, having destroyed the Confederacy, the British rendered the people of the Gold Coast less able to defend themselves against their enemies. In 1874 there was a strong feeling in the Colonial Office that since Britain had thus prevented the Fante from administering their own affairs and protecting themselves, it was the duty of the British to provide the inhabitants with administration and pro-tection,[2] hence the establishment of the Protectorate.

Thus after the war in 1874 a Conservative M.P. called Hanbury opened, in the British Parliament, a debate on the motion 'That in the interest of civilisa-tion and of commerce it would not now be desirable to withdraw from the administration of affairs of the Gold Coast'.[3] There was growing popularity for the views of Knatchbull-Hugessen, the strongest defender of expansion. Carnarvon, the new Secretary of State, announced that, as it was impossible to withdraw from the Coast, Her Majesty's Government had decided to exercise more direct authority in the 'Protectorate'. He decided on the declaration of a British Protectorate and Colony by Royal Proclamation.[4]

By the proclamation, Her Majesty's power on the Gold Coast was defined to extend to:

1. Preservation of public peace, protection of individuals, life and property.
2. Civil and commercial jurisdiction. (This involved the establishment of Superior Courts of Justice and the regulation of Native Courts, enactment of laws relative to crimes; property rights, etc. arrest and trial of criminals, supervision of native prisons.)

1 *Ibid.*, pp. 258 and 261

2 C.O. 806/3, Minute by Fairfield, 24 March 1874, quoted in Metcalfe, *Great Britain and Ghana*, p. 364

3 Hargreaves, p. 170

4 *Ibid.*, p. 171. It was the forts and settlements which became the Colony, and the Pro-tectorate referred to the rest of present day Southern Ghana west of the Volta.

3. Extinction of human sacrifices.
4. Abolition of slave dealing.
5. Measures with regard to domestic slavery and pawning.
6. Establishment of police force, administration of health, education and the raising of revenue.[1]

The declaration of the Protectorate was unilateral. Carnarvon's decision not to consult the chiefs was based on his fear that some of them might withhold their consent.[2] He was definitely expecting opposition. The fact that the chiefs and people raised no objections to the proclamation of the Protectorate is therefore puzzling. Unfortunately we do not have sufficient evidence to be able to explain this strange acquiescence. We can only speculate. There is no doubt that the Asante invasion of the Coast in 1873 was very impressive. We have seen how their army defeated the coastal states in several battles and how terror and panic seized Cape Coast itself.[3]

When the British announced the Protectorate and Colony in July 1874, the coastal states could not have completely recovered from their fear of Asante. Consequently they might have thought that they needed the protection of Britain against future Asante invasions, especially since the British had just proved themselves conquerors of Asante. It is probably this which accounts for their acceptance of the Protectorate.

One of the first measures of the British after the declaration of the Protectorate was to abolish slavery, and this aroused bitter opposition among the chiefs and people of the country. The Governor, Strahan, called a meeting of the kings and chiefs of the Western Districts on 3 November 1874 in the Palaver Hall of Cape Coast Castle. As soon as the Governor broached the question of abolition, King Edu of Mankessim asked that they should be allowed to go and deliberate till the next day for an answer. Strahan objected, but gave them a short time during which they withdrew from the hall. When the chiefs returned they raised strong objections to the slaves being permitted to go free if they chose without there being any cause shown, and likewise to pawns not being allowed.

> After some discussion, it was decided that no slave could leave his or her master or mistress unless there was proof of cruelty or maltreatment when such slave would be entitled to his or her freedom; and the question of pawns was settled by the debtor being held liable for the amount that the pawn had been given as security for and that the amount should be recovered on the pawn leaving.[4]

In December the chiefs followed their verbal protests with a formal petition. The petitioners were the 'Kings of Mankessim, Aborah, Eccumfie, Inkosokoom and Gomoah', as well as two chiefs of Saltpond and twenty-three chiefs 'mostly of small dependencies of Mankessim and Aborah'.[5] The petitioners explained

1 Proclamation defining the Nature and Extent of the Queen's Jurisdiction on the Gold Coast.

2 Claridge, Vol. II, p. 176   3 See above pp. 47–8

4 *Daily Telegraph*, 3 December 1874

5 Further Correspondence respecting the Abolition of Slavery on the Gold Coast, Strahan to Carnarvon, 3 January 1875

that their grievances stemmed from Her Majesty's message on the subject of abolishing slavery and pawn-holding. They argued that nine-tenths of their slaves had descended to them by the laws and customs of the country which the British recognised. They complained that to emancipate their slaves would impoverish them. They therefore requested that the Government should allow them to retain their slaves and pawns as was agreed at the November meeting.[1]

At the November meeting the chiefs won the first round when they compelled Strahan to agree that slaves could only leave their masters when cruelty was proved. But since the British could not put up with slavery in their colony they began to look for new ways of destroying the institution. By the beginning of December 1874 Strahan began, in spite of his November promises, to give slaves manumission papers to leave their masters, and on the 17th, he got two ordinances to be enacted in the Legislative Council in Cape Coast, declaring slavery permanently abolished.[2]

1. An ordinance to provide for the Abolition of Slave Dealing called 'Gold Coast Slave Dealing Abolition Act 1874'.
2. An ordinance to provide for the Emancipation of persons held in slavery called 'Gold Coast Emancipation Ordinance 1874'.

The first made buying, selling or importation of slaves into the Protectorate unlawful. The chiefs had no quarrel with this. The second, however, implied that no rights over slaves could be legally enforced and that the relation between master and servant as existing in England could alone be recognised on the Gold Coast.[3] This clearly was not in accordance with the spirit of the November agreement, which guaranteed the existing relation between master and slave.

As was to be expected the people were bitterly opposed to the ordinance. This time it was not only the Western Districts which protested. The chiefs and people in the Eastern Districts also opposed these measures and continued to hold slaves contrary to the ordinance. When in the 1880s the British executive tried to get the Eastern Districts to give up their slaves as required by the ordinance, the people planned to send a deputation to the U.K. to complain directly to H.M. Government about their grievances, which included the question of abolition. But the deputation was delayed and by the time they left the Coast it was clear to the people that H.M. Government would not welcome discussion on the subject, which was anyhow overshadowed by the land question. So they dropped the abolition issue.[4]

Plans for consolidation and expansion

The proclamation of the Protectorate was a result of the Asante War. But perhaps even more indicative of the nature of the British reaction to the Fante and

1 *Ibid.*, encl.

2 Further Correspondence respecting the Abolition of Slavery on the Gold Coast, Strahan to Carnarvon, 7 January 1875

3 Further Correspondence respecting the Ashantee Invasion, Strahan to Carnarvon, Telegraphic, 3 November 1874

4 See below pp. 144–5

Asante rising was their determination to extend the territory which had just been brought under the Queen's jurisdiction. This is evident from the plans for expansion they drew up soon after the war.

Naturally these plans began with the consolidation of British power over the territories already occupied. There was a clear indication as early as 1874 that the Government was anxious to give practical effect to the principles upon which the new Protectorate was established. As Dr Coombs has shown, Carnarvon assumed that the Protectorate, no less than the settlements, involved Britain in formal rights and obligations, and pointed out to the House of Lords that as long as Britain stayed on the Gold Coast she would exercise effective control over the protectorate. That this was a new departure in British Gold Coast policy could no longer be in doubt when Kimberley further clarified Carnarvon's meaning by adjuring their Lordships 'not to imagine that under the name of Protectorate we do not assume all the responsibility of managing the affairs of the colony'.[1]

In the matter of consolidation, the most immediate problem was in Akyem, where Dr Skipton Gouldsbury was made Special Commissioner. We learn that Akyem was bent on causing defection in Asante, which must simply be a reference to a continued alliance between Akyem and Juaben. There was some danger of Akyem being embroiled in another conflict with Asante before long, a factor which could not fail to unsettle the newly established Protectorate. Therefore, when Carnarvon gave orders in June 1874 that Akyem should be checked in the most decisive manner,[2] and when earlier in May, Captain Lees had similarly instructed Dr Gouldsbury,[3] it must be understood that what the British were after was not Asante unity but the consolidation of their own power south of the Prah.

The Volta districts, too, needed attention and Captain Lees instructed Gouldsbury to go there after Akyem. He was to contact King Sackitey of Eastern Krobo at Odumase and there invite the King of Akwamu to come and sign a treaty of friendship with the British. This was designed to keep the Volta open for trade. Even the distribution of Asante war medals to the local levies was to be utilised to the advantage of the Protectorate. The issue of the medals was to be based partly on good conduct since the war, and disobedience to the British by any local levy annulled his claim to the medal.[4]

Plans for expansion beyond the Protectorate seem to have received similar attention from the British authorities. We are told that the logic of the changed situation on the Gold Coast led Carnarvon to favour the ideas of acquiring sovereign rights over an extended coastline on either side of the Protectorate. The Colonial Office was indeed anxious to initiate negotiations for the surrender of French rights and territories which stood in the way of this new policy.[5] The French Government, too, was ready to welcome a territorial exchange, especially since at first it appeared that all the British wanted was an exchange of the Gambia for the Ivory Coast and Assinie adjacent to the Gold Coast. But

---

1 Coombs, *The Gold Coast*, p. 137

2 Further Correspondence respecting the Ashantee Invasion, Carnarvon to Lees, 11 June 1874

3 *Ibid.*, Lees to Gouldsbury, May 1874   4 *Ibid.*, W.O. to C.O., 11 June 1874

5 Hargreaves, pp. 173, 174

when in December 1874 Carnarvon outlined the full British plan of expansion, involving the whole territory between the Gold Coast and Lagos, it became clear that the French would be requested to renounce all claims between the Benin rivers and some point north of Sierra Leone, and that the British would do likewise from this point to the Moroccan border.[1]

The Foreign Office was even more ambitious, requesting that the vast Niger areas should be reserved for Britain, thus suggesting that the limit of the British area might be extended from the Benin River to the Gabon. The French naturally recoiled from entering into any such agreement which might mean their losing so much territory.[2]

Even so, it looked in 1875 as though France would accept the British terms, pressed as they were by British officials. Merchant opposition to the exchange of the Gambia was, however, gathering strength, and British politicians were beginning to think that if they could acquire the French possessions and at the same time retain the Gambia, it would probably be desirable to do so. It was at this time that Carnarvon took up the earlier suggestion of the Foreign Office of extending the British terms still further to include the Gabon area, as this 'would tilt the balance of actual territory more strongly in Britain's favour'.[3] A clearer tendency toward territorial expansion there could not be.

It is interesting to note that in the British plan of expansion, Asante and the interior territories, too, came in for consideration. Even though immediate expansion into the hinterland of the Gold Coast could certainly not be easy, the territory found its due place on the extension programme. This was why the Asantehene's gesture in again paying 200 ounces of gold for the Fomena Treaty in June proved very satisfactory to the Colonial Office officials.[4] Carnarvon wrote: 'It is of importance politically even more than financially that the King should be induced to adhere to the treaty of Fommanah, and to perform the engagements which he has contracted.' He went on to express the view that friendship with Asante should be pursued,[5] and:

I should hope that, as a result of the mission to Ashantee which I have contemplated, much available and particular information may be obtained respecting the tribes to the north of that country, of whom at present very little is known and the mission may also tend to the establishment of our future relations with the Kingdom of Ashantee.[6]

British anxiety at this time to improve the roads from Cape Coast to Prahsu,[7] too, although primarily an economic measure, had some political significance. To open the way to Asante must have been to the British a first step towards the successful implementation of their new policy towards the Gold Coast hinterland.

The first essential of the British plan was the establishment of defence

1 *Ibid.*, pp. 177–8   2 *Ibid.*, pp. 178, 180   3 *Ibid.*, p. 186

4 Further Correspondence respecting the Ashantee Invasion, no. 51, Carnarvon to Officer Administering the Government, 3 July 1874

5 *Ibid.* See also *ibid.*, no. 54, Lees to Carnarvon, 9 June 1874.

6 *Ibid.*, no. 51, Carnarvon to Officer Administering the Government, 3 July 1874

7 Encl. in *ibid.*, no. 60, Lees to Carnarvon, 19 June 1874

measures. These would provide for the security of the Gold Coast and its ex-pected extension. The security problems facing the Gold Coast authorities included the strengthening of the forts against African assailants, maintaining order among the people, holding such points 'as will give us an effective command of the country both as regards military and commercial operations',[1] and preventing the Kings of Accra from plunging the Eastern Districts into another war.[2]

To solve these problems it was necessary to maintain redoubts and protect ammunition stores at Prahsu, Manso, etc. It also became necessary to con-tinue the temporary arrangement under which the military and civil command had been united in one person during the late war.[3] But the most important security measure was the organisation of the Gold Coast Hausa Constabulary.

British authorities were very anxious to see the Hausa Constabulary estab-lished on the Gold Coast. Kimberley in a series of letters urged Kennedy to raise a corp of Hausa soldiers to be permanently stationed on the Gold Coast.[4] Kennedy followed these instructions after some hesitation because of the diffi-culties involved. From then on the Hausa force became an established institu-tion on the Gold Coast and the execution of the British defence and security systems came to depend largely on the conduct of these sturdy men from beyond the Middle Niger.

The Gold Coast Government employed the Hausa force in several ways. First, they were sent on missions to hold down the local populations. In Sep-tember 1874 Strahan sent Dr Gouldsbury with a force of Hausas to collect fines imposed on the Ahanta people for their disloyal part in the late war, and which they had refused to pay. Dr Gouldsbury marched the Hausa force all the way through Komenda, Shama and the Ahanta country to Dixcove, easily sup-pressed the people and extracted the fine of 70 ounces of gold.[5]

Next, Strahan dispatched Dr Gouldsbury with fifty-three Hausas to Twifu Denkyira to discipline the King who was holding a number of Asante as slaves and had refused to give them up. Firm action in Denkyira had some effect on the King of Western Wassa, who sent to Cape Coast, without being asked, twenty-four Krepis left there by the Asante.[6] That the Hausa force was sent on another mission to the Eastern Districts was due to the great faith Carnarvon had in their usefulness. Not only did he accept Captain Lees's recommendations that a detachment of armed police should go to Ada and remove the Kings of Accra who were provoking the Anlo and Akwamus there,[7] but he himself suggested that it was 'a matter for consideration whether it would not be desirable to move a body of Hausas to Accra, or some other convenient place from which to watch, if necessary repel, any hostile movements on the part of

1 *Ibid.*, no. 51, Carnarvon to Officer Administering the Govt., 3 July 1874

2 In 1874 they were at Ada trying to provoke Akwamu and Anlo.

3 Further Correspondence respecting the Ashantee Invasion, no. 84, Carnarvon to Berkeley, 27 March 1874

4 Adm. 1/461, no. 74, Kennedy to Kimberley, 25 July 1870; no. 105, 6 October 1870

5 in Further Correspondence respecting the Ashantee Invasion, no. 108, encl. 2 in Strahan to Carnarvon, 4 September 1874

6 *Ibid.*, no. 115, Strahan to Carnarvon, 24 September 1874

7 *Ibid.*, no. 55, Lees to Carnarvon, 9 June 1874, C.C.

the Eastern tribes'.[1] In July he repeated his requests, so strong was his faith in the Hausa troops.[2]

Another aspect of the British plan of consolidation concerned the improvement of health conditions on the Gold Coast. First, since they decided not merely to stay on the Gold Coast but also to expand their influence, it became necessary to find a healthier seat of Government than Cape Coast. For a time, Elmina was thought a possible alternative but eventually Accra came to be regarded as 'the only healthy station on the West Coast of Africa'.[3]

The chief advocate of Accra was Major A. F. Elliot, Acting Colonial Surgeon of the African Medical Service, who argued that it was better than Elmina because the European residents there looked healthier than their counterparts in other parts of the West Coast. Another advantage of Accra, he maintained, was the Akwapem Hills behind it, with most attractive climatic conditions which prolonged the life of the Basel Missionaries living there in Akropong.[4] Others supported the choice of Accra for the same reason. Sir J. H. Glover, for instance, wrote: 'What Simla is to Calcutta, Akropong must become to Elmina, Cape Coast Castle and Lagos.'[5] So Accra was eventually chosen as a seat of government. The Colonial Office wrote to the War Office on 22 October that:

> Among the many important questions connected with the government and future well-being of the newly constituted Colony of the Gold Coast and Lagos, there is none to which his Lordship is disposed to attach greater importance than to the execution with the least possible delay such public works as are required, not only to develop the resources of the country but also to improve to the utmost the conditions of health.[6]

The chain of events following the Fante Confederacy thus caused Britain to assume greater territorial responsibilities on the Coast. The Asante invasion of 1873 which followed the Confederacy was in itself a climax of African activities arising over local issues, and was at first directed against the Fante, but later maintained against the British, to whom Elmina was finally ceded. Even though these early activities of the Asante cannot rank in importance with the later ones by which Asante sought to preserve her independence, yet they affected British policy enormously. In 1865 Britain set her face against expansion. But by 1874 Britain took over Elmina and the other Dutch possessions in the Western Districts, proclaimed the establishment of the Protectorate and consolidated her political power on the Coast. We have seen African politics, including protest, compelling Britain, at every turn, to make these changes in her policy. These, therefore, are clear examples of how local events affected the formulation of British policy on the Gold Coast.

1 *Ibid.*, no. 48, Carnarvon to Officer Administering the Govt., 24 June 1874

2 *Ibid.*, no. 62, Carnarvon to Lees, 16 July 1874. The establishment and employment of Hausa Corps aroused serious opposition from the people. There is a full discussion of this in the next chapter.

3 *Ibid.*, no. 54, encl. in Officer Administering the Govt. to Carnarvon, 9 June 1874

4 *Ibid.* Surgeon-Major A. F. Elliot wrote, 'I saw an old man at Accra the other day who had resided there, I think, for thirty years, and had the fresh pink colour of a country clergyman in England'.

5 *Ibid.*, no. 81, Glover to Carnarvon, 3 August 1874

6 *Ibid.*, no. 112, C.O. to W.O., 27 October 1874

CHAPTER THREE

The rise of opposition in the east

In the last chapter we saw that by 1874 Britain had initiated a policy of expansion on the Gold Coast. This they extended to the area east of the Volta where the desire to expand their influence involved them in formulating fiscal and territorial policies. The fiscal policy meant applying to the area the revenue system operating on the other side of the Volta since 1873 in the form of *ad valorem* duties on certain imports. These duties ranged from two shillings and sixpence per gallon on spirits to sixpence per pound on cigars and tobacco. Ten per cent duties on the invoice price were imposed on other items such as guns and gunpowder. The number of taxable commodities was gradually increased till in the 1880s there was a ten per cent *ad valorem* duty on twenty-four different articles.[1] These duties the British planned to impose on the Anlo.

The territorial policy also involved the British in reoccupying the Anlo country, which they had abandoned in 1859.[2] When the British reoccupied Keta in 1874, the people knew that they were there to pursue the fiscal and territorial policies already in operation west of the Volta.

It is important to note that even before 1874 the Anlo had been anti-British. Since the British takeover of the Danish possessions in 1850, the Anlo had steadily resisted the spread of their influence. Their reason was the help which the British frequently gave to enemies of Anlo. In 1866, for instance, the British supported the Gas in their war against Anlo. After the war, the Accra merchants, disappointed with the result, actually persuaded the British to bombard the Anlo villages on the sea-board.[3] Consequently the Anlo never liked the British and as soon as they reoccupied the coast in 1874, resistance movements were organised.

We need to consider the nature of the protests against the British east of the Volta. Since all of them were concerned with questions of the people's trading system, of their independence, or of British interference with their rights, they must be regarded as occurring over national issues. It is true that not all the subdivisions – Anlo, Somme and Aflao – came together to fight the British simultaneously, but the issues involved were such that there was never any disagreement among the people themselves over them. Also, though some of

1 C.O. 96/118, no. 167, Lees to Carnarvon, 10 August 1876

2 Adm. 1/687, no. 90, Ussher to Kennedy, 8 July 1870. The British occupied Anlo in 1850 when they bought the Danish possessions, but in 1855 they withdrew the garrisons from Keta and Dzelukofe and in 1859 abandoned the whole country.

3 *The African Times*, 22 September 1866

these outbursts were spontaneous and concerned with isolated incidents, they were more often carefully planned protests over such important issues as independence. At such times a picture emerges of the entire Anlo–Somme and Aflao sea-board fighting for a national cause. In the last analysis, these protests should be classified as a planned struggle for freedom. They constituted, in fact, a protonationalist movement of no small magnitude.

Let us first consider the protests connected with the preservation of independence, then those arising from the trading system, and lastly those which dealt with British interference with the rights of the people.

By 1874 the Anlo were already set in their habits of protest. As soon as the British reoccupied Keta, therefore, the Anlo decided, even before the Gold Coast Government had time to implement its policies, that they had to grapple with the task of preserving their independence. They looked at Asante and Dahomey, still politically free and independent, and wished to emulate them. The methods they employed in doing this were (a) attacking British stations and establishments on the coast to warn British officials against interference in their policies; (b) sending petitions to the British authorities, requesting them to confirm that Britain recognised the sovereign and independent status of Anlo.[1]

One of the earliest attacks on British establishments took place on 12 February 1878, at Denu, where the neighbouring people set fire to the factory of Messrs Alexander Miller Brothers and Company of Glasgow. While the factory was burning the inhabitants, all armed, plundered it, causing damage worth about £500.[2] Later that year on 19 and 20 October the principal chiefs of Anlo assembled in Council at Anloga, the capital, to discuss whether to make war on the Government. Chief Domey, the second chief of Woe, who reported this in Keta on the 21st, said that the Council of War had dissolved on the 20th leaving the final decision to their new king, who was still observing the customary period of confinement for new kings.[3] Three days later he completed this custom and gave his decision in favour of war against the Government. All Anlo began to mobilise in preparation for the struggle. Even before the King's decision was known, the people of Tegbi, half-way between Keta and Anloga, assaulted and drove out of their town Private Kwamina Gyan of the Gold Coast Constabulary, whom the District Commissioner had sent to arrest a prisoner who had escaped from custody in Keta. The Chief of Tegbi, when requested by the District Commissioner to find out those most prominent in assaulting the Constable, refused to do so. The sea-board inhabitants, particularly those of Woe and Tegbi, sent their wives, children and property across the Lagoon to the islands and mainland for safety.[4] But while this general mobilisation was reaching its climax, Ellis, the District Commissioner, was taking ruthless measures to suppress it. As a result the Anlo postponed the start of the general war they had planned.

East of Anlo, in Somme, the fight for independence had to take a slightly different form. As soon as the British came back to the coast in 1874 the Somme

---

1 C.O. 96/123, no. 48, Freeling to Hicks Beach, and encl., 9 March 1878; C.O. 96/126, no. 6, encl. 3 in Lees to Hicks Beach, 12 January 1879

2 *Ibid.*   3 C.O. 96/124, no. 213, encl. 1 in Lees to Hicks Beach, 28 October 1878

4 *Ibid.*, encl. 2

realised that they had plans for expansion beyond Keta. When they saw Captain Baker landing in Adafienu (1874), they guessed his intention and protested. They warned him that, since their country had never been part of the Danish possessions on which Britain's original claim was based, he must keep his hands off Somme.[1] They emphasised that Danish jurisdiction had been confined to Anlo. 'We beg to say', they continued, 'that our country must not be confounded[2] with that of Anlo – we are a distinct people; and our country is quite distinct from theirs. We are in no way connected with them, either by treaty or alliance.'[3] They further explained that Anlo territory stopped at Kedzi and theirs began from Blukusu, extending as far as Denu.[4]

By 1878, in spite of Somme protests, the British occupied Adafienu and Denu. Thus the Somme protests, from 1879, were no longer efforts to prevent occupation of their country, but attempts to get the British to withdraw from their towns. In January 1879 the chiefs and headmen of Somme sent to the Gold Coast Government a petition, in which they stated: 'The seizure and annexation of our country we are at a loss to understand.' They concluded the petition: 'We therefore beg to submit that, as the taking of our country was forcibly and unjustly done, we feel that it is in the bounds of reason and duty, to ask for its restoration.' They preferred not to enjoy British protection.[5]

In reply to the petition, the local Government intimated that it would consolidate its position in Somme rather than withdraw.[6] So the chiefs and headmen looked for other ways and means of terminating British occupation of their sea-board. In November 1879 they opened negotiations with the captain of an American trading barque, belonging to Messrs Upton and Steave, for the cession of their coastline to America. According to the agreement reached, in consideration of a sum of money paid down and an annual consideration of $500, they ceded to these traders, for ninety-nine years, the whole of the Somme sea-board, including Adina and Adafienu, then in occupation by the British.[7] It was rumoured after some time on the coast that the U.S.A. had ratified the treaty of cession. The Agbozume chiefs then told Turkson, the Assistant Examining Officer at Adafienu, that they had sold the land to the U.S.A. Government,[8] and Agbozume territory 'did not belong to the British Government', so he must withdraw to Keta.[9] But the British occupation of Somme continued.

East of Somme was the Aflao country. The 1879 protests in Aflao were meant to prevent the British occupation of the country; for as late as December

---

1 C.O. 96/126, no. 6, encl. 3 in Lees to Hicks Beach, G.C., 12 January 1879

2 They must mean 'confused'.

3 The Somme and Anlo were one people, i.e. of the same origin. But it is true that at the time it was said the Somme would have nothing to do with the Anlo. See Fisher's report in C.O. 96/182, no. 305, Fraser to Governor, 21 July 1887

4 C.O. 96/126, no. 6, encl. 3 in Lees to Hicks Beach, 12 January 1879

5 *Ibid.*   6 *Ibid.*, encl. 2

7 C.O. 96/127, no. 254, encls. 2, 3 and 4, Ussher to Hicks Beach, 30 October 1879

8 C.O. 96/128, no. 269, encl. 3 in Ussher to Hicks Beach, 11 November 1879

9 *Ibid.*, encl. 4. Ussher wrote that the American traders also requested British officials to withdraw to Kedzi and that they landed 400 puncheons of rum in Denu to be smuggled into British territory, at a loss of £5000 to the Revenue.

that year, there was yet no effective occupation of this coastline. But about 10 December, the British began preparations to occupy both Aflao and Gbagidah. At once the inhabitants protested and opposed Captain Hay's attempts to hoist the English flag in their towns. When Captain Hay proceeded to the Aflao beach and sent the interpreter into the town, half an hour's journey inland, to request the chiefs to meet him and reach an agreement on the occupation of their sea-board, they refused. Hay sent the messenger a second time, but they again refused. The British had to bring in a man-of-war, threatening to destroy the town, before the inhabitants acquiesced in the hoisting of the British flag and the occupation of their town by customs officials, etc.[1]

The inhabitants of Gbagidah were more successful in preventing British occupation of their country. Before the attempted occupation began, Captain Hay discovered the mistake he had made earlier in thinking that Gbagidah was in Aflao territory. So when his emissaries, led by Captain St Clair, went to Gbagidah in 1881 their first task was to negotiate cession with the chiefs to make occupation possible. But a large section of the people were opposed to the suggestions of the British, and the opposition was strong enough to prevent the agreement being signed.[2]

G. B. Williams, the chief trader in Gbagidah, played an important part in organising the people of Gbagidah against the British. While Captain St Clair and the British officials who had arrived in the town to treat with the chiefs and headmen were in one house, this Williams was in another, giving the people rum and tobacco, and using his best endeavours to prevent them from giving up their sea-board.[3] He won the day.

At the same time that the Anlo were trying to safeguard their political and territorial rights, they were also concerned with the preservation of their trading system, which was unique and based on smuggling. In the 1870s and 80s a number of merchants lived in Keta, including Tamakloe, Akolatse, G. B. Williams, G. R. Turnbull, C. Rottman, J. B. Cole and Ditchfield.[4] About 1878 G. B. Williams established a factory at Denu a mile and a half from Adafienu, outside British jurisdiction. Other Keta merchants joined him, and Chief Antonio of Adafienu himself lived there doing good business in trade. Again, it was the Keta merchants who established another trading post at Gbagidah.

Now, the arrangement in Keta was that when the Anlo traders came, instead of taking goods directly from the merchants they received orders for goods and spirits on the merchants' stores at Denu, in exchange for produce they handed in at Keta. The Anlo traders then smuggled the goods into the Protectorate, either by running their cargoes into British territory during the night, or by taking the goods to the other side of the lagoon and shipping them to the Volta. This second method was facilitated by the lagoon behind the coastline of Anlo and Agbozume, leading on one side into the River Volta, and on

1 C.O. 96/128, no. 311, encl. in Ussher to Hicks Beach, 11 December 1879   2 *Ibid.*

3 C.O. 96/135, no. 294, encl. 2 in Rowe to Kimberley, 17 November 1881. In line with their contention that they were independent the inhabitants of Anlo and Somme refused to bring their cases, including those of murder, to British Courts. C.O. 96/140, no. 269, encls. 1 and 3 in Moloney to Kimberley, 27 June 1882

4 C.O. 96/125, no. 229, encls. 2 and 9 in Lees to Hicks Beach, in November 1878 and no. 252 and encl., 18 December 1878

the other extending nearly to the termination of British jurisdiction. This made it possible for the traders to carry their goods from Denu to the northern banks of the lagoon without passing through British territory, and once on the lagoon, the traders found it easy to distribute their wares. By this means they evaded the British customs and revenue posts, established in 1879, and consequently conducted a prosperous business. With such a profitable trading system, naturally the inhabitants of Anlo, Somme and Aflao were opposed to British policy.

Several incidents occurred as a result. The first of these took place on 24 September 1879, when the people of Srogboe treated the District Commissioner, Cecil Duddley, with violence and indignity[1] as he was examining the channel to the windward of Atokor in search of a suitable site for a station, where, no doubt, a detachment of Hausas would reside to check smugglers ferrying their goods from the lagoon into the Volta. As Duddley and his party approached the mainland shore of Srogboe, their canoe struck a line of rushes and came right upon another canoe and six casks of rum, concealed in the vegetation. Meanwhile a lot of people had been watching them from the opposite shore, and soon several canoes put off and speedily went to the place and carried off the casks of rum. The District Commissioner then ordered his canoemen to pull back to Atokor, and they had to go by the narrow channel which at that point ran very close to the village.[2] It was in these circumstances that the population of Srogboe treated the District Commissioner with indignity. 'Until my arrival at the outskirts of Attoko,' wrote the District Commissioner, 'my canoe had simply to run the gauntlet of a shower of coconut husks, sticks and clods of earth – thrown by the younger and adult portion of the population of Shrogboe.'[3] The use of coconut husks as missiles meant that they had a very low opinion of the District Commissioner.

The second incident occurred the following November, when a master plan of revolt against British rule was hatched. On the 9th the people of Anyako, Atiave, Sarame, Tsiame, Afiadenyigba and Glime held a council of war after having sent messengers to Anloga, the capital, for consultation with the authorities there. The messengers were to obtain the permission of the King for the resumption of war preparations, which were suspended in the previous year. The permission was given, and so the people proceeded with the preparations. The man organising the movement was none other than Tenge, the powerful Chief of Anyako. Tenge was the deputy of the Awamefia or King of Anlo on the islands. He was supported in this new move by Atikpo also of Anyako, the chief of Atiave and Kwawukume of Abolove. The great warrior was determined to fight so as to compel the British to change their financial policy.

Tenge sent Kwawukume and others to distribute casks of rum and large quantities of powder to the people on the islands. The people proposed to divide their forces into two, so that, when the District Commissioner left Keta

1 C.O. 96/128, no. 265, Ussher to Hicks Beach, 11 November 1879

2 The geographical features described by Cecil Duddley are exactly the same today. They are such that there can be no mistaking the exact spot where he struck the rushes and exactly where his canoe passed when the missiles were thrown at him.

3 C.O.96/128, no. 265, encl. 1 in Ussher to Hicks Beach, 11 November 1879

in one direction, an attack could be made from the opposite side. But unfortunately the people hesitated to attack Keta, as Chief Tamakloe 'has too much property here'. Chief Tamakloe, not yet estranged from his people by British policy, was himself moving closely with the leaders of the revolt and acted as a spy for his people, watching and reporting all the movements of the District Commissioner to them. Instead of attacking Keta, the people made a plan to trap the District Commissioner, but he eluded them.[1]

Another example of African activity designed to circumvent the British policy of checking smuggling, was the establishment of trading settlements such as Lome east of Aflao. As the British extended their influence eastward to Aflao in order to check smuggling and increase their revenue, the merchants and the local traders moved further east beyond British jurisdiction, to thwart the British plan. When the British annexed Aflao late in 1879 it was Chief James Quaminah Bruce's consent to cession that they obtained. But even Bruce could not afford to see the smuggling trade stifled.

In handing over Aflao to the British Government, Bruce swindled them by not leasing one part of the Aflao territory, which he handed over to the Chief of Bey, arranging with him to keep the matter secret. On this land he established business with American traders, thus evading British customs officials. This smuggling depot he called Little Sierra Leone.[2] A mile to the east, another trader, G. B. Williams, soon started a new settlement. His factory was speedily followed by the Bremen factory, and this new depot known as Bey Beach gradually merged with Little Sierra Leone to form the beginnings of Lome, which by 1881 became the headquarters of the smuggling enterprise.[3] All the principal firms in Keta, both European and African, with Chiefs Akolatse and Tamakloe, Aguagoo, Roberts and Antonio established agencies there.[4] The interior traders, too, supported the firms to make the smuggling effective. In October 1881, the new District Commissioner of Keta, R. H. Wilton, observed that 'people are constantly passing through Addafia and Danoe with empty demi-johns on their heads going to Lomi. None of these empty demi-johns ever return the same way full. I saw while standing outside the Bremen Factory at Danoe no less than 150 demi-johns empty pass in this way'.[5]

From 1881, therefore, no local trader from the interior went to Keta, but all to a man repaired to Lome for their merchandise.[6] This development involved a considerable loss of revenue for the local British Government.[7] It was a silent but a most effective measure against the Government.

The last example we shall discuss here of the attempts of the Anlo to preserve their system of smuggling took a more violent form and was nothing less than a general uprising of the communes in arms to crush the Government.

1 C.O. 96/128, no. 266, encl. in Ussher to Hicks Beach, 12 November 1879

2 C.O. 96/135, no. 294, encl. 2 in Rowe to Kimberley, 17 November 1881

3 *Ibid.*, encl. 1

4 C.O. 96/141, no. 329 and encl. 1, Moloney to Kimberley, 21 July 1882

5 C.O. 96/135, no. 294, encl. 1 in Rowe to Kimberley, 17 November 1881

6 C.O. 96/134, no. 40, encl. in Griffith to Kimberley, 11 February 1881

7 C.O. 96/141, no. 329 and encl. 1, Moloney to Kimberley, 21 July 1882

It all started when early in 1885 Geraldo, the champion of smugglers, who had been active at Denu and Aflao, fell into the hands of the British and was being led to Accra from Keta, through the sea-board villages. The Anyakos rushed to Wuti in the hope of intercepting Geraldo's escort and rescuing him; they failed.[1] His removal seriously threatened the smuggling system, so the Anlo, who had already been planning a general war speeded up their preparations. 'The whole of the Awoonahs and Anyakos, and the many tribes that paid them feudal allegiance . . . entered into a compact by fetish bond to be loyal to each other, and to attack Quittah from two directions.'[2] The creation of hostile combinations against the British was the assignment of Tenge himself and Akrobotu, Chief of Srogboe. Internally they brought together Chiefs Nanevi and Gate of Srogboe, Morte of Wuti, Kwawu Kuku of Atokor, Zametsi and Agbeko of Dzita and Kodzo Safo, all of the sea-board villages, who resolved to stand by each other and the mainland chiefs until British forces were crushed. Then the insurgents looked for external assistance. They dispatched messengers to Akwamu and Asante to ask for help against the Government.[3]

The next stage of the preparations was the acquisition of munitions of war. The Anlo had to do this outside British jurisdiction in Little Popo. Here Pedro Kudjo, a store-keeper, sold them Snider rifles and ammunition on easy terms. Within a few weeks in March (1885) Tenge obtained about 100 Snider rifles and ammunition on credit, and Pedro Kudjo actually said that he need not pay until he finished his war with the British.[4] The financial aspect of the preparations then received particular attention, and a collection of cowries (eight strings from men and two from women) was imposed on the Anlo population generally. The final stages of the preparations included Tenge's application to Aholu, the supreme commander of the entire Anlo fighting forces, to make available to the insurgents the ancient war sword of Anlo, since Aholu would not personally be in command of the approaching campaign.[5] There was some difficulty, however, and the Anlo authorities could not produce the sword.

The Anlo forces had to move in support of Geraldo before they were absolutely ready to fight. They then numbered 3000 under Tamakee and Tsigui, Tenge's lieutenants. This force faced the District Commissioner of Keta, Captain Campbell, with a party of thirty-eight Hausas. From Wuti the force pushed the D.C.'s party towards Keta by way of Taleto, a small lagoon close to the sea between Wuti and Anloga. Near this lagoon the Anlo poured a heavy fire into the ranks of the retreating party. Two Hausas were killed and Captain Campbell received serious wounds. The Anlo nearly succeeded in routing the Government forces but they got away to Keta with great difficulty.[6] The Anlo could not attack Keta without further preparation, so the campaign was temporarily suspended.

The Anlo resistance was not resumed until 1889. The 1889 campaign was really the climax of Anlo protests not only to prevent the implementation of

1 C.4477, encl. 3 in Young to Derby, 19 January 1885. See also African no. 277.

2 C.4477, encl. 3 in Young to Derby, 6 February 1885

3 C.O. 96/166, no. 178, encl. 1 in Griffith to Derby, 6 June 1885

4 *Ibid.*, and encl. 3   5 *Ibid.*

6 C.4477, encl. 1 in Young to Derby, 19 January 1885. See also African no. 277.

British policy towards them, but also to forestall the ruthless manner in which, knowing the past record of the British, they feared it would be implemented.

The Anlo–Somme and Aflao resistance on this account began as early as 1878, when the inhabitants initiated a series of petitions arguing that, from what they knew of the British, they feared there would be further raids of Government forces on their villages, and that the brutality of the Hausas in the course of checking smugglers was likely to increase. One of these protests occurred in July 1878 when the chiefs and elders of Somme appealed to His Excellency, Governor Lees, to withdraw the Hausas from their borders because they feared they would soon begin 'their brutal usage of people, their murders and other unbecoming behaviour, etc.'[1]

The most bitter petition, however, was presented in the following January. The Somme now addressed themselves to the Secretary of State for the Colonies, pointing out that the local authorities had failed to heed their requests in the earlier petition. But they were still convinced that as long as the Hausas continued in occupation of their territory,

> our towns and villages may at any moment be burnt and sacked without cause and our wives and children subjected to the same barbarous and inhuman treatment to which our neighbours the Awoonahs have recently had to submit at the hands of the Hausas comprising the Garrison of Quitta Fort, we have no other recourse than to appeal to Her Majesty's Imperial Government through yourself, Sir, for the redress which it would seem had been withheld from us hitherto only because our right is powerless against the might of the Gold Coast Colonial Government, but which we are satisfied will not be denied us one moment after the facts of our case came to be laid before that distinguished body of Englishmen, of which you, Sir, are a prominent member – we pray, in fine, that the Gold Coast Government may be instructed to withdraw its Hausas from our territories and its Custom House Officers from our ports.[2]

Government in Whitehall was no more sympathetic to the cause of the Agbozumes than the local Government, except that a decision was now made to pay the Somme chiefs subsidies in lieu of withdrawing the Hausas from their territory. This was unsatisfactory to the people. They realised that they could not achieve freedom from impending Hausa brutality through petition alone. So they began to organise armed attacks on the Hausas themselves.

The Sommes and Aflaos used to set traps for the Hausas and to attack them when they fell into them. One of the earliest of these incidents occurred in 1881. Some women, disguised as smugglers, went past two unarmed Hausa soldiers cutting grass on the outskirts of Adafienu. As soon as the Hausas summoned the 'smugglers' to give up their goods, a party of armed men appeared in support of the women and, when the Hausas began to run away, shot one of them dead.[3] Later that year, on 22 June a Somme man set a new trap for the Hausas when he carried a demi-john of rum towards a group patrolling round the town of Adafienu. Immediately they saw him the man threw down the rum and ran away. Naturally one of the Hausas followed him, and when they were out of sight of the others, the man turned round and wounded his pursuer with a cutlass.[4]

1 C.O. 96/126, no. 6, encl. 3 in Lees to Hicks Beach, 11 January 1879   2 *Ibid.*, encl. 2

3 C.O. 96/135, no. 294 and encl. 4, Rowe to Kimberley, 17 November 1881

4 C.O. 96/135, no. 294, Rowe to Kimberley, 17 November 1881

The third incident took place at Aflao. Here on 6 October the Aflao decided to have a row with the police, whom they deliberately provoked later by sending a party of 'smugglers' along Aflao beach instead of along the road through the bush from Lome which genuine smugglers used. In this way on 5 November about 6 a.m., three fake smugglers passed in full view of the police station and the patrolling Hausas, Lance-Corporal Anthony and Private Mensah. The smugglers were carrying three demi-johns of rum and a small case of gin, which Anthony seized and took to the police station. The men told the police that the contraband articles belonged to Chief Quacoe of Denu. They then reported the incident to the chief, who together with thirty men and six women came down on the police station, set upon the two policemen and took away the rum. Lance-Corporal Anthony was wounded and Private Mensah had to flee to Adafienu. The native officer in charge of the Adafienu Hausa Detachment, Abudu Karimu, sent ten Hausas under Sergeant Mada to Aflao. But a large number of armed Aflaos set upon the Hausas, the women inciting the men. They attacked Sergeant Mada with cutlasses and tracked him down, dispersing the entire party of Hausas.

When after this Captain J. R. H. Wilton, the District Commissioner, decided to punish the Aflaos, the Hausa force he sent there had the worst of it. As the force approached the town they heard the Aflaos drumming as though for entertainment and unaware of the approaching danger. But all of a sudden the Aflaos opened fire on them from all sides and in the first two minutes two Hausas were shot dead, one through the kidneys, the other higher up the chest, which confirmed that they were completely surrounded. The District Commissioner had to withdraw the force to Adafienu with great difficulty. He later gave orders for the town to be shelled from the sea but before this could be done, the inhabitants had retreated with their belongings into the unknown interior.[1]

All these activities culminated in the 1889 campaign mentioned earlier. After the 1885 campaign Tenge went to Little Popo to buy arms in preparation for a more deadly struggle with the British. He returned to Anyako in 1888 and set up his headquarters some twenty miles east of that island. Here he and his lieutenants Tsigui, Akrobotu, Dzaho and others continued to mobilise their forces when the Government, alarmed at the situation, sent forces to capture Tenge and the others. Tenge's forces began to move eastward and soon clashed with the Government troops at Kitarme. The Government troops had superior ammunition and succeeded in breaking through Tenge's forces which dispersed. Tsigui and other leaders of the rebellion fell in action. Tenge himself managed to escape and finally retreated into German Togo, where he and a few of his followers lived until their return to Anlo some years later. Thus he was never arrested by the Government. But the decisive defeat of his forces in 1889 brought the Anlo resistance to an end.

If we look back on these events and try to put them in their true perspective, the picture which emerges is of a movement deliberately planned to prevent the British from establishing their hold on the Anlo–Somme country. It was also planned to forestall the cruel conduct of British officials towards the sea-board people. By this movement, therefore, the subdivisions tried to preserve their rights as a free and independent people.

1 *Ibid.*, encls. 3 and 4

The Anlo protests had an important effect on British policy east of the Volta. Before their arrival on the Anlo coast in 1874 the British had already decided on a policy of expansion. But we know that, in the past, Britain had exercised great caution in the execution of her policies. As a result, she had been very slow in making her power felt on the Coast. A clear example was that although she had taken over the Danish possessions east of the Volta in 1850, she had made very little impact on the Anlo country, and as we have already seen, had actually abandoned the territory in 1859. But during this second occupation in 1874, they carried out their policy of expansion in quite a different manner.

Thus we find that the policies of territorial and fiscal expansion were carried out with great haste and with unnecessary cruelty, no doubt because the British were anxious to nullify the consequences of the protest movement or to crush it altogether. Thus we can see clearly that, unlike the Fante Confederacy, the Anlo protests east of the Volta affected not the formulation but the execution of British territorial and fiscal policies and the personnel employed in their implementation.

The territorial policy had to be implemented in great haste. The reason given for this was that the protests of the people made it necessary. On 22 June 1874 the British signed the Treaty of Dzelukofe with the King of Anlo. In summary the terms were:

1. The River Volta should be kept open for all lawful traders.
2. The Government was to have the right to occupy Keta, Dzelukofe and any other towns that might be deemed necessary in order to bring the whole of the Anlo country under British control.[1]

Captain Lees signed for the Government. On the Anlo side it was Chief Adjabe who deputised for the King, and he was supported by fourteen other chiefs and captains including Foli of Dzelukofe, Tamakloe of Wuti, Akrobotu of Srogboe and Tenge of Anyako.[2] The Anlo authorities were reluctant to enter into this agreement, pointing out that the British had not honoured their agreements in the past. But the British threatened to use force and so the Anlo reluctantly signed.[3]

Almost at once protests began, and the Gold Coast Government consequently hurried to carry out an effective occupation of Keta. Anlo activities affecting the collection of the revenue in particular worried the British. In April 1879 Captain Hay, after a tour of inspection in the Keta District, suggested to

---

1 Further Correspondence respecting the Ashantee Invasion, no. 61, Lees to Carnarvon, 23 June 1874, 'Active' at sea

2 *Ibid.* The other chiefs were:
   Kwakume for Aholu, War Captain of Anlo
   Kposu, Captain of Dzelukofe
   Atiku   ,,   ,, Anyako
   Agudogo ,,   ,, Fiaxo
   Letsha   ,,   ,, Sadame
   Agblevo, Chief of Atiave
   Nyaho   ,,   ,, Sadame
   Saba   ,,   ,, Afiadenyigba
   Mogolu   ,,   ,, Weta
   Amedomey for Antonio, Chief of Woe

3 *Ibid.*

Administrator Lees that the occupation of the Coast up to and including the village of Gbagidah would promote the better protection of the revenue of the colony, by preventing the smuggling of goods and spirits into the Protectorate.[1]

When this suggestion reached the Colonial Office it found ready support. Before taking action, the Colonial Office explained to the Foreign Office 'that the present boundary is an unsatisfactory one' because, during the rainy season, the lagoon which ran parallel to the sea extended somewhat beyond British jurisdiction, affording facilities for smuggling. Since the annexation of the suggested extension would create an effective barrier to the contraband trade, which as we have seen, was inimical to British plans[2]: 'Sir M. Hicks Beach proposes therefore to instruct the Governor to negotiate with the Afflahow Chiefs for the cession of the strip of land in question, but before doing so he would be glad to know whether Lord Salisbury is aware of any objection to such a measure.'[3] Lord Salisbury was aware of none and so Ussher, who took over the administration of the Gold Coast on 1 July 1879, was accordingly instructed to proceed with negotiations.[4] Ussher's method was to send a Danish mulatto, Mr Lutterodt, to persuade the Aflao chiefs to ask for the stipends, which they were alleged formerly to have received from Denmark, and voluntarily to surrender their coast-line to the British.[5] The Aflao chiefs did not move and Ussher, in a hurry to achieve the desired goal, compelled their representatives, as well as those of Agbozume (Somme) to attend on him at Keta. There, under pressure, he got them to cede Agbozume and Aflao coast-line to the British on 2 December 1879.[6] At once the Government proceeded to effectively occupy Denu and Aflao, which they now regarded as Her Majesty's territory. Governor Ussher introduced strong security measures, including a fortified block house built in Aflao with a camp on the border.[7] When they took possession of Aflao, the British realised that Gbagidah, the easternmost limit of Captain Hay's proposed extension, did not belong to Aflao; and so early in 1881 preparations began 'to try and get Bagieday through the chiefs'.[8] But since there was not much to expect from this method, Captain Graves, D.C. of Keta, recommended taking by force the entire Bey territory in which Gbagidah was situated.[9]

A complication arose over the Bey issue, however. From 1881 to 1883 the Chiefs of Bey and Porto Seguro steadily refused to cede their territories. Never-

1 C.O. 96/126, no. 90, Lees to Hicks Beach, 21 April 1879   2 See above p. 67

3 C.O. 96/126, G.C. Conf., Hicks Beach to Salisbury, 25 June 1879

4 C.O. 96/126, no. 153, Minute of 9 August 1879 by Antrobus on Ussher to Hicks Beach, 8 July 1879

5 C.O. 96/127, G.C. Conf., Ussher to Hicks Beach, 30 August 1879

6 C.O. 96/128, no. 305, Ussher to Hicks Beach, 3 December 1879; *Standard* 10 January 1880; *Daily News* 10 January 1880. Those who represented Agbozume were Klu for the King, Anthony Chief of Adafienu, Soha Chief of Denu, Defor for Kudjo, Chief of Adina.

7 C.O. 96/130, no. 25, Ussher to Hicks Beach, 26 January 1880

8 C.O. 96/134, no. 40, encl., Griffith to Kimberley, 11 February 1881

9 *Ibid.*, no. 5, encl., 4 January 1881

theless, in 1884, while British officials were preparing to force cession on Bey,[1] it was learned at the Colonial Office that France, too, was becoming interested in this part of the Coast. The Colonial Office was anxious to avoid conflicts with France in the neighbourhood of the Gold Coast, and so it was agreed that negotiations should be entered into with France over the issue.[2] While the British were waiting for the results of these negotiations Germany suddenly annexed the entire Bey country, to the surprise of both France and Britain. Had it not been for these complications Britain would have extended her territory beyond Aflao. It was nevertheless remarkable that within six years of the reoccupation of Keta (1874), Britain acquired the entire Coast from the Volta to Aflao. The speed with which this territorial expansion was achieved was clearly the result of persistent African protest.

Similarly, the hurried manner in which the British executed their fiscal policy was due to the protest movement. Whenever the Anlo claimed ownership of their own lands, warning against the posting of British customs officials in their towns,[3] the British, anxious to beat down these protests, established new customs posts on the Coast.[4] Again, whenever the people established new trading posts outside British jurisdiction,[5] the British extended their customs posts eastwards to those areas.[6] By 1880 therefore, the Gold Coast Government had set up customs posts all along the Coast at Atokor, Dzelukofe, Keta, Adafienu, Denu and Aflao.[7] Thus, it was as a counter measure to African activities, that Britain's commercial and financial policies towards the Anlo–Somme country were so quickly executed.

Perhaps an even more important effect of these protests on British policy east of the Volta was the cruel manner in which British agents executed that policy. The chief agents employed by the Gold Coast Government to carry out its policy were the District Commissioner of Keta and Detachments of the Hausa force.

As soon as the British occupied Keta and Dzelukofe in June 1874 the Gold Coast Government stationed in Keta a District Commissioner with responsibility for the execution of Government policies in the district. The District Commissioners tended to be ruthless in the execution of their duties; they believed that this was the best way to crush the protests of the people, and prepare the way for a successful implementation of British policy. A. B. Ellis, D.C. of Keta District from 1878 to 1879, in particular, discharged his duties with unnecessary cruelty. Anlo authorities, including the King and Chief Antonio of Woe, accused Ellis in November 1878 of having seized spirits from Anlo traders, plundered the town of Tegbi and shot down three people at Abolove

1 C.O. 96/157, no. 255, Young to Derby, 29 April 1884, Minutes of 21 June by Hemming on above

2 *Ibid.*, Minutes of 8 July 3 See above p. 64

4 C.O. 96/126, no. 6, encl. 11 in Lees to Hicks Beach, 12 January 1879

5 See above p. 67

6 C.O. 96/128, no. 223, Minutes of 22 January by Lowther on Strahan to Carnarvon, 22 November 1875

7 C.O. 96/128, no. 311, encl. in Ussher to Hicks Beach, 11 December 1879

where he went to check smuggling.[1] Although Ellis's report that he was first provoked by the Abolove people on his landing there, was denied by an eye-witness,[2] it indicates the sort of effect that the protests had on British officials. Elsewhere Ellis was found to have acted ruthlessly, and in particular he conducted continuous raids on Anlo villages in his pursuit of smugglers.[3]

The District Commissioner had to rely on the Hausa force at his disposal for the performance of his duties. The manner in which the Hausas, in turn, discharged their duties caused even greater offence. As soon as the British reoccupied Anlo, they stationed the Hausa force in the area, and by May 1876 there were detachments at Atokor, Dzelukofe, Keta, Adina and Adafienu.[4] In 1880, after the boundary was extended to Aflao, Hausa posts were established in Denu and Aflao as well.[5] The frequent use to which the District Commissioner put the Hausas meant that force was the Government's normal method of increasing control. Early in November 1879, for instance, Ussher reinforced the Hausa detachments in the Keta district, and he himself with Captain Hay, Acting Colonial Secretary, Captain Wilton, Assistant Inspector Gold Coast Constabulary, and 120 non-commissioned officers, went to help Duddley, the District Commissioner of Keta, to quell the inhabitants of the district, who were breaking the customs regulations.[6] While in Keta the Governor sent a detachment of fifty men of the Gold Coast Constabulary (Hausa) under Captain Wilton and 'native' officer Ali to Adafienu.[7] The force was provided with a seven-pound gun, a rocket-thrower, and enough gunners to work the gun; each man carried eighty rounds of ammunition.[8] When they reached Adafienu they succeeded in brutally suppressing the people and checking smuggling.

According to the inhabitants, the Hausa force, which was frequently used, was guilty of theft, extortion, robbery and, above all, drunkenness, raiding and sheer brutality.[9] The Sommes and the Aflaos gave several examples of the Hausas illegally seizing spirits outside British jurisdiction.[10] Even more brutal was their conduct at Kedzi on 29 October 1878. On that day a number of Hausas from Keta without orders 'attacked the defenceless village of Kedgie, fired the native houses and shot down the women and children as they rushed through the flames'.[11] In this way they killed six persons, one of them a baby, and

---

1 C.O. 96/125, no. 219, encl. in Lees to Hicks Beach, 6 November 1878; no. 229, encl. 4 in same to same, 18 November 1878

2 C.O. 96/125, no. 229, encl. 9 in Lees to Hicks Beach, 18 November 1878

3 Ibid., no. 217, encl. 2, 5 November 1878

4 C.O. 96/118, no. 115, encl. 2 in Lees to Carnarvon, 8 May 1876

5 C.O. 96/130, no. 25, encl. 1 in Ussher to Hicks Beach, January 1880

6 C.O. 96/128, no. 280, Ussher to Hicks Beach, 17 November 1879

7 Ibid., no. 287, 23 November 1879   8 Ibid., encls. 1 and 2

9 C.O. 96/120, no. 55, Freeling to Carnarvon, 20 February 1877

10 C.4477, encl. 2, Rowe to C.O., 16 August 1884

11 African Times, 30 October 1878, quoted in Minutes by Hemming, 5 December 1878 on C.O. 96/125, no. 219, Lees to Hicks Beach, 6 November 1878

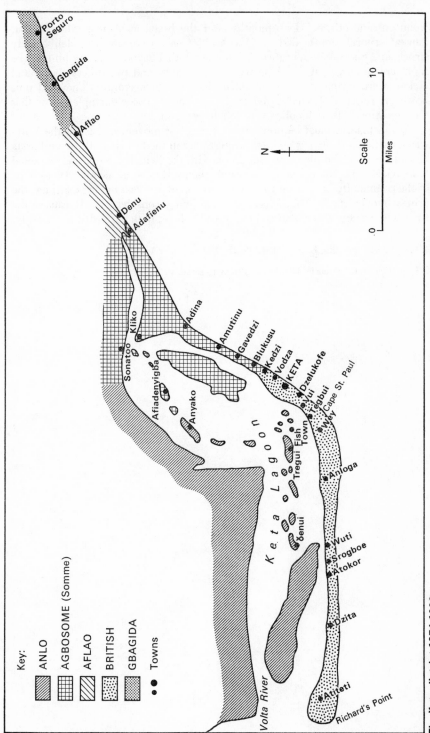

Key:

	ANLO
	AGBOSOME (Somme)
	AFLAO
	BRITISH
	GBAGIDA
●	Towns

Porto Seguro

Gbagida

Aflao

Denu

Adafienu

Adina

Amutinu

Gavedzi

Blukusu

Kedzi

Vodza

KETA

Dzelukofe

Kliko

Sonatoo

Afiadenyigba

Anyako

Tui

Tegbui

Wey

Cape St. Paul

Tregui Fish Town

Anloga

Denui

Wuti

Srogboe

Atokor

Dzita

Atiteti

Richard's Point

K e t a   L a g o o n

Volta River

N

Scale

Miles

10

0

The Keta district 1874-1900

wounded nine others.[1] Two months after the Kedzi incident another Hausa, Lance-Corporal Imoru Bade of the Gold Coast Constabulary, deliberately struck an Agbozume man called Ackummey with a bayonet, killing him on the spot. This occurred at Adafienu where Ackummey and two others, Issay and Geloo, were trying to smuggle spirits into the Protectorate. They did not, however, resist when challenged by Imoru Bade.[2] These examples show that the execution of British policy was definitely harsh.

To conclude, it must be noted that the protest movement east of the Volta was a particularly strong one. Its strength lay in the fact that all the outbursts of protests involved direct confrontation with the British agents and none led to a division of opinion among the people themselves, as in Asante. All sections of the community agreed on the same national objectives. Being so strong, the protest movement in Anlo affected British policy considerably. It caused the British to execute their fiscal and territorial policies both hurriedly and harshly.

1 C.O. 96/125, no. 229, Lees to Hicks Beach, 18 November 1878

2 C.O. 96/126, no. 6, encls. 10 and 11 in same to same, 12 January 1879

CHAPTER FOUR

Asante activities and British interference 1875–1890

At the same time as the Anlo were organising opposition to British rule, the Asante were also busy trying to thwart British policy in their own country. But these activities in Asante (1875–90) were different, both in origin and organisation, from those in Anlo. They occurred over internal disaffection in the Asante Empire.

The Asante Empire consisted of the Amantoo states and the Amansin states. The Amantoo states were the inner chiefdoms, forming metropolitan Asante; Kumasi, Juaben, Kokofu, Bekwai, Nsutah and Mampon. The Amansin states were the provinces added to metropolitan Asante either through conquest or moral influence: Salaga, Nkoranza, Gyaman, Sefwi, etc. From 1875 onwards secessionist movements began in both metropolitan and provincial Asante, and the Asante Central Government was therefore busy trying to restore unity. There were thus local issues at stake during the period when Asante politics were partly geared (1875–90) towards influencing British action there. This is clear from the fact that the Central Government of Asante had to fight against a number of metropolitan and provincial states – such as Juaben, Adansi, Salaga, etc. The Kumasi authorities never launched a direct attack on British troops or officials during this period, as did the protesting Anlo.

But although these Asante activities were not solely concerned with the British, they were to a considerable extent directed against them. This was because the British encouraged the secessionist movements in Asante. Besides, in spite of the lack of a united front in Asante, activities hostile to the British were nevertheless carefully planned, using twin weapons of diplomacy and the military force. Normally they started with negotiations, and when these failed force was used. Though the immediate objects of these campaigns were the secessionists, they left deep marks on British policy. The aims of these attacks were not just to prevent secession, but also to scare the British away from interfering in Asante politics and extending British influence into the Asantehene's dominions.

And Asante achieved her aim. Through victorious campaigns, Asante succeeded in causing a delay in the execution of British policy there. It is interesting to note that, whereas Anlo protests led to a speedy execution of British policy east of the Volta, Asante activities had the opposite effect. This was due not only to the fact that expeditions against Asante were definitely more expensive, but also that the Kumasi fighting forces, which spear-headed the activities of the Asante traditionalists, were among the most formidable in western Africa. The British had to move very slowly in face of active campaigns by such an army.

It has been fashionable for almost every writer on British policy in Asante before the 1880s to describe it as one of non-intervention. Claridge, in his *History of the Gold Coast and Ashanti*, called it one of non-interference in intention, if not in practice.[1] Ward, following Claridge, maintained generally that Britain pursued a policy of non-interference, stating, for instance, that the Gold Coast Government did nothing to interfere in Asante during the Kumasi–Juaben War.[2] Even a recent author like David Kimble appears to have embraced this tradition and, giving instances of British officials holding back from open intervention, calls it a disinclination on their part to intervene in a decisive manner.[3] However, it is clear from the available evidence, that short of territorial control, the British did have a policy of intervening in Asante affairs by (*a*) trying to break up the Amantoo, and (*b*) seizing control of the trade routes through encouraging defection in provincial Asante. When British officials thus interfered in Asante affairs, Asante first availed herself of the diplomatic machinery built up since the eighteenth century to achieve an amicable settlement with both the British and the people concerned. When diplomacy failed, the Asante Court had to resort to police action.

Juaben, Salaga and Gyaman

Juaben was the first place where Asante needed to take police action to restore normal conditions for trade and re-establish the political control of the Asante Central Government. We have already referred to the defection of the Juabens in the 1874 War. It may be useful, however, to go into the circumstances which tended to cause disaffection in Juaben, which both Professor Ivor Wilks and Professor Adu Boahen, in their recent surveys of Asante, describe as the most powerful of the Amantoo states. Dr Boahen has analysed the tremendous increase in the power and wealth of Juaben and how this brought about conflict with Kumasi.[4] He has shown how the Asantehene in the nineteenth century became increasingly concerned with the growing threat from Juaben to the power and prestige of his dynasty. Ahuren tradition puts this Kumasi–Juaben conflict even earlier, to the time when Juaben men captured Ntim Gyakari, the Denkyirahene, thus gaining the prestige of being the saviours of Asante.

It is said that Kumasi fought the Juabens several times without success to regain the relics of this Denkyira war.[5] This suggests that Juaben's wealth and power in the nineteenth century was not the only cause of conflict with Kumasi. It was the early Kumasi–Juaben contests which were extended into the nineteenth century, when they were aggravated by the changing fortunes of Juaben. The immediate cause, however, of the 1875 conflict was the non-aggression pact with Akyem, which, as we have already seen, resulted in

1 Claridge, *A History of the Gold Coast and Ashanti*, Vol. II, p. 198

2 Ward, *A History of Ghana*, p. 285

3 Kimble, *A Political History of Ghana*, pp. 277–8

4 Boahen, *Juaben and Kumasi relations in the nineteenth century*

5 Ahuren tradition, Bekwai D.R.B.

Juaben's disobedience to the orders of Kofi Karikari during the British invasion of Kumasi.[1]

The Asantehene Kofi Karikari was anxious that Juaben should be restored to Asante rule by negotiation. He was aware of the increasing British influence in Juaben and so he referred the matter to the Gold Coast Government. In July 1874 both Kumasi and Juaben messengers were in Cape Coast, pleading for intervention by the Government. The Asante embassy led by Euchin stated that the King wanted Britain to intervene because he 'does not wish the place to be in bad order, but wishes peace and is much concerned about this matter'. Governor Strahan's reply, as he himself later indicated, was

You have requested my interference to settle matters between Coomassie and Juabin by sending messengers to the Kings, but you intend that my inter- ference shall be such as to induce the Juabins to return to Ashantee rule. I have already informed you that although steps have been taken, and taken successfully, to send back Ashantees who were being detained in the pro- tectorate against their will, the Queen will not interfere to induce, much less to compel, anyone to return to the Ashantee rule. If this, then, is the object you have in view by asking my interference, what use is there in my sending a messenger?[2]

This reply of the Governor came after Euchin, the Asante of rank, and the rest of the embassy had 'begged' Strahan to intervene in Kumasi–Juaben affairs.

But the British did not, in fact, stop there. They actually decided to support Juaben defection, seeing that would lead to the break up of the Amantoo and at the same time weaken Asante control of the trade routes to the northeast. Moreover British officials became convinced that if Kumasi succeeded in turning the tables on the Juabens, 'a momentary success on their [Asante] side would lead to a renewal of the prestige they have lost, and revive among the western tribes of the Protectorate a spirit of disaffection which has now been success- fully overcome'.[3] For these reasons intervention was imperative, and Juaben could be the tool for this intervention. By strengthening Juaben the Gold Coast Government could prevent any such developments in the affairs of Asante.

With these ends in view, Governor Strahan sent Captain Lees to Kumasi and Juaben about the middle of 1874.[4] Upon reaching Kumasi Captain Lees realised that the situation was grave indeed. He learned that the peoples of 'Sootak, Kokofoo and Bequi' had sided with Juaben and were seizing Kumasi men. He wrote: 'The King appeared to me to feel that the state of affairs was critical and to appreciate fully the gravity of the situation.' The King begged Captain Lees that the King of Juaben might either come to Kumasi or send a representa- tive, that the headmen of the villages which had thrown off their allegiance might be sent for, and that 'I would then exert myself to bring them again under

---

1 See p. 54. Kukurantumi tradition, Birim D.R.B.

2 Further Correspondence respecting the Ashantee Invasion, no. 85, Strahan to Carnarvon, 13 July 1874

3 *Ibid.*   4 *Ibid.*

his authority'.[1] When the King persistently repeated this request, all that Captain Lees did was to threaten to leave Kumasi forthwith. He eventually left for Juaben.[2] He had gone to Kumasi first, because he wanted to assess the situation there so as to know what line of action to take when in Juaben. Now that he was so impressed by the dangers facing Kumasi, he became convinced that in a contest between the two states Kumasi would be defeated.

In Juaben he was confirmed in this conviction, as the city's bald-headed war captain assured him by his attitude that he did not lose wars but won them. He straightaway reached an agreement with the Juaben authorities; first that Juaben should be independent of Kumasi; secondly Juaben was to live in peace with Kumasi and not incite others to molest Kumasi men, and finally that Juaben should open roads through her dominions to all lawful traders of any nation whatever.[3] It is this last clause which shows that one of the aims of the British in these negotiations was to terminate African control of trade routes in the interior whether it was by Kumasi or Juaben.

Captain Lees sealed his activities in Juaben in the following way: First he gave an English flag to the King of Juaben,[4] Asafu Agyei, thus extending British protection to the state. He then feverishly sought assurances from the King whether through his royal influence this agreement could be extended to some other states, thereby strengthening the supposed tendency of these states to bind themselves together against Kumasi. To strengthen the power of the Juabenhene vis-à-vis the Asantehene even further, the British presented him with a yellow stool, which he was to use as the Golden Stool of the Juaben Confederation, to bring these allegedly rebellious states even closer together against Kumasi. What the British sought to achieve in this respect was to create, or at least help to create, a block of states independent of Kumasi, in alliance with Juaben, and therefore under British influence, to constitute a permanent check upon the power of Kumasi.[5]

Alarmed by the growth of British influence in Juaben, and annoyed by Asafu Agyei's arrogance, Kumasi decided to resort to force after diplomacy had failed to halt these developments. This was done with great vigour. Soon after Captain Lees left Kumasi and was known to have entered Juaben, scheming to establish British influence there, the Kumasi chiefs staged a minor revolution, deposed the hesitating Karikari, and placed Osei Mensah, his younger brother, on the throne. The new king, anxious to end the Anglo–Juaben threat to peaceful trade and Asante power, sent two forces against Asafu Agyei, for whom the English flag and support constituted licence for disorderly behaviour.[6] After six days' fighting in Juaben, this ancient city lay in smouldering ruins.

Asafu Agyei's account of his defeat was that he managed to hold back the

1 Ibid., no. 106, encl. in Strahan to Carnarvon, 3 September 1874

2 The Asantehene had already sent Bonnat to Juaben on a similar mission without success. See M. Johnson, Kumasi, Juaben and M. Bonnat.

3 Encl. in Strahan to Carnarvon, 3 September 1874

4 C.O. 96/120, no. 31, Freeling to Carnarvon, 20 January 1877

5 C.O. 96/116, no. 210, encl. 1 in Strahan to Carnarvon, 25 October 1875

6 C.O. 96/116, no. 226, encl. 5 in Strahan to Carnarvon, 26 November 1875

Asante until his powder ran out.[1] The Asante added that the tide was even turning against Kumasi. But the Kumasi chiefs, especially Adu Boffo, who spear-headed this movement against Juaben, refused to yield. When the Asante army was on the point of retreat, Adu Boffo ran into Juaben and sat on his stool in the middle of the street in the very centre of the town, which meant, according to the practice of Asante warfare, that the troops had to fight and defend him to the death. In this way, the Asante army regained its waning morale, the result being the total destruction of Juaben.[2]

The Asante attack on Juaben was an important event not only to the Juabens but also to Britain. First, the behaviour of the Juabens shows this. In spite of their earlier confidence,[3] when the Asante danger became a reality, messengers from Juaben kept dashing into Eastern Akyem, asking King Amoako Attah for his assistance against Kumasi.[4] Secondly, King Amoako Attah, too, was very much shaken by these events. After the war, fugitive Juabens began to pour into Akyem at such a terrific rate that the King had to send troops to guard his frontier on the Prah. He also wrote to the District Commissioner of Accra, asking for ammunition for the purpose of keeping his territory inviolate.[5] Thirdly, Governor Strahan in Cape Coast was also impressed by this Asante achievement. As soon as the news of Asante victory reached him, he sent 150 Hausas and ammunition under Captain Ashe, requesting Assistant Inspector Hay to take over command in Kibi, and in concert with Dr Gouldsbury, then on a mission to Asante, to employ it in support of Akyem. He was thus assisting Amoako Attah to enable him to resist an Asante incursion into the Protectorate, in pursuit of fugitive Juabens.[6] The Governor then wrote to Dr Gouldsbury, issuing the complementary instructions that he should abandon his mission to Asante and return to Akyem to act in concert with Captain Hay, so as to prevent the explosive situation there from plunging the Protectorate into another Asante war.[7]

Clearly, therefore, the Juaben episode was important to the British. Even more significant were the effects of this episode on the implementation of their policy in Asante. This policy, which, as we have seen, was one of 'divide and rule', was to be implemented through Juaben. The defeat of Juaben, therefore, helped to bring about two significant changes. First, the policy of 'divide and rule' failed in the 1870s, though resumed later. Secondly, the pro-Juaben policy was changed to an anti-Juaben policy.

The records leave us in no doubt whatsoever about the failure of the British policy in Asante in 1875. On the eve of the Kumasi–Juaben contest, Dr Gouldsbury emphatically wrote 'that any marked success of Asantees would be followed by the submission of the seceded tribes to Ashanti rule, if not by that of Juaben itself, a consummation certainly not to be desired'.[8] Less than a week later

1 *Ibid.*, encl. 4   2 Kukurantumi tradition, Birim D.R.B.

3 C.O. 96/116, no. 221, Strahan to Carnarvon, 16 November 1875

4 *Ibid.*, no. 220, encl. 2, 13 November 1875

5 *Ibid.*, no. 221, encl. 4, 16 November 1875

6 *Ibid.*, encl. 5   7 *Ibid.*, encl. 6

8 C.C., C.O. 96/116, no. 220, encl. 2 in Strahan to Carnarvon, 13 November 1875

Juaben fell; and with this, Britain's hope of breaking up Asante evaporated. 'I confess', wrote Governor Strahan, 'that from the self-reliant tone of the King of Juabin's communications to me as well as from other circumstances I expected the Juabins would have made a much stronger stand than now appears to have been made.' If they had succeeded, they might have made it easier for him to intervene. But now it would appear that Juaben miscalculated its powers. 'And', he concluded, 'it is thus with regret that I have had now to inform your Lordship of the fall of Juabin as it will tend, I believe powerfully, to restore the former power of Ashanti Kingdom.'[1]

The Asante success in Juaben not only contributed to the failure of British policy, but also helped, in two ways, to cause a long delay in its resumption. First, military victory in Juaben increased Asante's reputation as a fighting people so much that British officials were scared of her. We find R. H. Meade, the Under-Secretary of State of the Colonial Office, writing in December 1875: 'The possibility of future complications or hostilities with the Ashantees appears to Lord Carnarvon to be a matter of such great importance. . . .'[2] Augustus Hemming at the Colonial Office was also overwhelmed by the Asante victory, fearing, with Captain Strahan and Dr Gouldsbury, 'that this defeat of the Juabins may be the precursor of trouble for the colony from the reviving power of Coomasie'.[3] Because the Asante defeat of Juaben scared them so much, British officials did not dare to resume the policy of breaking up Asante until much later, in the 1880s.

Secondly, when the Juabens fled from Asante arms into the Protectorate, they decided to use the Protectorate as a base for revenge against Asante, and the British had to employ all their resources to stop this. So, even though they tried in 1876 to pursue their policy of breaking up Asante in Salaga, British officials could not devote all their attention to the implementation of this policy, hence the delay.

While fugitives in Accra the Juabens, led by King Asafu Agyei and his captains, decided that they would launch an attack on Asante. One of Asafu Agyei's captains, Poku Ansuragya, went to Gyaman, a province of Asante, with twenty companions and captured about thirty Asante whom they plundered.[4] Besides, since their arrival in the Protectorate late in 1875, the Juabens had been collecting muskets, powder and lead in different parts of the Protectorate, and by August 1877 they were only waiting in the interior for Asafu Agyei to arrive from Accra to lead them against Asante. The Juaben intriguers also enlisted the support of King Tackie of Accra against Asante.[5]

When the Asantehene learned of these intrigues, he threatened to invade the Protectorate. He sent an embassy to Cape Coast to inform the Governor that Asante was prepared to fight King Tackie of Accra, and that until the Juaben

1 C.O. 96/116, no. 221, Strahan to Carnarvon, 16 November 1875

2 C.O. 96/116, Under-Secretary of State to F.O., 28 December 1875

3 C.O. 96/116, no. 221, Minute of 14 December 1875 by Hemming on Strahan to Carnarvon, 16 November 1875

4 C.O. 96/121, no. 142, Freeling to Carnarvon, 29 May 1877

5 Ibid., no. 199, 10 August 1877

intriguers were put down, he would close the roads and stop all trade to and from the coast.[1]

The prospect of another Asante War caused great concern in British official circles. Augustus Hemming referred to the Juaben activities as creating a dangerous situation on the Gold Coast.[2] Carnarvon agreed with him, adding that the incident should be regarded as 'another of the many illustrations which we have had of the insecure position of our Government on the Gold Coast'.[3] Governor Freeling, too, on the coast, was in a frantic mood. On 7 August 1877 he took Amoako Attah of Eastern Akyem to task for not preventing the Juabens from collecting arms.[4] A week later, he treated the Rev. W. Eisenschmidt of the Basel Mission at Akropong in a similar manner, censuring the missionaries for not discovering the Juaben intrigue.[5] The British were greatly concerned about the activities of the Juabens, and accordingly spent a great deal of time and energy in suppressing them.

First, in an effort to prevent the threatened Asante invasion, Governor Freeling sent conciliating messages to the King of Asante, explaining that he had already fined King Tackie for his part in the Juaben intrigues. Then, the Governor proceeded to arrest those of the Juaben leaders who were living in Accra. He made a state prisoner of Asafu Agyei himself. Then he arrested and imprisoned Ankah and Yowmanuah, two of the leading spirits of the movement against Asante.[6]

Freeling then sent forty Hausas, all he had, under Wyatt, the only available officer, with Reinecker, the Auditor, as special Commissioner to enquire into these matters, to endeavour to seize the arms and ammunition and to bring the Queen, Asafu Agyei's daughter living in Akwapim, into custody.[7] So serious was the situation that the Governor took the trouble to find out as much information as he could about the plot, as could be seen in the detailed instructions issued to Reinecker. He was told, for instance, of the exact places where powder was supposed to have been kept by Juabens. These were Amanu or Amamakrom, Obosomasie and Brewassie in Akwapem and Kukurantumi in Akyem. The instructions gave details of the positions of all these places as well as that of Mampong, where the Queen of Juaben was to be found. A Chief Captain was said to be at Obosomasie with followers, one at Adafu, three hours beyond Akropong, and one at Kukurantumi in Akyem. Reinecker should go to Quow Daddy of Akropong, warn him against helping the Juabens and get him to help collect the powder and store in one place.[8]

---

1 *Ibid.*   2 Minute of 5 September 1877 by Hemming on above

3 Minute of 7 September on above. I have had to edit this minute slightly using full words for Carnarvon's abbreviations to effect easy reading.

4 C.O. 96/121, no. 199, Freeling to Carnarvon, 10 August 1877

5 *Ibid.*, no. 209, encl. 2, 14 August 1877

6 *Ibid.*, no. 199, 10 August 1877   7 *Ibid.*

8 *Ibid.*, encl. It was General Hay whom Gov. Freeling sent to Eastern Akyem (Kibi) for a similar purpose. He seized a total of 1037 guns and rifles, 26 kegs of powder. By 13 September Quow Daddy sent down 79 guns to Accra making a total of 1116. It was said that the reason for this small number being secured was that the Juabens had sent a large number out of the Protectorate. C.O. 96/122, no. 226, Freeling to Carnarvon, 13 September 1877. See encl. 2, instructions to General Hay.

After this, Freeling found that he had to make further arrests. On 13 August 1877 he captured Asamoah, one of the most influential Juaben chiefs. The following day the Queen was brought down to Accra, a prisoner.[1] By the 23rd, three more principal chiefs had been arrested in Akwapem: Quamina Piah Mor, the Queen's husband, Asafo Boateng, the King's son, and Yao To, the King's head linguist.[2]

In this way, the British pro-Juaben policy was completely reversed. The delay in resuming their policy of breaking up Asante was thus due partly to the time and resources they expended in putting out the Juaben fire.

Thus by contributing to the failure of British policy in Asante in the 1870s the Juaben episode was an important factor in delaying its implementation.

In Salaga, as in Juaben, Asante activities began over local issues, constituting an attempt by Asante to retain control of the north-eastern districts of the Empire, in face of Juaben intrigues there. This dispute between Kumasi and the northern districts gradually came to involve the British as well. We can illustrate the nature of this Asante activity in the north by discussing the local issue at stake and how this changed into a wider issue involving the British.

The local dispute actually started with Juaben activities, directed towards terminating Asante influence in the north. *The Liverpool Mercury* of 12 January 1876, for instance, reported that since the rebellion of the Juabens against Asante, a little while after the English expedition, the Salagas, at the instigation of the fetish priest of Krachi, Dente, in the service of Asafu Agyei, King of Juaben, revolted against the Asante monarch and killed hundreds of Asante traders. This act appears to have been committed by the people of Bagyemso, whom Theophil Opoku, the Basel missionary, described as allies of the King of Juaben. Marion Johnson holds the view that the Krachi people were at this time determined, above all, to retain for themselves alone the trade which brought them enormous profit. Besides, there were specific references to an embargo having been placed on trade, soon after the Juaben upheaval, by Dente at Krachi, and this would seem to imply that the Asante traders, many of whom had already been put to the sword, were now debarred from leaving Krachi even for the purpose of seeking refuge, let alone retaliation.[3]

The Juabens extended their activities against Asante to the Atebubu road. For example, when Bonnat, the French adventurer, insisted on reaching Salaga through Kumasi and under Asante protection, the Juabens were determined to stop him, for such a journey by a white man would do much to strengthen Asante authority. Juaben was in a strong position to present a challenge here, because of their effective occupation of the Kete Krachi–Salaga district, particularly Bagyemso and the Bassa villages, so that the deeper Bonnat travelled into this area the greater his difficulties, as the Juaben population increased and placed obstacles in his way.

First, when Bonnat reached Mampon he met King Djeomo and was obviously expecting a royal entertainment from the Mampon authorities when suddenly Kojo Kuissa, a subject of the Protectorate, giving himself out to be a policeman

---

1 C.O. 96/121, no. 209, Freeling to Carnarvon, 14 August 1877

2 *Ibid.*, no. 213, 23 August 1877, C.O. 96/122, no. 226, encl. 1 in same to same, 13 September 1877

3 M. Johnson, *Bonnat on the Volta* (I.A.S. Legon)

sent by His Excellency, arrived with the message that the Mampons, etc. should 'not listen to what I said – because I was a lier [liar] and a begger [beggar] – that they should drive me out of Mampon as I had been driven at Juabin, and that they should not allow me to go into the interior'. Bonnat had seen this very man with Asafu Agyei in Juaben,[1] so the source of obstruction was clear to him. On his arrival at Atebubu he found a considerable number of Juabens, who promptly arrested his Asante escort, and he himself was given over to a Juaben chief. The following day a fresh party of 106 armed Juabens arrived in the town to kill the Asante members of the escort, who were only saved by the intervention of the King of Atebubu. The Juabens were preparing to seize Bonnat himself when the King again intervened. The King of Atebubu was eventually persuaded to allow them to arrest Bonnat, who was then brought to Akyem where the Juabens were at the time, and where he was further mal-treated. He met three Hausas believed to have gone there with His Excellency's authority, and these tried to tie him up and send him to the coast.[2]

Although it was originally a local conflict between Kumasi and the Salaga district, this episode in the north gradually grew into a wider issue involving activities hostile to the British. There were two reasons for this development. First, before the Juabens became a nuisance to them in the Protectorate, the British had encouraged the Juaben intriguers to terminate Asante influence on the Kumasi–Atebubu road. The Juabens, who arrested Bonnat in Atebubu, declared that they enjoyed the 'marked favour of the English Government'. They further took upon themselves the responsibility of 'assuring the King [of Atebubu] that all they were doing was approved by the Govern-ment'.[3]

The second reason was that the British decided to gain control of the Volta–Accra trade route, thus interfering with Asante control. They did this in two ways. The first was to build up Salaga armed resistance against Asante. The second was to send a Commissioner of great experience to get the Salagas to trade directly with the coast by way of the Volta.

To build up the resistance of Salaga against Asante involved supplying the poorly armed Salagas[4] with arms and ammunition. Even though they them-selves did not ask for these, yet the Colonial Office draft despatch of 25 August 1876 stated that 'it is obviously for the advantage of these people that they should be in a position to resist the King of Ashantee, should he attempt to attack them'. To make it easier for the Salagas to import arms through direct trade with Accra,[5] the embargo which had been placed on the importation of arms into the Gold Coast was lifted.

The second method, which involved sending a Commissioner to persuade the Salagas to forge a direct link with the coast independent of Asante, was favoured by the political situation in Salaga. The Salaga constitution made allowance for a kind of second king, who in 1876 was being supported against

---

1 Ussher to C.O., 29 July 1879, *The Salaga Papers* collected by M. Johnson, I.A.S. Legon

2 C.O. 96/116, no. 210, encl. 1 in Strahan to Carnarvon, 25 October 1875   3 *Ibid.*

4 The principal ammunition of the Salagas consisted of bows and arrows, there being scarcely twenty guns in the whole district.

5 Carnarvon to Lees (draft) 25 August 1876

the first one by Asante.[1] The British, therefore, decided to support the first king, Dose. They sent Dr Gouldsbury, loaded with costly gifts of cloth, to Salaga in January 1876 and he, showering the gifts on King Dose, made overtures of friendly relations to him. King Dose, too, afraid of the Asante move against him, responded favourably to British overtures. This Salaga–British friendship grew very rapidly. By July, King Dose had already made a second request for arms from the Government.[2] A year later, the King returned the friendly gesture, which the Government had earlier extended to Salaga, by sending to the Governor presents of ivory and ostrich feathers. The result was that the direct route which the British wanted was opened between Salaga and the Coast by March 1877.[3]

When Asante activities in the north became more concerned with the British, the Asantehene and his great chiefs decided to reassert Asante authority in the whole of the north. One way of doing this was to appoint a commissioner who would reorganise the administration of the northern districts. It was essential to appoint someone who could command the respect of the inhabitants of these regions. Secondly, it was vital to have someone who could be trusted. Bonnat had both qualifications. Being a white man, he was bound to wield great influence among the Africans of the Volta states. Secondly, he had lived in Asante for some four years and the Asantehene, having had the opportunity of watching his conduct, now had implicit faith in him. The mere fact that Bonnat himself decided to go into the interior under Asante protection in preference to that of Juaben was much in his favour at the Asante court. Bonnat made no secret of the fact that he was greatly impressed by the Asante control of the trade of the Brong peoples. Indeed so great was his impression that not even Strahan's strong objections to his proceeding into the interior by means of Asante permission and escort could induce him to alter his plans.[4] Such loyalty to the Asante cause could not have escaped the notice of the astute monarch and his court, and in choosing Bonnat to be their representative they were absolutely sure that they were employing the right weapon against British intervention. So, when Bonnat further demonstrated his loyalty by swearing allegiance to the King and agreeing to pay a percentage on all goods from the interior which passed through his hands,[5] he was duly appointed Governor of Akrosso,[6] where, above all things, he was expected firmly to re-establish Asante control in the north-eastern districts.

Next, the Asantehene closed the trade routes north of Asante, no doubt to make sure that British intrigues did not create havoc there as they had done elsewhere, and resisted every effort by Dr Gouldsbury, who was on his way north, to open these routes to British influence.[7]

The strength of Asante resistance on this occasion can only be gauged by the subterfuge to which Gouldsbury was compelled to resort. He set out south from

1 'L'Explorateur 111, Paris 1876', *The Salaga Papers*

2 C.O. 96/118, no. 186, encl. 2 in Lees to Carnarvon, 6 September 1876

3 C.O. 96/120, no. 87, Freeling to Carnarvon, 28 March 1877

4 C.O. 96/116, no. 210, encl. 1, in Strahan to Carnarvon, 25 October 1875

5 *Ibid.*   6 M. Johnson, *Bonnat and Salaga* (I.A.S. Legon)

7 C.O. 96/116, no. 234, encl. in Strahan to Carnarvon, 11 December 1875.

Kumasi, giving all to believe that he was returning to the coast; he reached the first village on his way south, but suddenly returned through Kumasi with Hausa soldiers 'travelling up in our territory they say to Saraha our market town, without given [giving] us any notice, or the least information respecting the object of his travelling thither and with Houssa soldiers'. The Asantehene could not control his anger at Gouldsbury's behaviour. He and his chiefs wrote to Governor Lees in April 1876, describing Gouldsbury's conduct as offensive, and pointing out that he had not treated them justly and 'therefore we do protest against his proceedings'.[1]

So far the Asante court has been seeking to have these matters peacefully settled. But after Gouldsbury's departure for the north-eastern districts, there did not seem to be any alternative now but to clear the areas around Salaga and Kwahu that were infested with Juaben warriors, former agents of British strategy. In August, therefore, the Asante were rumoured to be moving on Salaga and Kwahu.[2] There are no records of actual clashes, but this in itself could not disprove an Asante campaign in 1876. In fact, the Asante appear to have crushed their opponents at least at key points along the newly opened British trade route. It is significant that not long afterwards this trade route was reported closed again. Clearly Asante was able to re-establish her control over the Volta trade route and it was not until 1880 that British agents again found the route passable between Salaga and the coast.

The Salaga episode represents yet another successful effort of Asante to delay till the 1880s the execution of the British policy of seizing control of trade routes in the interior.

Gyaman was the third region in which the Asante were active during the 1870s, their aim being both to prevent Gyaman secession and to forestall the extension of British influence there. Here, too, we find the British encouraging the Gyamans to secede from the Asante Empire. To achieve this objective, the British gave the Gyamans help both directly and indirectly. Indirectly the Gold Coast Government encouraged Asafu Agyei and his refugee Juabens (before they became a problem in the Protectorate) to organise a war party in Gyaman in the hope of defeating Asante in the field. So it was that Asafu Agyei while in Accra was allowed by the Government to send Poku Ansuragya and Guentil to Gyaman on a mission of war.[3] Poku, the 'sword-bearer of the Defeated King Asafu Aidjay', and Asaidoo of Fanti became the leaders of the Juaben intriguers who were trying to cause confusion in Gyaman. They collected some of their followers from among the refugee Juabens, some from Sefwi and the remainder from Gyaman itself. With these followers the Juaben emissaries moved into Bonduku and informed King Agyeman of Gyaman that they were sent by the British Government which was helping Asafu Agyei soon to make war on Asante with white troops. They were therefore requested to call the Gyamans to arms since Asafu Agyei himself had already started with Sniders through Krachi to attack Asante. Asaidoo of Fante, who represented himself 'as whiteman in general', then formally declared war on Asante. 'Be it known to all Gyamans and its dependencies,' he was reported to have declared, 'and to whom these presents shall come on all the prairie countries that we Asaidoo of

1 C.O. 96/118, no. 186, encl. 1 in Lees to Carnarvon, 6 September 1876   2 *Ibid.*

3 C.O. 96/120, no. 32, Freeling to Carnarvon, 20 January 1877

Fantee are ordered by the said Government and the Governor of the Gold Coast Colony to proclaim war against the Ashantees.'[1]

The Juaben adventurers and their followers then invaded Asante territory. They were joined by Kobina Fofea, the runaway chief of Techiman, who had rebelled against Asante, and who now asked Asaidoo for military assistance. Together they attacked Berekum and went even deeper into Asante territory.[2]

The result of these attacks on Asante was the seizure of thirty Asante traders.[3] Apart from this, Asaidoo and his followers wrought a great deal of havoc during this period. They plundered Asante traders, and molested and kidnapped some, selling them for guns and powder. They seized Prince Ansah's gold, plundered Gyaman villages, killing sheep, robbing fowls, taking people's wives and fining people heavy sums of money under false pretences.[4] But apart from this havoc, the war party led by Asaidoo against Asante achieved no permanent results, as the invasion of Berekum was repelled by its inhabitants.

The direct assistance that the Gold Coast Government gave Gyaman was to send a Commissioner to their country to help them plan their resistance against Asante. This was in response to a request that Gyaman and Sefwi messengers made in January 1877 to the effect that a white ambassador must go to Gyaman to give weight to their authority *vis-à-vis* Asante. Furthermore they asked for powder and military assistance.[5] The despatch of Hausas and a commission into Sefwi and Gyaman was readily supported by Carnarvon at the Colonial Office,[6] and after some delay, John Smith, District Commissioner of Palma and Leckie, and a 'native' of Accra on leave of absence, set out in May 1879 for Gyaman, as head of the mission. His instructions made it clear that he was to endeavour to create a direct link between Gyaman and the coast by urging the villages along his route to keep the roads clear and safe,[7] and also by assisting Gyaman to prepare for war against Asante.[8] Smith and his mission went through Sefwi to Gyaman where he tried to encourage the Gyaman war party, but to no avail. His failure was due to Asante activities.

Asante tried first to settle these matters peacefully by sending envoys to Cape Coast and then to Bonduku. As early as January 1877 an Asante embassy arrived in Cape Coast to plead with the Government to desist from interfering in Sefwi and Gyaman,[9] and to prevent Asafu Agyei and his Juabens from carrying out their plans in these states. The Government paid no heed and the Cape Coast mission failed.

The Asantehene then sent another mission to Bonduku. The leader of the mission was the Danish military instructor of the Kumasi forces, Charles

1 C.O. 96/128, no. 251, encl. 2 in Ussher to Hicks Beach, 8 November 1879   2 *Ibid.*

3 C.O. 96/121, no. 199, Freeling to Carnarvon, 10 August 1877

4 C.O. 96/128, no. 251, encl. 2 in Ussher to Hicks Beach, G.C. 8 November 1879

5 C.O. 96/120, no. 39, Freeling to Carnarvon, 26 January 1877

6 C.O. 96/120, no. 408, Carnarvon to Freeling, 9 March 1877

7 C.O. 96/126, no. 106, Lees to Hicks Beach, and encl. 1, 5 May 1879

8 Minutes of 6 June 1879 by Antrobus and 1 November 1879 by Hemming on above; also C.O. 96/126, no. 172, Ussher to Hicks Beach, 24 July 1879

9 C.O. 96/120, no. 31, Freeling to Carnarvon, 20 January 1877

Nielson, who would have no difficulty in convincing the Gyamans that he was 'more European' than Asaidoo of Fante and that his mission was more important than that of the Juabens. Huydercoper, a Fante, was chosen as interpreter to Nielson. Unfortunately for the mission, it arrived after Asaidoo had had ample time to establish an influence on King Agyeman. Agyeman was thus prevailed upon to act shamefully towards the Asante mission 'by making us fool running about in the bushes after him', and because of too much exposure to the sun Nielson died. Huydercoper then took over the leadership of the mission. His appointment was duly confirmed by the King of Asante. 'Know all men', goes the citation, 'by these presents I Osei Mensah King of Ashantee, and its dependencies in my name, and in the name of our chiefs, do hereby nominate, constitute, and appoint S. L. Huydercoper as our Commissioner and headman of, our Mission of Peace to the King of Gaman.'[1]

Armed with these credentials, Huydercoper and his mission plunged into work. He was instructed:

1. To restore Ansah's gold usurped by 'Gyamans'.
2. To deliver the revolted Kobina Fofea, Asaidoo and Poku Ansuraidja, since these three men were against the Mission of Peace in Gyaman; and were fighting against Asante's allies 'Inquransay, Banna, Baidoo Krom, Braicoom, etc. (The only reason why the Mission wanted them, it was emphasised, was that if they remained in Gyaman no peace could be made.)
3. To make 'Gyamans' open the roads to trade and not plunder Asante traders' gold as they had been doing.
4. To help Prince Korkorbo, the Asante partisan and energetic half-brother of the vacillating Agyeman, to seize the throne of Gyaman.[2]

When the mission arrived in Bonduku, Agyeman realised it was a top-ranking one. Apart from dodging it he could not obstruct it in any other way, in spite of the excessive propaganda of the Juabens. These must have suggested the arrest and imprisonment of the members of the mission, hence the spread of rumour on the Coast that they were actually imprisoned. In fact the King of Gyaman had no power to do this. The only real impediment in the way of the Asante mission now was John Smith and his Hausas. When these approached Bonduku, the Asante mission broke off its engagements there and withdrew into Banna in Asante territory with Prince Korkorbo and three of the most powerful Gyaman chiefs.

The results of the work of the Asante mission were spectacular. Even before the mission's arrival the war party consisted only of King Agyeman, Princess Akosuah Ayansuah of Gyaman, Kwaku Kye, King of Sefwi, Kobina Fofea of Techiman and the King of Tarkwa. All the principal chiefs of Agyeman refused to support the war effort 'showing clearly their reluctance to throw off their old allegiance to Ashantee'.[3] So there was some disunity between the King and his chiefs before Huydercoper's arrival in Gyaman. But the arrival and message of the Asante Commissioner created such a disaffection against Agyeman that all hopes of union between the King and his chiefs were shattered.

Another important result of the Asante mission was that the Asante party

1 C.O. 96/128, no. 251, encl. 1 and 2 in Ussher to Hicks Beach, 8 November 1879

2 *Ibid.*   3 *Ibid.*

in Gyaman was greatly strengthened. It was this development that foiled Smith's mission and the aims of the war party in Gyaman. The people simply ignored him first and then openly rejected his requests. It was with great difficulty that the King could get some of his chiefs and elders to agree to meet the Commissioner on 7 August 1879. When Smith arrived at the meeting-place at 1 p.m. he found only the King and one of his chiefs there. After waiting for two hours in the blazing sun he was informed that one chief was drunk and fast asleep, another had a bad leg and could not walk and a third was making fetish, and consequently could not attend that day. Another meeting was held next day without any more success. At a third meeting on the 15th, the chiefs rejected Smith's requests that they might cooperate with their King to open a direct route to the coast and throw off Asante commercial control. Instead they complained to Smith about Agyeman receiving the Kings of Juaben, Techiman and Tarkwa, formerly allies of Asante, into a Gyaman alliance against Kumasi. Because of this they would never serve him again. Smith tried at three subsequent meetings, on the 20th, 21st and 23rd, to win them round, but they refused to fall in line with the British plan or to be reconciled with their king. So the British mission failed and Smith had to leave Bonduku on the 24th. Immediately Korkorbo re-entered the Gyaman capital to seize the stool.[1] It was a diplomatic victory for Asante.

When John Smith returned to the coast with these reports, Governor Ussher realised immediately that Asante had once again thwarted the British plan of inland penetration. He was compelled to write that 'the only attitude for this government is the one of friendly neutrality'[2] in the affairs of the interior. At the Colonial Office everyone was impressed by the diplomatic victory of Asante in Gyaman. Both Wingfield and Herbert entertained serious doubts whether anything good could ever result from such a costly expedition.[3] Herbert became even more blunt in his criticism and stated that Ussher must be informed that in future no such missions should be sent without the express approval of the Secretary of State for the Colonies.[4] No one in the Colonial Office seemed to remember that it was Lord Carnarvon himself who urged the despatch of the recent mission into Gyaman.

Clearly, therefore, Asante activities in Gyaman followed the general pattern, except that here the diplomatic victory was complete, and consequently, no military expeditions became necessary. Here, too, we find that Asante was seeking to solve a local problem of secession, as well as to forestall the execution of British expansionist policies. Asante action, which took the form of sending a full diplomatic mission into Gyaman to build up an anti-British party, was indeed successful, as can be seen from the reactions of the Colonial Office officials to the Smith mission. In fine, the conclusions these officials reached was that the implementation of the policy of commercial expansion should be delayed. This, therefore, was the manner in which Asante activities in Gyaman affected British policy.

The events in Juaben occurred in 1875, those in Salaga in 1876, and those in Gyaman in 1877–79. After the Juaben episode, the British were discouraged,

1 *Ibid.*   2 C.O. 96/128, no. 251, Ussher to Hicks Beach, 8 November 1879

3 Minute of 18 December 1879 by Wingfield on above. The mission cost the Government £450 17s.

4 Minute of 19 December 1879 by Herbert on above.

but thought they could still try to implement their policy in Salaga. Before their failure in Salaga was certain, they hoped that they might still try to carry out their policies in Gyaman. It was their failure in Gyaman which finally crushed their hopes of implementing their policy of inland commercial penetration in the 1870s. The cumulative effect of the Jauben, Salaga and Gyaman episodes, therefore, was to prevent the execution of British policy in the 1870s.

Adansi, Kumasi, Mampon and Nsutah

When the British resumed their attempt to carry out their policy in Asante in the 1880s, Asante activities again caused its failure, postponing once more the successful implementation of this policy until the 1890s. These activities occurred in Adansi, Kumasi, Mampon and Nsutah and followed the pattern of the 1870s.

The nature of activities in Adansi was exactly like those in other parts of Asante. The central question was the restoration of Adansi to Asante rule. But to achieve this, Asante realised that she had to forestall British intrigues. It was in Adansi that the British, in the 1880s, first tried once more to execute the policy which had been thwarted in the 1870s; their interference began with the provision in the Treaty of Fomena that Adansi should be independent of Asante. Later Captain Moloney was sent to strengthen the Adansis in this resolution.[1] The British continued throughout the 1880s to interfere in Adansi, and we shall soon be discussing their activities in this connection.

But in Adansi there was a second factor leading to unrest and instability. This was the activities of concession-mongers. These were people to whom the documents refer as 'scholars'[2]; they came from the coast into Asante, at this time, promising to help the secessionists against Kumasi, in return for gold-mining concessions in various parts of Asante, especially in Adansi. To boost their own prestige these concession-mongers introduced themselves as agents of the Gold Coast Government. The Kumasi authorities, too, believed that they were agents of the Government.[3] This increased the already strong feeling of the Asante central government against the British. Thus, although the efforts of the Asante central Government were in the 1880s primarily directed towards the restoration of Asante rule in Adansi, they were at the same time concerned with the activities of the British there.

Since 1874, when the British recognised the independence of Adansi, the Asantehene had realised that an independent country so close to his borders could become a real threat to peace. In spite of the Fomena Treaty he continued to regard any efforts of Adansi to assert their independence as acts of rebellion. Moreover, the King decided, soon after the Fomena Treaty, to restore Adansi to Asante rule. By February 1879 the Asantehene's efforts in this direction were intensified.[4]

1 C.O. 96/118, no. 32, Strahan to Carnarvon, 19 February 1876

2 An example of a 'scholar' was Dawson, who became the 'political agent' of the French G.C. Company, one of the earliest gold-mining companies in the Tarkwa district. He wielded considerable influence with the chiefs of the district. He held courts, at first nominally as deputy of the chiefs of Tarkwa, but afterwards clearly on his own account.

3 Claridge, Vol. II, p. 148

4 C.O. 96/126, no. 32, Lees to Hicks Beach, 25 February 1879 and encl. 1, and also no. 83, 14 April 1879

The first method Asante used to end the Adansi rebellion was to send a diplomatic mission. According to Cudjoe Obboebbo, a Captain of King Nkansa of Adansi, the first Asante embassy empowered to end the Adansi secession had been resident and at work there since the last war.[1] The influence of the mission was certainly being felt by 1879, for apart from Nkansa, who complained, in that year, of the presence of its members in Fomena against his wishes, Captain Lees also referred to their activities in his despatches of February 1879 to the Colonial Office.[2] Later that year the Asantehene decided that, because of British opposition, the Adansi problem required a more powerful mission to solve it. He accordingly withdrew the Fomena mission and sent to Twumasi a new mission, including representatives, not only of Kumasi, but also of the other inner kingdoms of Mampon, Kokofu and Bekwai. The head of this mission was Yao Agyei, a high-ranking chief at the Kumasi Court.[3]

These Asante missions in Adansi had instructions to perform several duties in the hope of ending the rebellion. First, they were to supervise the trade route through Adansi. This was necessary because of the turbulent excesses of Kotoko, Nkansa's chief linguist, who led 'the Adansis in stopping trade by robbing, beating, panyarring and otherwise ill-treating traders passing from or to Asanti and the coast'.[4] Secondly, they were to investigate political matters affecting the Asantehene's exercise of authority in Adansi. Thus, for instance, when Nkansa deposed the Chief of Twumasi, the Asantehene instructed the embassy to proceed to that town and reassert Asante political influence. Yao Agyei himself led the mission there, and when he left for Kumasi on business, no less a personality than the court crier, Assan Yao, was instructed to watch over affairs in Twumasi, whose deposed chief, Ampoful, he must not let out of his sight.

The missions were also requested to reinstate the chief of Twumasi and Dompoasi as well as Fossu Oduro, all of whom had been deposed by Nkansa for their Asante sympathies.[5] Again to assert Asante political authority, the missions were to win over Nkansa himself to Asante allegiance and prevent him from allying with Sefwi. Lastly, they were to prevent the Rev. Picot from building a school in Adansi without permission from the Asantehene.[6]

The normal way in which an Asante mission of this nature went about its assignment was to approach the chiefs of the secessionist region, and to try to persuade them to return to Asante allegiance. When this was successfully done, the Asantehene then paid monies to these chiefs to show that he was once again their overlord. This procedure was adhered to in Adansi, and in 1879 the Asantehene sent £8 2s (about £32 in present day value) in gold dust to Yao

---

1 C.O. 96/126, no. 83, encl. 1 in Lees to Hicks Beach, 14 April 1879

2 *Ibid.*, no. 32, encl. 1 and 2, 15 February 1879   3 *Ibid.*, no. 83, encl. 1, 14 April 1879

4 C.4906, Griffith to Granville, 1 April 1886

5 C.O. 96/127, no. 32, encl. 1 in Lees to Hicks Beach, 25 February 1879

6 C.O. 96/126, no. 83, encl. 1 in Lees to Hicks Beach, 14 April 1879. Picot had gone earlier to Kumasi and asked permission to build a school house in the capital but this was refused. On his way back to the coast he stopped in Adansi for the same purpose and Nkansa granted him permission to build a school. The Asantehene considered this to be an affront to his authority.

Agyei to be distributed to a number of Adansi chiefs who had been won over. Those who received the money included two chiefs of Fomena, Inkie Cobbina and Kwaku Saubine, Fossu Oduro of Edubiasi, Ogwah, chief of Dompoasi and Quassie Oduro, nephew of Ampoful, who received £2 0s 6d. Other chiefs and captains were also known to have received monies from Kumasi.[1]

As a result of all these efforts the Asante embassy scored a number of successes. A 'loyalist' movement came into existence in Adansi, led by the chiefs of Edubiasi, Dompossi and Twumasi.[2] These three chiefs had a large following,[3] showing how popular the Asante cause had become. Indeed, when Nkansa deposed them, there was nearly a riot.[4]

That Nkansa deposed the three chiefs was surprising, because such vigour was not typical of the Adansi court. Indeed, the whole series of Adansi reactions to the work of the Asante embassy cannot be understood until we realise that the British were helping Nkansa. After deposing the chiefs of Twumasi, Edubiasi and Dompoasi, the King very quickly filled two of the vacant stools, those of Edubiasi and Dompoasi, with fresh nominees of his own. The King then sent a party under the chief linguist, Kotoko, to arrest Ampoful, the ex-chief of Twumasi, whom the Asante were supporting. Ampoful escaped but they got Kofi Aboagye, the stool-bearer, with the stool and sword and brought him to Fomena. Again, Nkansa and his chiefs at once proceeded to elect one Adarbo to fill the vacant stool. Then, with surprising energy, the King of Adansi began negotiations for an alliance with Sefwi.[5]

That the British supported the Adansis in their rebellion against Asante was definite. First Captain Moloney, representing the Gold Coast Government, helped Nkansa to succeed to the Adansi throne and thereafter supported him so as to prevent him from returning to Asante allegiance. It was in line with this policy that the British now supported Adansi to obstruct the work of the Asante embassy. In 1879 Captain Hay forced the Asante envoys at Twumasi to return to Kumasi. He then ordered the arrest of Quassie Oduro, Ampoful's heir to the Twumasi stool, so as to forestall Asante perpetuating her control over Twumasi and other Adansi towns.[6] British interference thus reversed the trend of affairs in Adansi. When the British terminated Asante efforts to win back Adansi by getting the embassy out, the Asantehene had to resort to force.

When the time came to substitute force for diplomacy in Adansi, Kumasi itself was not blessed with a king. However, a confederation came into existence led by Bekwai, a true representative of traditional forces of Asante, and one of the most powerful of the inner kingdoms of the empire. Apart from Bekwai itself there were in the confederation, Manso, Sewuah, Mampon, Nsutah, Agona and Kumasi.[7] With its full backing, Karikari, the King of Bekwai, moved swiftly to humble Adansi. First he sent messengers to Fomena to demand the customary 240 pounds of gold dust as a mark of servitude and repentance. But Nkansa refused to pay. This was followed by Karikari's request that Nkansa should repatriate a Bekwai fugitive, Deabaah by name, then living with Kwaku Asante of Edubiasi.[8] But Nkansa refused to submit, principally because he was

---

1 *Ibid.*, encl. 2   2 *Ibid.*, encl. 1   3 *Ibid.*, encl. 2

4 *Ibid.*, encl. 1   5 *Ibid.*, encl. 1 and 2   6 *Ibid.*

7 C.4906, encl. 1 in Griffith to Granville, 1 April 1886

8 *Ibid.*, encl. 2

expecting British military aid,[1] and the Bekwai Confederation invaded Adansi with a force of 10,000 men about the end of 1885.[2]

In the face of the vigorous move of the confederation Nkansa sent for assistance from the Gold Coast Government before the end of January,[3] but by 10 February the *Western Echo* had to report that Adansi was defeated.[4] There seemed at this point to have been a lull in the contest which was vigorously resumed in March. From then onwards, the feeble resistance of Adansi having been squashed, the whole affair turned into a punishment for that state. All accounts[5] agree that Adansi was severely beaten, that 100 high-ranking Adansis had been captured by the Bekwais, who also killed thirty Adansi chiefs, and that the remaining Adansis and their King, together with the King of Dadiasi, fled across the Prah into the Protectorate.

The Adansi war had great effects on the implementation of British policy, because it created a difficult refugee problem as did the Juaben episode.

When Asante forces drove the Adansis across the Prah into the Protectorate in 1886, the fugitives caused considerable trouble to the British. Mark Hayford, clerk and interpreter at Prahsu, frequently reported the attempts of the fugitives to avenge their defeat. These fugitives were all over the Protectorate. Karsang, one of the defeated chiefs, was reported, in January 1887, to be attacking villages belonging to the King of Bekwai. More Adansis were causing trouble in Denkyira. In another report, soon after the first one, Hayford described how some fugitives again attacked traders at Kurisa, forty-five miles from his station.[6] The Daniasis, who also fled with Adansis, were reported to be in Upper Denkyira, where they killed some Bekwai captives in their power, selling the rest. The chief of the Daniasis, Gyamfi, in particular, was very turbulent. According to reports from Akyem and Bekwai residents in the town of Tamfudie in Denkyira (ten miles from Akyem), as soon as Gyamfi arrived in the town, he caused them all to be made prisoners, threatened to cut off their heads, but fined them instead.[7]

The British had to deal with these problems, for they were endangering the peace and security of the Protectorate and a great deal of time and energy was spent in resettling the fugitives in places where they could be under the control of the Government. First, Governor Griffith sent Inspector Duddley to tackle the problem; he travelled to Jukwa, the Denkyira capital, to Assin, to Upper Denkyira, etc.[8] Secondly, Captain Lonsdale was appointed Commissioner for Native Affairs in 1887, with instructions to study the problem in all its aspects.

---

1 *Ibid.*, also encl. 3

2 *Ibid.*, encl. 1. The 10,000 mentioned by Griffith's dispatch as all the force the Bekwai Confederation brought against Adansi is a surprisingly small figure. The Confederation must have had a much larger fighting force. It may be that the 10,000 were just the men in the division of Asaidoo, the Supreme Commander of the Confederation's forces.

3 *The Western Echo*, 30 January 1886   4 *Ibid.*, 10 February 1886

5 See C.4906, Admiralty to C.O., 17 July 1886; *The Western Echo*, 17 March, 29 May and 30 June 1886

6 C.5357, encl. 1 in White to Holland, 16 February 1887

7 C.5357, encl. 8 in White to Holland, 19 February 1887

8 C.5357, encl. 1 in White to Holland, 16 February 1887

He travelled all over the Protectorate and prepared a detailed report, which revealed exactly where the refugees were and what they were doing. He made recommendations for their immediate removal to the coast,[1] to make it easier for the Government to supervise their activities. The Adansis, he said, should be settled in the Agona country.[2] Lonsdale also suggested that some turbulent individuals should be moved from near the Asante border. Assistant Inspector Barnett was instructed to take chief Mensah and some other Nkwanta chiefs to Elmina, and to send down Gyamfi of Daniasi and some of his chiefs.[3]

The effect of the defeat of Adansi on British policy was tremendous. After their failure in the 1870s, in the 1880s their policy of penetration might at last succeed. But this defeat of Adansi by Adante was once again to cause the failure of British attempts to exercise influence in Asante.

Apart from these Adansi defeats events in Kumasi, Mampon and Nsutah, where the British entertained great hopes of establishing their influence, also contributed to the failure of their policy in Asante. Towards the middle of 1882 Governor Rowe became convinced, following his interviews with some messengers from the interior, that the power of the central government of Asante had declined.[4] The British decided, therefore, that the time was ripe for them to exercise influence in Kumasi and the other metropolitan states.[5] This was to be achieved by sending travelling commissioners to carry out the details of the Government's plans. In May 1882 Governor Rowe was talking about cultivating 'intercourse with Ashanti by sending a European officer' to see the King; and he was looking forward to such a mission as an event which could take place 'with considerable advantage to the influence of this Government'.[6]

The detailed plans of the Government which these travelling commissioners were to carry out included establishing influence over the Asantehene, either by helping to install him on the throne, if and when the dynastic dispute was resolved, or by helping to intensify the division among the metropolitan states by supporting the Achereboanda party against Prempeh, if the dispute continued. It was Hemming at the Colonial Office who advocated the first alternative, when in 1883 he suggested that the Gold Coast Government should install a king in Kumasi. Later he went further and proposed that Britain should assume the role of supreme arbitrator among all the interior peoples. He suggested that a solemn durbar should be held at Prahsu to which all kings and

---

1 *Ibid.*, encl. 1. Those to be moved near the coast included the following chiefs and their people: Kwasie Mensah, Chief of Nkwanta (Mansu), Gyamfi, Chief of Daniasi; and Kwakye Nketia, ex-chief of Nkwanta.

2 C.5357, encl. 2 (15 June 1887) in White to Holland, 15 June 1887

3 C.5357, encl. 1 (13 June 1887) in White to Holland

4 C.O. 96/139, no. 144, Rowe to Kimberley, 5 May 1882

5 C.5357, encl. 3 (23 July 1887) in White to Holland

6 C.O. 96/129, no. 144, Rowe to Kimberley, 5 May 1882. The London Chamber of Commerce was also advocating the appointment of Travelling Commissioners at this time, arguing that they would be most useful in the extension of British influence into the interior. Hemming also wrote in 1885 'the method of keeping up close relations with the country [Asante] is by sending frequent missions'. Minute by Hemming on Griffith to Derby, C.O. 96/166, no. 185, 9 June 1885.

chiefs of neighbouring states should be invited. The Governments should arrange terms of peace among them and they should sign a treaty in the Governor's presence which he would ratify and confirm by his signature.[1]

The second alternative of intensifying Asante division which the travelling commissioners started to carry out in 1886 involved the Government in secretly supporting the minority party against Prempeh. In October the King of Bekwai gave wide publicity, in Asante, to a message he claimed to have received from Yao Awuah, an Asante living in the coast towns, to the effect that the Government did not wish Yaah Kyia's son, Prempeh, to be placed on the Stool, but Yaah Afrey's son, Achereboanda.[2]

The first travelling commissioner, whom Governor Moloney (in place of Rowe on leave) sent to Kumasi in 1882 was none other than Lonsdale, who was already experienced in local affairs. Lonsdale began his work of establishing British influence in Asante by trying to humour them. He got the Asante to observe the Queen's birthday in Kumasi in 'a becoming manner'. He invited the King and all the chiefs for the occasion and they all went. At noon, a *feu-de-joie* was fired by the Hausas. Lonsdale then made a speech and asked them to join him in drinking Her Majesty's health and they all agreed, including the King, Queen Mother, and the King of Kotoku. They went off in a high good humour, saying this was a splendid custom, and 'enquired if the Queen had more than one birthday in the year'.[3]

The task of helping to install a king in Kumasi exercised Captain Lonsdale's mind, but he never had the opportunity to carry it out. When in March 1887 Mr Badger of Accra, another envoy to the Kumasi Court, reported that the time was ripe for such a ceremony,[4] Lonsdale, now in Sefwi, offered his services to Governor Griffith to go to Kumasi for the purpose.[5] But again events did not permit this.

The question of assuming the role of peacemaker or arbitrator among the states of the interior was also tackled. Lonsdale committed the Government to settle disputes between Asante and Gyaman (now that the earlier British policy of war had failed in Bonduku). In 1882 an Asante army was marching to Gyaman, and it is said that it was the Nkoranzas who appealed to the Asantehene to halt the troops,[6] but it was Lonsdale who first suggested to the Asantehene and the Gyamanhene to make up their differences.[7] Lonsdale actually

---

1 C.O. 96/151, no. 295, minute of 12 October 1883 on Rowe to Kimberley, 21 August 1883. It may appear as though this first alternative contradicted the British policy of breaking up Asante. In methods it did, but not in the ultimate aims of the British. The reason they wanted to break up Asante was to seize control there, which they could not do if the state was strong and united. If the British succeeded in playing the role of supreme arbitrator, then they would have seized control in Asante all the same, though by a different method. What is more, if the British were to benefit by their control of Asante and carry on peaceful trade, then peace must be restored first.

2 *The Western Echo*, 9 October 1886. The Government later punished Yao Awuah for thus publicising their secret plans.

3 C.O. 96/140, no. 248, Moloney to Kimberley, 14 June 1882

4 C.6357, Griffith to Stanhope, 4 March 1887   5 *Ibid.* and encl. 1

6 Nkoranza Tradition; informants, Nana Kwame Baffo III and Kwadjo Baffo

7 C.O. 96/143, no. 429, Moloney to Kimberley, 12 September 1882 and Minute of 29 October by Hemming on dispatch, also African no. 249

travelled from Kumasi to Gyaman to effect the peaceful conditions he had proposed,[1] and succeeded in preventing an Asante–Gyaman conflict at this time.

Later in 1887, seeing that Prempeh was still going all out to get Mampon and Nsutah reconciled to himself,[2] the Gold Coast Government decided to make another attempt at peacemaking in Asante. So in the early part of 1888 the Government dispatched Assistant Inspector Barnett as travelling commissioner for Asante, to try to reconcile Mampon and Nsutah to Kumasi. When Barnett arrived in Asante the Mampons and Nsutahs were in arms against Kumasi and so he rushed to their camps and tried to get them to break up and go home. But he failed. In April Barnett was still in Asante, trying to carry out his instructions of reconciling the states to Kumasi. The British extended their activities in this connection to Kokofu, but everywhere they failed.[3]

Soon the local Government came to realise that the task of making the people of the interior look up to the British for leadership and of making 'them comprehend it is much wiser for them to do as the Government desire',[4] required something more than just visits of a travelling commissioner. So, urged by Lonsdale in particular, the Gold Coast Government suggested to the Colonial Office the establishment of resident commissioners in Asante. But the British Government hesitated because of costs.[5] This hesitation did not damp the zeal of the local Government, nor that of Lonsdale, who, as late as 1888, was still recommending the appointment of a resident commissioner. He hoped to get himself appointed to the post and, as Augustus Hemming commented, might even be hoping to be elected King of Asante.[6]

When the Government thus interfered, both Mampon and Nsutah protested against white men meddling in their affairs. First, when the Government's emissary, Assistant Inspector Barnett, went to Mampon to arrange the differences between that state and Kumasi, Sekyere, the Mamponhene, decided that he did not want to be dictated to by any white man. Though he had no intention of listening to Barnett, Sekyere called a meeting in the afternoon of 25 September 1887; he so organised the meeting that the etiquette of hand-shaking lasted till dusk (6.30 p.m.) after which he informed Barnett that he was tired and his followers were drunk; consequently nothing remained to be done that day except to break up the gathering and go home, which he promptly did. Barnett, disappointed, had to go home without having his say. On the next occasion, 28 September, when he tried to deliver his message, the King refused point blank to fall in line with his views and was extremely rude. Barnett had to proceed to Nsutah where again he received impudent answers to his queries,

1 C.O. 96/143, no. 344, Moloney to Kimberley, 29 July 1882

2 The cause of these differences between Kumasi on one hand and Mampon and Nsutah on the other was that Mampon, not being an Oyoko Stool, was left out of discussions in Kumasi at this time. The Mamponhene's pride was hurt, so he allied with Nsutah and attacked Kumasi. Kona Tradition: informant, Nana Kofi Mensah.

3 C.5615, encl. in Griffith to Knutsford, 30 June 1888

4 C.O. 96/143, no. 344, Moloney to Kimberley, 29 July 1882

5 *Ibid.*, no. 429, 12 September 1882 and Minute of 29 October by Hemming on dispatch; also African no. 249 and C.3687 of July 1883

6 C.O. 96/191, no. 119, Griffith to Knutsford, 13 April 1888 and Minute of 8 June by Hemming

the King saying if he had come to fight he was ready, and that he had not asked any white man to interfere. 'He then jumped up and left the palaver hall without any intimation. A message was then brought telling me to clear out of the town at once.'

When later Barnett sent Thomas Halm, one of his assistants, into Mampon to try once more to reconcile Mampon and Kumasi, young men drummed and uttered abusive words against the mission. In Kokofu, too, the people rose up in protest against British interference. Before C. W. Badger, the Government interpreter, arrived in Kokofu to advise them, the Kokofus had themselves decided to cooperate with Kumasi. But when they realised that the Government was now trying to tell them what they themselves had already decided to do they became abusive and arrogant and changed their mind about cooperating with Kumasi.[1]

Apart from rejecting British mediation, the states of Asante tried to heal the cleavages themselves. As clearly as 1885, the King of Bekwai doubled his efforts to solve the problem of disunity in Asante. Kirby was impressed, during his tour of Asante in that year, by the great cohesion that the state was achieving.[2] The following year the King of Bekwai was known to be actually preparing to put a king on the throne,[3] seeing that his efforts at uniting Asante under Prempeh appeared to be about to succeed.[4] The 'inner Kingdoms of the former Ashanti Kingdom, Insutah, Becquai and Mampon, are satisfied to unite under the rule of Quacoe Duah'.[5] Although this happy trend of affairs did not persist, it was clear evidence of the great efforts of Asante to solve her own problems. In any case, it had gone far enough to render ineffective the first alternative method by which the British had hoped to gain the upper hand in Asante affairs.

The Civil War which raged from 1884 to 1888 between Prempeh and the supporters of Achereboanda threatened, in the event of Kumasi's defeat, to weaken the Central Government of Asante. Such an event was the second alternative that the British hoped would place Asante in their power. So, when they were not pursuing the first alternative of assuming the role of arbitrators, then they were working for the defeat of Kumasi by the Achereboanda party, whose leader was, from 1888, in their power.

Prempeh fought the war with a reformed and victorious army which he inherited. The reform of the Kumasi fighting forces was in line with nineteenth-century Asante policy[6] and began much earlier in the century. In the late 1870s the Asantehene began to modernise the army, not merely by supplying it with Snider rifles instead of the old flintlocks or Dane guns, but also by enabling the forces to acquire new techniques of warfare, and thus raise their efficiency. For this reason, the Asantehene offered double pay to Hausa deserters from the

---

1 C.5615, encl. in Griffith to Knutsford, 30 June 1888

2 C.4477, Young to Derby, 21 April 1884

3 C.4906, Griffith to Granville, 14 July 1886

4 C.5357, Griffith to Stanhope, 30 October 1886

5 C.O. 879/21, African (West) no. 277, Rowe to Derby and encl., 23 February 1884

6 See Wilks, *Ashanti Government*

coast, who were more suitable than raw recruits because of their training in modern techniques in the Gold Coast Constabulary. It was because he insisted on this qualification of modern techniques, that the Asantehene declined to accept the 2000 Hausas whom Nielson was reported to have recruited direct from Salaga and offered to the Asante Court.[1]

Reports which reached the Coast in March 1879 indicated that sweeping reforms were being effected in the Asante fighting forces. According to one report coming from Abuda Karima, Prince Ansah, in the service of Mensah Bonsu, seems to have set on foot a gigantic military organisation which he himself directed. He was reported to have had a large share in the formation of the Hausa Corps in Asante, of 300 to 400 strong at the time of the report. The men were armed with Sniders and wore fez caps of red cloth with a blue tassel. The greater portion of the corps was composed of slaves of Hausas, so the report goes, of Moshi, Dagomba and Grunshi nationality, requisitioned by the King from his chiefs. It was reported that Prince Ansah first attempted instruction with the aid of a drill book; but that they now had someone from Accra (Nielson undoubtedly). The chief posts in the army were not held by Hausas for fear of betrayal.[2]

Another report coming from Prince Brew of Dunquah confirmed the first, affirming that Prince Ansah was at Kumasi superintending the drilling of the Hausa force there. Prince Brew further indicated that the King of Asante was trying to induce Hausas on the coast to desert from the Constabulary and join the Kumasi force; that their pay ranged from 12 to 16 dollars a month, and that on the authority of Yow Damtsi, a sub-chief of Kumasi, the Hausas at Kumasi received double the pay they got on the coast, besides rations.[3]

A third report, by Osei Yaw, grandson of the Asantehene, maintains that the force that Prince Ansah was drilling numbered 500 men armed with Snider rifles; that the Prince was himself general of the fighting forces, Owusu Kokor Kuma the sergeant, and Kuma the Captain. Owusu Kokor Kuma also assisted in drilling the men. This report also tells us how the troops were paid: every twenty days the 500 men were given either 9s or 4s 6d.[4]

The results of these reforms were considerable. By January 1881 it was learned that the King of Asante had 1000 Sniders and a good supply of ammunition and guns.[5] The Basel missionaries in Kumasi reported seeing 5000 men all armed with Sniders, bayonets and flintlock guns. They estimated the total fighting power of Asante at between twenty-five and thirty thousand men.[6]

Prempeh inherited not just a reformed army, but also an army which had had brilliant successes. Before Prempeh, the Asante court had formed the Hausas in the army into two regiments, and there were suggestions that it was with these that Asante effected the closure of the Volta route with such alacrity as we have already noted. Because of their success in gaining the physical control of the

---

1 I received this information from Mrs M. Johnson, Librarian, I.A.S., Legon.

2 C.O. 96/126, no. 83, encl. in Lees to Hicks Beach, 14 April 1879

3 *Ibid.*   4 *Ibid.*

5 C.O. 879/18, African (West) no. 232, encl. in Griffith to Kimberley (Confidential), 6 February 1881

6 *Ibid.*, 27 and 28 February 1881

river between Salaga and Kpong, the troops, with the aid of local chiefs, laid embargoes on goods and produce passing to and fro,[1] although it appears that the King could not afford to keep them there after 1882. A similar surveillance was instituted for the Gyaman road, where the King posted Owusu Kokor Kuma, who had been assisting in training the troops, with 300 men armed with Sniders. The question of guarding the Gyaman road obviously became so important that early in 1881, 3700 more men, armed with guns, were added to those with Sniders, making a total of 4000 men for Gyaman alone.[2] By 1884 the achievements of the Kumasi fighting forces had made a deep impression on contemporaries.

With a reformed army flushed with victory, Prempeh was able to win the war through determination and wise judgement. He entrusted Bekwai with the conduct of the war and the command of the Kumasi forces. His opponents were led by Kokofu, so that for most of the time the Civil War appeared, and was referred to, as a contest between Kokofu and Bekwai. The Bekwai–Kokofu duel, if we may so refer to the Civil War, was an exciting contest. The Kokofu side, led by Sem Akempon, and consisting of Mampon, Sewuah and Kokofu, could not match the Asante reformed forces to which the great powers of Bekwai and Kumasi contributed. Indeed it would appear that the only reason why Sem Akempon, an Asante general of importance, placed himself at the head of the Kokofu army up to the day of his arrest, was that he did not want to, or could not, hand over the treasure of the Asante royal family of which he was caretaker.[3] It was Prempeh's mother, who now demanded that Akempon would have to disgorge the 3200 ounces of gold dust and other valuables which the ex-king, Mensah, had given him for safe keeping.[4] In the third week of December 1886 reports reaching the coast indicated that Sem Akempon and the King of Bekwai were about to fight,[5] but it was not until about a month later that the conflict took place. In the very week that Bekwai, at the head of Asante forces, under Prempeh's orders, launched a campaign on the Kokofu side, Sem Akempon was taken prisoner by the King of Bekwai, and the King of Kokofu fled to Akyem. Akempon's captor laid down the conditions under which his life would be spared: he was to deliver up the treasure and other property of the royal family entrusted to him for safekeeping. Sem Akempon had up to 14 February to decide between losing his head or giving up what was demanded.[6] The *Western Echo* made it abundantly clear that by February the military opposition to Prempeh showed signs of waning: that everyone had reached the point of submission except Akempon, whom circumstances prevented from following suit. But Akempon was 'now out of the running',[7] being a prisoner in log, who at any moment might lose his head. It was indeed the military might of his opponents which had pushed Sem Akempon, the previous November, into such a tight corner that he was disposed publicly to withdraw his support of Achere-

1 C.O. 96/130, no. 100, Ussher to Hicks Beach, 5 March 1880

2 C.O. 879/18, African (West) no. 232, encl. in Griffith to Kimberley (Confidential), 6 February 1881

3 *The Western Echo*, 10–27 January 1887   4 *Ibid.*, 14–28 February 1887

5 *Ibid.*, 16–23 December 1886   6 *Ibid.*, 10–27 January 1887

7 *Ibid.*, 14–28 February 1887

boanda if only he could be assured that the new king, Prempeh, would not 'relieve him of his head'.[1] Now that he was in the power of his opponents, he could only save himself by satisfying the conditions laid down for his release, and since he failed to do this by 31 March, the inevitable had happened and this pathetic figure was hurried into the next world.[2]

The elimination of Akempon turned out to be the first step towards the total annihilation of the Kokofu forces. The defeat of Kokofu seems to have been achieved in two stages. Early in May 1887, Mark Hayford, the Government interpreter and clerk at Prahsu, reported that the Bekwais had completely routed the Kokofus.[3] Exactly a year afterwards, the final assault on the Kokofu army was to begin. But during this protracted period of tragedy for the Kokofu side, they put up a tremendous effort which brought them a temporary victory over Bekwai, resulting in the death of King Djimah of Bekwai late in May 1887. The campaign which ended in this way was actually the one in which Bekwais had earlier carried all before them, as Mark Hayford reported. But the failure of the Nsutah forces to appear on the right flank of Bekwai, at the hour agreed upon, gave the Kokofus the chance to turn the tables and to rout the small force of Bekwais in charge of the Bekwai camp. When these fled and conveyed the intelligence to their king in the front, he had no alternative but to seek safety in flight, unfortunately leaving his baggage and females to fall into the hands of the Kokofus.[4] Though only temporary, the Kokofu victory must have been impressive. At least the Kokofuhene, Asibe, looked upon himself as a great conqueror and haughtily sent messages to Awuah of Bantama and the chiefs of Kumasi requesting the handing over to him of Yaa Kyiah and her sons as well as those who had had a hand in the deposition of the late kings, Karikari and Mensah. He also requested that the King of Juaben should be sent to him so that he might spare Kumasi the horror of a capture or his sacking it with his victorious troops.[5] Indeed, if he had known Charles V, Asibe would have pictured himself as playing the role of this great Emperor whose victorious forces sacked Rome in 1527.[6] Asibe carried this arrogant conduct to the Kumasi Conference which was held shortly after his May victory.

But in fact Asibe's destruction was close at hand. When a new king, Abbebresseh, mounted the Bekwai throne, Prempeh confirmed his assumption of the generalship of the Asante forces. Abbebresseh, after closing the Kumasi conference and arresting the obstructionists, swore that he would have the King of Kokofu dead or alive and immediately proceeded, within a couple of months of the Kokofu victory, to attack Asibe and his forces and to drive them out of Bekwai in a headlong flight.[7]

This was the beginning of the end for the Kokofu side. From this time onwards it was one punishment after another, and about a year later, reports came

1 *Ibid.*, 9 November 1886   2 *Ibid.*, 16–31 March 1887

3 C.5357, encl. in White to Holland, 9 June 1887

4 *The Western Echo*, 31 May 1887. It was the strain of this flight which told on the health of King Djimah of Bekwai and caused his death.

5 *Ibid.*, 16–30 July and 15–30 June 1887

6 W. Kirchner, *Western Civilisation since 1500*, pp. 43–4

7 *The Western Echo*, 16–30 July 1887

pouring in from the interior which indicate that the tragedy was reaching its climax. By the end of June, Hutchinson, a representative of a European trading firm in the interior, sent in a report to say that the Bekwai side had defeated the Kokofus.[1] It must be remembered, however, that the Kokofu defeat followed their very vigorous efforts in the previous May to strengthen their defence measures. The King had done this by occupying deserted villages or building new ones about a mile or two from the main Adansi road.[2] Judging from the vigorous manner in which the Kokofus fought against Britain in 1900, they must have proved a tough side for Kumasi during the Civil War.

And yet by 5 July reports on the Kokofu–Bekwai duel indicated that the conflict had assumed a most serious nature and that the Kokofus were not only defeated, but actually driven across the Prah into western Akyem.[3] A week later this was confirmed, when fresh reports explained that it was the combined Kumasi–Bekwai forces that had expelled the Kokofu forces out of Asante. Prempeh had used the reformed forces well, and he was now determined to make the King of Kokofu a prisoner.[4] Distance prevented him from achieving this, but for all practical purposes the Kokofu opposition had been crushed.

Prempeh then turned to the King of Mampon, whose dissent, as we have seen,[5] was probably due to his pride having been hurt for not being consulted in Kumasi in these crucial matters, especially since without him no enstoolment of the Asantehene was possible. But at the time explicit obedience was vital, and Prempeh could not afford to have these 'over-mighty subjects' next door. Mampon resisted and attempted to enlist Nkoranza military assistance. King Kofi Fa of Nkoranza refused. But Mampon succeeded in securing the support of Nsutah. The Mampon and Nsutah forces were dispersed by Asante, and they fled north, mainly to Atebubu where they remained for some time, the Atebubus being sympathetic to them.[6]

Nkoranza, too, came in for attention, as the exigencies of the time made it necessary that Prempeh should be sure of the loyalty of Kofi Fa, King of Nkoranza.[7] Again Atebubu and the Brong Confederation found themselves in conflict with Asante for the same reason.

But all this belongs to the second phase of the struggle of Asante to maintain her independence and we shall discuss this in another chapter. For the moment it is sufficient to state that the first phase was won by Asante. Governor Rowe had submitted as early as 1885 a report on the Coast, indicating the probability that Kumasi would use armed force to reassert its control on the surrounding countries.[8] Events proved him right and some three years later the army succeeded, where diplomacy had failed, so much so that it was possible to enstool Prempeh in Kumasi.[9] The King had brilliant success and in a comparatively short period of time Prempeh stamped out opposition and unified the kingdom.

---

1 C.5615, Griffith to Knutsford, 30 June 1888   2 *Ibid.*, encl.

3 C.5615, Griffith to Knutsford, 5 July 1888

4 C.5615, *ibid.*, 12 July 1888   5 See above p. 97 n 2

6 Nkoranza tradition; informants, Nana Kwame Baffo III, Nkoranzahene and Kwadjo Baffo, an elder at the Nkoranza Court

7 *Ibid.*   8 C.4477, Rowe to C.O., 16 August 1884

9 C.O. 96/256, Maxwell to Ripon (Confidential), 13 June 1895 Governor Maxwell writing in June 1895 paid tribute to Asante efforts at unity in the following words: 'Their efforts

These activities in Asante, therefore, reveal how the Central Government of Asante continued at every turn to thwart British efforts to exercise their influence in the interior. These activities were, however, primarily concerned with secessionists in Asante. The events of 1875–90 in Asante cannot, therefore, be classified as proto-nationalist movements. But by using its traditional weapons of diplomacy and the army, the Asante Central Government twice frustrated British plans. We know that the British decided to extend their influence into Asante as early as 1875, but it was not until 1895 that this was achieved.

---

have been crowned with conspicuous success. As far back as 1888 their aim to secure unity and peace has resulted in the election as King of Ashanti of a sovereign whose rule has been characterised by firmness, tact and wisdom.'

CHAPTER FIVE

Inland states of the Protectorate and British interference

Asante activities thus held British influence at bay. In the Protectorate, however, the British had already established legal control over the chiefs and people in 1874. All that they needed to do from 1875 onwards was to organise economic exploitation of the country. But when they tackled this assignment, they came up against strong opposition from the people.

The activities of the states *vis-à-vis* the British in the Protectorate could be classified into two categories. The chief feature of the first category was the presenting of a united front against the British, such as occurred in Wassa and Akwapem. In these states the people protested directly against British interference in their politics. On such issues the entire population was united. The traditional rulers were the leading spirits in these protest, and they were supported by their people. The protests took the form of carefully considered petitions, as in Wassa, and spontaneous acts of disobedience, as in Akwapem.

The second type of activity occurred in places where the people were already divided over local issues. In such places only a section of the population were against British interference and then only because they supported their rivals. Examples were Akyem, Krepi and Kwahu. In these places local politics were not directly concerned with British activities. In Akyem, for instance, Chief Okyere's main concern was to get the ferry at Oda, and he disliked the British only because they prevented him from achieving his ends. In Krepi, Bella and the Taviefes opposed the restoration of Kwadjo Deh's rule, and their hatred for the Gold Coast Government was due to the fact that the British supported it. In Kwahu, too, there was no national programme of protests against the British, for there was a primary dynastic issue between Chief Boama and his rivals.

Briefly, therefore, there were two types of activities in the Protectorate. The first type was directly concerned with the British, and took the form of protest, as in Wassa and Akwapem. The second type arose largely over local issues, as in Akyem, Krepi and Kwahu.

Wassa and Akwapem

In Wassa, a series of events led to countrywide protests, carefully organised against the British. The ruler of Eastern Wassa in the 1870s was Ennemil Quow who lived in Manso. The British were anxious that he should submit to them, but he steadily refused. In 1875 Governor Strahan imposed on him a fine of 30 ounces of gold for a flagrant disregard of authority. A more serious offence was that the King contravened the slave-dealing abolition Ordinance of 1874. About February 1875 Ennemil Quow, disregarding the Ordinance, purchased seven persons from Asante, who were brought to Wassa. The act of purchase itself did not go much against the spirit of the Ordinance, if only the King, after the people had come into his possession, had at once manumitted them; he refused to do this, and kept them as domestic slaves for several months.[1]

For this offence Governor Strahan imposed a severe punishment on Ennemil Quow. He was to pay a fine of 100 ounces of gold, and be imprisoned for three years. The people of Wassa joined their King in protesting against this high-handed sentence. As soon as the Court's pronouncement was made, a deputation waited on Governor Strahan asking for a commutation of the prison sentence.[2] When Moloney, sent by Lieutenant Governor Lees, reached Manso, the Wassa capital, he observed that there was a strong party opposed to the decision of the Government. The members of this party favoured Ennemil's cause and were getting up a petition for his release and restoration to the throne.

From the petition which the people of Eastern Wassa submitted to the Secretary of State in April, it was obvious that the Government had attempted to impose a new ruler, and it was only the strong stand taken by the people which prevented Moloney from achieving this aim while he was in Manso earlier that month. Moloney talked about the meeting of chiefs and people in Manso preferring one Impira to Ennemil,[3] but according to the petitioners this statement had no foundation. They pointed out that on 25 February their King, Ennemil of Eastern Wassa, was sentenced by the Judicial Assessor's Court to a fine of 100 ounces of gold dust and three years' imprisonment, for contravening the Ordinance abolishing slavery on the Gold Coast. Following this, they pointed out, His Excellency resolved to depose him and 'your petitioners have learnt to their deep regret that one Quamine Oppira had been elected by the Governor to occupy and fill the stool of the Kings of Wassa'. What irritated them was not just the severity of the punishment, but the fact that the King 'is to be deposed from his stool, which is to be given to a nominee of His Excellency's while there are other members of the said Royal Family in direct succession to the said King'.

The question of succession has always been important in these communities and any arbitrary interference with it invariably generates protests. 'Your petitioners respectfully submit', they wrote, 'that they are, and have been, perfectly satisfied with the rule of the said King whilst he has been on the stool, and they could not recognise any other person outside the members of the said family as their lawful king, while there are some of them living who are in direct succession to the said King, who is the hundredth in direct descent from Geythuya Mansu, the first King of Wassay.'[4] A man, Adoo Pokoo, and several women, who were in direct succession to the King, were then living in Wassa.[5]

1 C.O. 96/118, no. 48, Strahan to Carnarvon and encl. 1, 4 March 1876

2 *Ibid.*   3 C.O. 96/118, no. 101, encl. in Moloney to Strahan, 22 April 1876

4 C.O. 96/118, no. 110, encl. 1 in Lees to Carnarvon, 1 May 1876

5 The members of the royal family were Adjuah Arduha, aunt of the King, Adoo Pokoo; her son, Accosuah; Baginah, the King's elder sister, who had two daughters; Abuah Beyduah, the King's younger sister who had a daughter. All these were in direct succession to the King.

As for Quamina Impira, the man elected by the Governor, he had been no more than a slave of the royal family and was actually at the time only retained there as one of the trumpeters or hornblowers. So they could not recognise Impira as their king, the more so because the election of a king was the right of his subjects. They therefore concluded their petition with the request that the Secretary of State should not depose their King and place anyone in his place. Apart from the royal family nineteen chiefs and captains from Eastern Wassa appended their names to the document.[1]

This petition served merely to confirm the Government in its determination to seize control in Wassa. To stop the agitation of the people on behalf of their King, Governor Freeling deported Ennemil Quow to Lagos.[2] When Ennemil's sentence expired on 24 February 1879, on the advice of Alfred Moloney, the Government ordered his further detention in Lagos[3] on the grounds that he had not paid the fine of £100.[4] As late as 1889, long after the expiration of his original sentence, Ennemil Quow was still detained in Lagos.

The action of the Government led to a new wave of protests. The people of Wassa renewed their agitation. They rejected Quamina Impira, who had been imposed on them. They quarrelled with him and finally seized the stool from him.[5] The people's support for Ennemil Quow, in opposition to the Government, was further demonstrated at a public palaver at Manso in 1889, called by S. Vroom, D.C. of Dixcove and Sekondi, on Governor Griffith's orders. Vroom was to ascertain, from the meeting, what their wishes were on the subject of Quow's return. The entire meeting categorically rejected Impira and asked for the immediate restoration of Quow. The chiefs bound themselves severally and collectively in the sum of £3000 'for the future good and loyal conduct, wise government and obedience to law and authority of Ennemil Quow'. The Government had no alternative now but to restore the King at once to his stool.[6] Before the end of 1889, therefore, Ennemil Quow was brought back from Lagos and restored to the Wassa stool.[7]

In Akwapem, from the 1870s, we find persistent protests against the Gold Coast Government, and determination to prevent the establishment of British control. Thus, although the protests were not as carefully planned as those in Wassa, being mostly spontaneous and isolated incidents, they revealed a com-

1 C.O. 96/118, no. 110, encl. 1 in Lees to Carnarvon, 1 May 1876

2 C.O. 96/121, no. 89, Freeling to Carnarvon, 5 April 1877

3 C.O. 96/126, no. 20, encl. in Lees to Hicks Beach, 7 February 1879

4 Minutes of 14 March by Meade and 20 March by Bramston on above. The C.O. subsequently raised the fine to £400, with what justification, we cannot tell.

5 C.3687, encl. in Moloney to Kimberley, 7 January 1882

6 C.O. 96/200, no. 57, Griffith to Knutsford, 26 March 1889

7 Ennemil Quow himself petitioned in 1887 for his release, maintaining that none of the new conditions of paying a fine and giving security in £1000, etc. had been laid down in the original sentence. He explained that according to the original terms imposed on him by Sir David Chalmers he was to serve two years imprisonment and pay £400, or in lieu of that a further three years imprisonment. By 1882, therefore, he had served the three additional years, so his further detention (till 1889) was illegal. C.O. 96/179, no. 36, Griffith to Strahan, 25 January 1887; also C.O. 96/180, no. 127, Griffith to Stanhope, 19 April 1887

mon agreement among the entire population that the white man's rule must, at all cost, be repelled.

It was in 1877 that the Akwapems went into action to forestall the consolidation of British rule. In that year, Quow Daddy, King of Akwapem, gave considerable support to the Juabens, who were then committing acts of disobedience against the Gold Coast Government. He protected the Queen of Juaben, then living in Mampong, a Juaben Chief Captain living at Obosomasie, and numerous other Juabens, who were in his kingdom. He also helped the Juabens to collect and keep powder in various Akwapem towns, including Amamakrom, Obosomasie and Brewassie.[1]

In the 1880s the protests against the British in Akwapem were led by Chief Ababio and his principal town of Adukrom. On 25 November 1886 a bailiff of C. Riby Williams, District Commissioner of the Volta District, travelled from Akuse to Adukrom and served a summons on a man who simply tore up the process and attempted to flog the bailiff. The man got away with it. On another occasion when Corporal French Mensah and Private Esiamah were trying to arrest certain persons charged with perjury, they were assaulted by people near Adukrom.[2]

After these incidents, C. Riby Williams, the District Commissioner, decided to go to Akwapem to talk to Ababio, the Chief of Adukrom. When he reached the town, he went to the Basel mission house and sent his Hausa orderly to call Ababio. Riby Williams informs us that the answer he got from the Chief was 'I was to go to his house and "salute" him, and that I must come myself to his house'. The Commissioner sent a second time and Ababio went. Asked why he had sent that reply, he answered that 'he was master of that town and that I must "come to him"'. The Commissioner pointed out that since he was the Governor's representative he was superior to any chief. The Chief retorted: 'Well! What do you want?' The District Commissioner replied that he wanted the Chief to trace the people who assaulted the police in his village. Ababio simply stared at Williams. The Commissioner repeated his requests. 'Then Ababio burst out "You may catch the people yourself as you are the one the Governor sent". Ababio then flounced out of his chair and in passing me shook his stick in my face and said "Go and arrest the people yourself" and went off with his people.'

Riby Williams was amazed. 'I never met with such impertinence and insubordination before', he wrote. The Commissioner had to go back to Akuse and issue new warrants for the arrest of the culprits. Sergeant Adams and five other constables went to serve the summons on the villagers near Adukrom. On their way to Akwapem they called on King Akrobetto of Srah, Yilo Krobo, who gave them handcuffs and a guide. When they arrested the first prisoner the people promptly rescued him. A headman called Lamptey led the resistance against the constables. They later reported in bad English: 'Lamptey is the man giving orders to go on "flog them, flog them" and he said "I will flog you, but if the Governor like, he must hang me"!' Lamptey is reported to have added that if they came to his village again he would kill them. The constables concluded their report: 'Lamptey told us to tell our master that he is a fool to send us to his village.' He refused to give them back the handcuffs.[3]

1 C.O. 96/121, no. 199, encl. in Freeling to Carnarvon, 10 August 1877

2 C.5357, Griffith to Stanhope, 28 January 1887   3 *Ibid.*

In 1887 the British discovered that Kwame Fori, the new King of Akwapem, was himself supporting the protests of his subjects against the Government. In that year he refused to supply Captain Douglas, who had been sent to arrest Ababio, with guides to find out the Chief's hiding place.[1] Consequently Douglas failed to find him. Thus Ababio continued his protests until 1893, when Governor Hodgson managed to arrest him.[2]

The protests in Wassa and Akwapem were thus directly against British agents. Throughout the period 1876 to 1893 there was not a single occasion when those involved in these anti-British protests were divided among themselves. Because of this, the protests in Wassa and Akwapim were really formidable, in spite of the fact that the latter were largely spontaneous rather than organised and premeditated. The effects of these protests on British policy were tremendous, but before discussing them, we must look at local politics in other parts of the protectorate.

Akyem, Krepi and Kwahu

In these places local pressure on the British was not as strong as in Anlo, Wassa, Asante or Fante, for the following reasons. Apart from the fact that these states were divided over local issues, those sections of their people who opposed the British did not possess armies as strong as those of Asante. Then, the organisation of local activities here was done by chiefs alone, without the skilled support of educated Africans, as in Fante. The chiefs had to rely entirely on traditional institutions in their dealings with the Government, and these were not as effective in the Protectorate as they were in Asante.

There were three phases of activities in Akyem. The first phase (1875–80) was dominated by Amoako Atta I of Akyem Abuakwa; the second (1887–88) by chief Okyere of Wankyi; and the third (1888–89) by King Atafuah of Akyem Kotoku.

About 1875 Amoako Attah I of Akyem Abuakwa was engaged in expanding his influence over Akyem Kotoku and Juaben.[3] Since the British were also trying at this time to extend their influence into these regions frequent conflicts arose. In 1875 Amoako Attah rejected the Governor's orders not to attack Asante forces and, had Governor Strahan not sent Hausas to stop him, would certainly have invaded Asante territory.[4] In August 1877 the King again refused to carry out Governor Freeling's orders about stopping fugitive Juabens from collecting arms in Akyem Abuakwa.[5] The King continued in his conduct, but in 1880 Ussher exiled him to Lagos.[6]

The activities led by Chief Kwabena Okyere of Wankyi (ten miles east of Oda) began about 1887, with a dispute over the ownership of the ferry over the River Birim and of the town, Oda, itself. The two claimants were Chief Okyere

1 *Ibid.*, encls. 2 and 3   2 C.O. 96/237, no. 333, Hodgson to Ripon, 7 October 1893

3 C.O. 96/116, no. 220, encl. 1 in Strahan to Carnarvon, 13 November 1875

4 C.O. 96/116, no. 221, Minutes of 14 December 1875 on Strahan to Carnarvon, 6 November 1875.

5 C.O. 96/121, no. 199, Freeling to Carnarvon, 10 August 1877

6 C.O. 96/130, no. 86, Strahan to Carnarvon, 25 March 1880

and Atafuah, King of Akyem Kotoku. The Oda ferry and the town lay on the borders of both Akyems, and since the ferry attracted a lot of trade from Asante, both rulers were anxious to acquire the profits accruing from its use.[1]

The British intervened on the side of Atafuah. In 1888 the Government sent first Assistant Inspector Lethbridge, then Dr Smith and finally Turton, the Colonial Secretary, to deal with the problem.[2] The decision they were to implement was that Okyere should cut a road from Wankyi to the main Asante road, so as to divert trade to a new Wankyi ferry which would be set up for the purpose. This was to be done on the understanding that Atafuah would close the Oda ferry. But the manner in which the agreement was hedged round by all sorts of conditions, such as Atafuah reserving the right to cross his own people by the ferry, revealed to Okyere and his followers that the British did not really mean to induce Atafuah to close the ferry.[3]

Okyere accordingly rejected the agreement. His opposition was thus against both Atafuah and the British. He had some very powerful supporters. The first was King Amoako Attah II himself. About the middle of 1888 the king was known to have complained that 'Chief Atcherie had spent all his substance without being able to obtain the river'.[4] The second supporter of Okyere was Chief Kofi Ahinquah of Akyem Swedru.

With the support of these people Chief Okyere organised his activities well. First he stated his claims to the ferry, as well as his objections to the proposed British settlement, and then he backed up his statements with force. In the middle of 1888 it was reported that the 'Chief of Wankie has rejected everything in the way of a settlement and insisted upon taking possession of the river and Insuaim (Oda)'. The Chief told Turton's interpreter 'that he would listen to nothing I might say unless I handed over to him the river and the land upon which Insuaim stands. If I was not prepared to do that I might return at once to Accra and leave him to get them in his own way'.[5]

To back his pronouncements with force Chief Okyere made a plan for getting his own people, the Abuakwas, supported by Amoako Attah's men and Kofi Ahinqua's agents, to launch a military attack on King Atafuah and the people of Oda. His final aim in this regard was the destruction of Oda. 'There can be no doubt', wrote Turton, 'that Wankyi and the towns of Eastern Akim west of this, together with Akim Swaidro, are acting in concert and the object can only be that of destroying Insuaim.'[6]

In executing his military plans, Chief Okyere taxed his organising abilities to the full. First he collected a large number of Abuakwas from all the villages adjacent to Wankyi, where they underwent rigorous preparations for the attack.[7] Then he invited Amoako Atta and Kofi Ahinquah to set up auxiliary services calculated to promote his military onslaught on his rivals. First Amoako Attah ordered Chiefs Asuan and Ambosu and their men to join Okyere, thus increasing the latter's fighting force. Then the King got Akyease people to shut the road from the sea-board to Oda, and not to allow tobacco, rum, ammunitions of war, or arms pass to Oda.[8] This was meant to weaken Atafuah and his supporters. Conversely, Chief Kofi Ahinquah cooperated with Amoako Attah

1 C.5615, Griffith to Knutsford, 17 May 1888   2 *Ibid.*   3 *Ibid.*, encl. 3

4 *Ibid.*, encls. 4 and 8, 14 June 1888   5 *Ibid.*, encls. 1 and 2

6 *Ibid.*, encls. 4 and 8   7 *Ibid.*, encls. 1 and 2   8 *Ibid.*, encls. 4 and 8

to strengthen Chief Okyere's military position. Both rulers sent their men to Mankessim to buy powder, guns and lead, 'which they stated were for Chief Atchere to fight with'.[1]

Briefly, therefore, Okyere did everything possible to make sure that he got the ferry. But the features of the Akyem episode, discussed above, were weaknesses in Okyere's system. His rivals gave valuable support to the British, and this proved too much for Okyere and his allies. They failed to destroy Oda. Eventually, Turton tricked Okyere, and persuaded him to go to Accra, explaining to the chief that the Governor was willing to re-open the question of ownership of the ferry.[2] But when Okyere reached Accra, he was detained in Ussher Fort as a political prisoner.[3] Before the end of 1888, the Governor deported him to Lagos.[4] This brought Okyere's resistance to an end.

It was ironical that the third and last phase of the Akyem episode (1888–89) was led by Atafuah, King of Akyem Kotoku, who had earlier supported the British against Okyere. The trouble in Akyem Kotoku was over the Kokofu refugees. In 1888 the Asantehene, Prempeh I, drove King Asibe and his Kokofus across the Prah into the Protectorate. To avoid the troubles they had had with earlier refugees the British decided to resettle the Kokofus in the Agona country, whence they could not easily organise raids on Asante towns. But Atafuah had a different plan for them, and indeed gave them land in Kotoku where they were right on the Asante border.[5]

The situation thus led to a clash of interests between Atafuah and the British. Atafuah now resisted British demands. First, he suppressed the Governor's instructions requesting the Kokofus to move from Kotoku to Agona. Even when Akers was sent to Kotoku as Commissioner to Akyem to persuade Atafuah to change his mind, the King still refused. In the end Akers had to send Police Sergeant Vandyke to inform the chiefs in Kotoku of his instructions because 'Attah Fua is not a man to be implicitly trusted in the future'.[6]

Next, Atafuah placed a food embargo on Oda, in the hope of starving Akers and his Hausas there. The Commissioner had to threaten that, if food was not brought to Oda, the Hausas would take it. But the King took no notice of the threat.[7] Then the Government requested the King to go to Accra; he refused. Akers, therefore, fixed a time and date on which the King should start for Accra. Atafuah secretly organised his men to resist his removal from Oda. At 8 a.m. on the second Monday in September 1888, when the King was to start for Accra, his drum was beaten and in less than five minutes 200 armed men appeared from Oda. Soon there were 1000 Kotokus against Akers's 20 Hausas. Akers had to use great tact before he could get Atafuah to go to Accra, where he was fined £1000 and kept a political prisoner until the fine was paid.[8]

The strength of Atafuah's activities could be seen in the fact that they inspired Asibe and his Kokofus to disobey the orders of the Governor. For

1 *Ibid.*, encl. 2, 17 May 1888

2 C.5615, encl. 2 in Griffith to Knutsford, 14 June 1888

3 C.5615, Griffith to Knutsford, 14 June 1888

4 C.O. 96/196, no. 449, Griffith to Knutsford, 18 December 1888

5 C.5615, encl. 2 in Griffith to Knutsford, 18 September 1888   6 *Ibid.*, encl. 3

7 *Ibid.*, encl. 4   8 *Ibid.*, encl. 2

instance, when Akers sent Sergeant Major Futah to bring Asibe to Oda, the King of Kokofu refused flatly. It was with great difficulty that Futah eventually brought him to Oda. At Oda, the Kokofu leaders, Asibe, Achereboanda and Addom, continued to give Akers considerable trouble. In the long run he agreed that the Kokofus should go to Akrosso, only three miles south east of Oda, instead of to Insanbang as originally planned.[1]

Thus, although Akyem activities did not rank with the protonationalist agitations, say, of Anlo, yet they gave the British considerable trouble.

In Krepi, as in Akyem, activities against the British arose from local disputes. Kwadjo Deh VI of Krepi was anxious to restore a rebellious section of his kingdom, Taviefe, to his rule, and, when the Taviefes refused to submit, the King decided to humilitate them. Between 1875 and 1877 the King of Krepi sent to Taviefe on the pretext that he wished to hold a palaver with them, and make friends at Ziavie. The unsuspecting chief of Taviefe sent between forty and fifty of his own people to Ziavie to meet the King. But it was a trap, and the King had all the Taviefes massacred in cold blood. The Taviefes never forgave Kwadjo Deh.

The British, looking for ways and means to make their power in Krepi (a part of the Protectorate) effective, decided to support Kwadjo Deh against his rivals. Before the middle of 1888, Dalrymple was sent with a Hausa force to compel the Taviefes to submit to Kwadjo Deh, and later Akers was sent on the same mission.[2]

The Taviefes decided to resist these developments. They wanted to prevent their restoration to Kwadjo Deh's Krepi kingdom and to prevent British interference in their affairs, and that in favour of their rivals. So they made allies of Adaklu and Waya, whose inhabitants were also opposed to Kwadjo Deh, so as to strengthen their military resistance to Kwadjo Deh and his Pekis, as well as to the Government troops. When on 9 May 1888, Dalrymple ordered Kwabla Bella, Chief of Taviefe, and his captains to go to Peki, Kwadjo Deh's capital, they refused. Dalrymple threatened to use force, so the Chief sent out his young men into secret ambushes around Taviefe, and then agreed to go to Peki. While the party was nearing the entrance to the Taviefe valley, the hidden Taviefes suddenly shot Dalrymple dead. Bella escaped with the other Taviefes and disorder broke out amidst the terrified Hausas.[3]

The Taviefes went further. When Akers entered Taviefe on a punitive expedition they simply disappeared from the valley and hid on the hills above. As soon as Akers marched out again, the people returned to their homes and were soon able to remobilise their forces. They planned guerrilla warfare against the Hausas and the Pekis left in the neighbourhood of Taviefe. On 4 June some of the troops, returning to camp with food, fell into an ambush on the Madze road, in which some were killed and others fatally wounded. Though the Hausas had guns, these proved to be of no avail. The sergeant-major in charge of the Hausa detachment, on Bennett's instructions, retreated upon Ho.[4] Akers had to return with reinforcements before the Taviefes yielded.

In one other place, Kwahu, a section of the people were opposed to the

1 C.5615, Griffith to Knutsford, 18 September 1888

2 *Ibid.*, 14 June 1888   3 *Ibid.*, encl. 28, 1 June 1888

4 C.5615, of December 1888, Griffith to Knutsford, 14 June 1888

attempts of the British to influence them. The resistance here also came to a head in the 1880s. The leaders were Chief Kwasi Boama of Aduamoa and Abankwa, chief of Obomeng. They were opposed in the first place to Kwadjo Akuamoa, whom the Government was supporting in a dynastic dispute against Yaw Donkor.[1] Chief Boama declared before Reinhold, a messenger from the Governor, that he would never obey the Governor's orders to submit to Akuamoa. All his chiefs did the same.[2]

At this juncture, we must examine briefly the fact that African opposition was also directed against the missionaries. This is a vast subject and cannot be treated in detail in a work of this nature, but it may be useful to present this factor in outline by citing two examples, from Akyem and Kwahu.

By 1864 the Basel missionaries reached Kibi in Eastern Akyem. Since the missionaries emphasised new values, they tended to undermine tribal society. Christian converts often considered themselves absolved from all obligations to their chiefs. Examples in Akyem included Yaw Buakye, a former unflinching supporter of Amoako Attah, who turned against his monarch on becoming a Christian. There was also the example of the chief to whom Amoako Attah entrusted a sum of 3500 ounces of gold before his deportation, but who joined the German missionary body in Kibi to avoid having to account for the money when the King returned from exile.[3] A third example was that when Amoako Attah was absent in Lagos,[4] three of his wives were married by other men. And although Agyeman, the King's linguist, said since it was 'man and woman's palaver he cannot tell' whether it was the wish of the women or whether they were forced,[5] it would not be surprising in the social condition of Akyem at the time, if the men took the King's wives by force.

In the political situation of the Gold Coast at this time, when missionaries were in a close alliance with the colonial authorities, these developments in Akyem appeared to threaten the very foundations of traditional authority. King Amoako Attah saw the whole missionary movement as a forerunner of European political intervention. He therefore organised a movement against the missionaries in Akyem. In 1886 he ordered Christians to be punished for the part they were playing in the decline of his power. The Queen Mother was an active member of the King's movement, so that even after his death on 2 February 1887, the persecution of the Christians continued, and she succeeded in banishing them from Kibi; she swore to leave the town if they returned. They never did in her lifetime. King Amoako Attah II, who succeeded Amoako Attah I at the close of 1888, also continued to oppose the missionaries. He insisted that they should never return to Kibi in spite of Inspector Lethbridge's orders that they should. Lethbridge wrote: 'I told the King that order must be obeyed and he replied that he refused to do so.'[6] So the Akyem feud with the missionaries continued.

In Kwahu, too, there was opposition to the missionaries. Here Chief Boama's

1 C.O. 96/209, no. 74, Griffith to Knutsford, 13 March 1890

2 C.O. 96/235, G.C. Conf., Hodgson to Ripon, 17 August 1893 and encl. 1

3 C.O. 96/165, no. 155, encl. 3 in Griffith to Derby, 12 May 1885   4 See p. 120

5 C.O. 96/165, no. 155, encl. 1 in Griffith to Derby, 12 May 1885

6 C.O. 96/189, no. 10, encl. in Griffith to Holland, 16 January 1888

resistance was organised not only against the Government, but also against the Basel Mission, whose leader, Ramseyer, became a councillor to the puppet King on the Kwahu stool. The Chief must have felt, and rightly too, that the work of the missionaries would increase the Government's influence, so he decided to get rid of the Mission and the Christians, who were increasing in number in several Kwahu towns. The Rev. Ramseyer himself tells us that Boama had once threatened that he 'would flog me one of these days'. Other chiefs were following Boama's example. Boama thus organised a strong opposition movement, in which were to be seen some of the most powerful chiefs of Kwahu. The chiefs of Nkwanta and Obo, for instance, were also active in the movement, and apart from disobeying the King, lent their support to the persecution of the Christians.[1]

The persecution of the Christians appears to have reached a climax on Easter Sunday, 2 April 1893. David Okyere, the catechist in charge of Nkwantia, noticed that two of his pupils from Aduamoa were not in church that morning. He later learned that they had been seized and put into fetters by Chief Kwasi Boama. The prisoners requested that their teacher should visit them, and Okyere accordingly travelled to Aduamoa; and begged to see them. As soon as he entered the door was shut behind him by the Chief, and he and his courtiers began to flog the catechist. The latter's followers tried to save him, but this only made things worse, as the Chief called out to his people to flog all the Christians.[2] These examples show that there was considerable opposition to the missionaries in the Protectorate because of their support for colonial expansion.

Between 1875 and 1890, therefore, there was considerable pressure in various parts of the Protectorate against the British. Although in places like Akyem, Krepi and Kwahu, local politics was not solely concerned with the British, the activities of the states of the Protectorate as a whole were strong enough to affect British policy towards the people.

The Native Jurisdiction Ordinance 1878–83

When from 1875 onwards the British came up against opposition in their attempts to consolidate their power over the Protectorate, they realised that their legal authority had to be transformed into physical authority before they could hope to achieve their plans. Their original policy was to send travelling commissioners, first appointed in 1875, to carry out the Government's decisions in the various parts of the Protectorate. But when African politics rendered this policy unworkable, the Government decided that the first thing to do was to transfer sovereign power from the chiefs and people to the Government. It was to achieve this transfer that the Native Jurisdiction Ordinance was passed in 1878. Thus the passing of the Ordinance, necessitated by the activities of the state, represented a change in British policy concerning the Protectorate. Secondly, the manner in which the Ordinance was implemented shows that it was designed mainly to counteract African political activity.

Before the Gold Coast Government reached the stage of passing the Ordinance, they went through a series of exercises designed to accomplish what the

1 C.O. 96/235, G.C. Conf., encl. 1 in Hodgson to Ripon, 17 August 1893

2 *Ibid.*, sub-encl. in encl. 1

Ordinance finally achieved. First, Sir David Chalmers, whom Governor Freeling appointed to look into the question of transferring the sovereign power, then residing in the people and exercised by the chiefs, to the Gold Coast Government, thought that the best way to achieve this was by a proclamation which would define the powers of the chiefs with a view to limiting them. This would leave the British to exercise the more important powers of the land.[1] Sir David later changed his mind about the proclamation and instead prepared a public notice, which would achieve the same purpose. But Carnarvon wanted to make sure that the Notice would serve the best interest of H.M. Government, and so invited Lees's views on it. Although it was implicit in the public notice that power now derived from the Government instead of the people, Lees wanted this fact to be explicitly stated. 'The better policy appears to me (he wrote) to be that the renewed powers of the chiefs should rest rather upon English authority, than upon their innate right.' To this end he advised a different plan. 'I would suggest as a convenient procedure to pass an ordinance stating generally the objects in view and empower the Governor-in-Council to annul, vary or add to the rules from time to time by means of further notice.'[2] Carnarvon concurred in Lees's arguments and requested Governor Freeling to proceed by way of an ordinance.[3] So it was that on 24 June 1878 the Legislative Council passed 'An Ordinance to facilitate and regulate the exercise in the Protected Territories of certain powers and jurisdiction by Native Authorities'[4] – the Native Jurisdiction Ordinance for short.

The terms of the Ordinance run into several pages and it is possible to reproduce here only the essential clauses.

3. It shall be lawful for the Governor, with the advice of the Executive Council, by Proclamation to be issued by him for that purpose, to declare from time to time as he may think desirable, that any Head Chief's division or part thereof, shall be brought from time to time to be named therein, within the operation of this Ordinance. On such Proclamation being issued, and in force, the said Division or part thereof, shall be subject to the provisions of this Ordinance, and the powers and jurisdiction of all Native Authorities therein shall be exercised under and according to the provisions of this Ordinance and not otherwise.

4. Every Head Chief's division or part thereof so brought within the operation of this Ordinance may be subdivided, if the Governor thinks fit, into such convenient groups of villages under the supervision of such Chiefs, subordinate to the Head Chief, as the Governor, with the advice of the Executive Council shall appoint. It shall be lawful for the Governor with the like advice from time to time to alter and amend any such subdivision. Except in so far as expressly so altered, all Native subdivisions of territory and grouping of villages for purposes of jurisdiction existing at the commencement of the Ordinance shall continue.

1 C.O. 96/121, no. 100, encl. 2 in Freeling to Carnarvon, 17 April 1877

2 C.O. 96/123, no. 18, encl. 2 in Freeling to Carnarvon, 24 January 1878

3 C.O. 96/123, no. 38, Carnarvon to Freeling, 29 March 1878

4 C.O. 96/124, no. 133, Lees to Hicks Beach, 3 July 1878

II. Power of making bye-laws:

5. It shall be lawful for the Head Chief of every division brought within the operation of this Ordinance, with the concurrence of the Chiefs, Captains, Headmen, and others who by Native Customary law are the Councillors of his Stool, to make such bye-laws, consistent with the laws of the Gold Coast, and subject to the provisions of this Ordinance, as he may deem expedient for promotion, the peace, good order, and welfare of the people of his division, and also by the bye-laws to be made to annex and appoint penalties in respect of the breach of any such bye-laws.

The matters respecting which such bye-laws may be made, and the nature and extent of the penalties which may be imposed for their enforcement shall be such as are declared by the Rules. The concurrence mentioned in this section and in section seven may be given by such majority of the said Chiefs, Captains and Headmen and others, or in such other manner as is sanctioned and authorised by Native customary law.

6. The bye-laws so prepared shall be forthwith reported to the Governor for the approval or disallowance thereof by the Governor in Council, and such of the bye-laws as shall be so approved shall be published in the Gazette, and shall thereupon become valid and effectual as if the name had been enacted in this Ordinance. No bye-law which the Governor in Council disallows shall have any force or effect whatsoever . . .

Section III is on Native Tribunals. Clauses 21 to 23 stress that appeals could be made from Native Courts to British Courts.

21. Cases beyond native jurisdiction to be referred to the 'Court' (Commissioner).

23. The defendant in any case brought before any Native Tribunal may apply to the 'Court' (Commissioner) for removal of the proceedings, and if the 'Court' (Commissioner) sees sufficient reason . . . 'it' (he) may stop the hearing or further hearing of the case before such Tribunal . . . and direct the trial to be by the Court . . . .

Section IV deals with miscellaneous matters:

26. Chiefs to have power (a) of conservators of peace; (b) of carrying laws and orders of Court into effect; (c) of apprehending offenders.

Withdrawal of powers:

28. Governor in Council may withdraw privileges of Ordinance.
29. Governor in Council may suspend or dismiss Chiefs.[1]

It can be maintained that the Native Jurisdiction Ordinance achieved the transfer of authority from the chiefs and people of this country to the British Crown. For instance, in Clause 3 reference was made to the British Crown. instance, in Clause 3 reference was made to the Governor bringing by Proclamation any Head Chief's division under the operation of the Ordinance. Now, we know what was to be in such a Proclamation, because Sir David Chalmers had already outlined this. As we have mentioned earlier, this Proclamation was to limit the exercise of the Chief's powers to minor spheres and Clause 34

---

1 Metcalfe, *Great Britain and Ghana*, pp. 300–93

lists them in detail, i.e. making of roads, wells, etc. The bye-laws which the kings and chiefs would make (see Clauses 5 and 6) were confined to only these spheres.

Clause 6 is probably the most important. 'No bye-law which the Governor in Council disallows shall have any force or effect whatsoever.' Clauses 21 to 23 also meant that the defendant in any case could easily apply to a British Court and the case would be stopped in the King's Court.[1] What was even worse for the Africans, Clause 29 states clearly that it was the Governor in Council who should now dismiss kings and chiefs. All that these stipulations boiled down to was that any king who refused to seek recognition of his power or the exercise of it by the Colonial Government would have no powers at all. It was in these ways that the Native Jurisdiction Ordinance ensured that the source of power was no longer the king and his people but the British Governor.

The activities of the states affected the implementation of the Ordinance in two major ways. First, it was applied to regions which were centres of opposition to British influence. Second, the manner in which the Ordinance was implemented varied from region to region and state to state, depending on the nature of political activity in the region or state concerned.

Thus, since there were three major regions of opposition to the British, the Tarkwa region in the west, Akyem region in the centre, and Akwapem-Krepi region in the east, the British decided to concentrate the application of the Ordinance on these regions. It was, therefore, in order to disarm the states obstructing the expansion of British power that in April 1880 Governor Ussher suggested the appointment of three civil commissioners of higher standing than travelling commissioners in three different districts – Tarkwa, Central Fante and the Volta Districts. With the establishment of these 'three centres of supervision' a certain degree of control would be steadily exercised over the 'native' chiefs, wrote Ussher. He concluded: 'Thus Tarkuah in the west, Mansue in the centre, and the Volta in the East, will serve as a starting for an essay of the "Native Jurisdiction Ordinance".'[2]

In the Volta River District the British decided that the best way to deal with the obstructing states was first of all to secure recognition for British jurisdiction in the district as a whole. The most appropriate way of doing this appeared to them to be to restore law and order to the district, and physically to take over the handling of civil and criminal cases there. This assignment was executed with great zeal. On 2 September 1880 the Government published a proclamation, declaring the creation of the Volta River District to include Manya Krobo and Yilo Krobo, Akwapem, Shai to Gave, and Krepi.[3] Odumase in Manya Krobo was chosen to be the headquarters of this District, and Captain Rumsey R.N. was appointed District Commissioner of the Volta River District with extensive powers.[4] By September the Commissioner was already on the Volta, trying

1 See C.O. 96/123, no. 18, encl. in Freeling to Carnarvon, 24 January 1878

2 C.O. 96/130, no. 243, Ussher to Kimberley, 25 September 1880

3 C.O. 96/130, no. 236, encl. 1 in Ussher to Kimberley, 11 September 1880. Kwahu was later to be included in the V.R.D.; C.O. 96/130

4 C.O. 96/13, no. 146, Minute of 10 June 1880 by Hemming on Ussher to Kimberley, 10 May 1880; Ussher to Kimberley, 11 August 1880

to restore law and order, and to stop evils such as the common practice of European traders, especially at Amedeka, flogging women for bringing impure oil for sale. He was also concerned with stopping similar evil practices at Kpong, 'a receptacle for all the rascals in the Eastern Division'.[1]

In April 1882 the Colonial Secretary wrote to Kirby, deputising for Rumsey, to proceed to the Volta by way of Akwapim and in accordance with clauses 21 and 23 of the N.J.O. which empowered the Government to take over cases from the local courts,[2] to look into the following cases:

1. Death of the son of King Sackitey of Eastern Krobo.
2. The seizure of a village called Asnoga by Juabens.
3. A complaint by the King of Akwapim against Lartey chiefs for refusing his orders.
4. The reported murder and robbery of Hausa traders at Agomenya between Adumasi and Kpong.
5. Report by a Krepi woman, Mansah Chewee, that four children were stolen from her by a woman called Larwey and that her husband was killed. That the stolen children were with Larwey in Krobo.

Inspector Kirby was instructed to inform Sackitey of Manya, and King Akrobetto of Yilo, Krobo that the last two cases would be investigated in Accra.[3] Kirby performed all these duties with great attention to detail.

Then the British paid attention to individual states in the Volta River District, where local politics were delaying the consolidation of British power. They turned first to Akwapem. As we have seen,[4] the basis of local politics here was the claim of traditional rulers like Ababio that they were the lawful rulers of Akwapem, implying that the British were usurpers. To overcome this protest, therefore, there was concentration in Akwapem on the aspects of the N.J.O. (clauses 3, 4, 5 and 21 to 23)[5] dealing with 'native' authority and tribunals. It was because of this that Captain Rumsey, under clause 4 of the Ordinance, was instructed to find out the exact boundaries of each district presided over by an ohene, and of the larger districts presided over by the head chief sitting with captains, headmen and councillors, who constituted a native tribunal under the Ordinance. The aim of the exercise was to find out exactly how the native tribunals worked, as a preparation towards seizing their control from the chiefs of Akwapem. Rumsey was in fact requested to inform the people, as he went through Akwapem, that the existing native tribunal would bed one away with, and its place would be taken by a new one.[6]

Rumsey worked with great vigour. He came out with the information that Akwapem was divided into four district, Akropong–Aburi, Amankrom, Adukrom and Late. He went into even greater detail, pointing out that the two districts of Akropong–Aburi and Amankrom were collectively called Amantenso, and the other two, Adukrom and Late (more correctly the district of

1 C.O. 96/130, no. 243, and encl. 2, Ussher to Kimberley, 25 September 1880

2 See p. 115   3 C.O. 96/139, no. 149, Rowe to Kimberley and encl., 10 May 1882

4 See p. 107   5 See pp. 114–15

6 C.O. 96/143, no. 351, encl. 3 in Moloney to Kimberley, 31 July 1882

Adukrom) were called Kyrepon.[1] The British thus gained a considerable knowledge of the traditional system of government in Akwapem; gradually they took over its running from the chiefs and people. When in spite of this, Ababio continued to oppose the Government, Governor Hodgson, in 1893, deposed him, in accordance with Section 29 of the Native Jurisdiction Ordinance, no. 5 of 1883.[2] The implementation of the Ordinance in Akwapem, and the manner of its implementation were clearly the British reaction to the African protest movement there.

This was also true of Krepi. Here, the objections to the spread of British influence were coming from Taviefe, Waya, Adaklu, Madze, etc. whose original grievances stemmed from their dislike of Kwadjo Deh's rule. In order to silence opposition to their own rule, the British thought that they should operate the Native Jurisdiction Ordinance in Krepi in such a way as to restore these rebellious states to Kwadjo Deh. They accordingly invoked clause 4, which empowered the Governor to place any village under any chief he liked. Thus, as soon as the implementation of the Ordinance was commenced in Krepi in October 1886, the Government sent flags to the various divisions in Krepi, and requested the chiefs of these divisions to travel to Peki to obtain them as a mark of loyalty to Kwadjo Deh.[3] It was because of this that Akers forced Madze, about the middle of 1888, to submit to Kwadjo Deh and the British.[4] Dalrymple, too, as we have seen,[5] tried to force Taviefe into a similar submission without success. It was, again, to weaken the obstructionists in Krepi that, from 1887 onwards, the British tried to get Madze, Waya, Adaklu and Taviefe to sign treaties with the Government. Only Madze agreed.[6] The British, therefore, decided to back up the implementation of the Native Jurisdiction Ordinance with a full military campaign against the rebellious peoples.[7] So Akers was sent back with reinforcements into Krepi. About 15 June 1888, Akers occupied Taviefe. This meant a great deal of suffering for the people there, who had to abandon their homes to the rapacious Hausas. For about a week some of them took no food. Chief Kwabla Bella had to surrender himself on 24 June to save his people from further suffering. He was immediately placed under arrest, and before his famished subjects could be allowed to return to their homes, they had to promise to:

1. Become loyal subjects of H.M. the Queen and obey all commandments of the Gold Coast Government;
2. pay a fine;
3. give up seven chiefs including Kwabla Bella, Jakpa, Takekuli, etc.;
4. keep all roads open.[8]

In the circumstances the Taviefes had no alternative but to accept these terms.

1 C.O. 96/143, no. 351, encls. 1 and 2 in Moloney to Kimberley, no. 351, 31 July 1882. Full instructions to the D.C. can be found in encl. 3.

2 C.O. 96/237, no. 333, Hodgson to Ripon, 7 October 1893

3 C.5615, encl. 9 in Griffith to Knutsford, 1 June 1888

4 *Ibid.*, 7 June 1888, encl.　　　　5 See p. 111

6 C.5615, encl. 3 in Griffith to Knutsford, 14 June 1888

7 See p. 111　　　　8 C.5615, Griffith to Knutsford, 7 July 1888

The Ordinance was now fully implemented in Krepi, and all activities hostile to British interests were crushed.

In Wassa, too, the protest movement had led to a number of developments which dictated the manner in which the Native Jurisdiction Ordinance was executed. The first development was that many chiefs in Wassa, because of the protest movement, had become jealous of their ancient institutions, especially those concerned with the preservation of the authority of the chief. This was a natural result of so many years of agitation for the restoration of their king, Ennemil Quow, who had himself exhibited such a flagrant disregard for British authority.[1] The British therefore decided that the first aspect of the Ordinance which should be stressed in Wassa was clause 3, which required all chiefs, in a declared region, to register themselves. It was stressed here that anyone who failed to do this could not legally exercise any power.[2] It was thought that if the chiefs submitted themselves to the Government in this way, they could not at the same time continue to defend their traditional authority as they had been doing.

One important issue arose out of this. It was realised that the larger the number of chiefs who were made to register under the Ordinance, the easier it would be for the British to crush the protests. It was to achieve this that several civil commissioners were appointed to travel through Wassa and cause as many districts as possible to be brought under the Ordinance. The first of these commissioners was Inspector Cecil Duddley of the Gold Coast Constabulary, who was appointed in August 1880.[3] Others were Assistant Inspector W. Thompson[4] and Assistant Inspector Torry,[5] both of the Gold Coast Constabulary. Through the work of these officers, the provisions of the Ordinance were soon being applied to a large number of districts. These included those under the authority of Chief Ennemil Kuma, of Chief Ango,[6] and of Chief Kwamina Bedu of Manso. The hinterland of Elmina, Sekondi, Dixcove and Axim was also brought under the Ordinance.[7]

A second development was that, since the protest movement in Wassa had led to the exile of Ennemil Quow to Lagos and the enstoolment of Quamina Impira, a great social upheaval occurred. The rejection of Impira by the people led to the growth of lawlessness, especially in the Tarkwa area. This resulted in the Government's growing concern about the restoration of law and order in various parts of Wassa. Thus in implementing the Ordinance in Wassa, the Government concentrated on projects calculated to restore law and order. The officers sent to Wassa to implement the Ordinance accordingly concentrated on clauses 26 and 21 of the Ordinance which dealt with how the chiefs should be assisted to conserve peace and maintain law and order in their states. The officers, therefore:

1 See p. 105   2 C.O. 96/151, no. 287, Rowe to Kimberley, 20 May 1883

3 C.O. 96/130, no. 162, Ussher to Kimberley, 25 May and no. 177, Ussher to Kimberley, 11 August 1880, Accra

4 C.4477, encl. in Rowe to Derby, January 1884

5 C.O. 96/157, no. 269, Young to Derby, 9 May 1884

6 C.O. 96/151, no. 287, Rowe to Kimberley, 20 May 1883

7 C.4477, encl. in Rowe to Derby, January 1884

(a) studied and reported on the exact definition of boundaries of 'native' chiefs;
(b) supported the chiefs 'in their efforts for proper management of their respective districts . . .';
(c) dealt with minor cases, transferring serious ones from the chiefs' courts to the D.C.'s Court.[1]

In various other ways these officers strove to bring some order into Wassa Society. The implementation of the Ordinance in Wassa, too, was thus largely determined by the nature of local politics.

Similarly, there was a high correlation between the way the Ordinance was implemented in the third region, the Central Fante District, created in 1881,[2] and local activities there. For one thing, the creation of this District came at the end of the first phase of Akyem activities led by Amoako Attah I himself.[3] Besides, when, in about 1883, Kirby completed the groundwork for the implementation of the Ordinance in the Central Fante District (hinterland of Saltpond, Essicummah, Akyem),[4] the British settled down to using it almost exclusively as an instrument for putting down the Amoako Attahs, Okyere, etc., all of whom had reason to dislike the Government.[5] The spirit of the Native Jurisdiction Ordinance as a whole, and of clause 29 in particular, empowered the Governor to destroy the power of these over-mighty kings and chiefs.

When, for instance, Amoako Attah I returned from exile in 1885[6] and resumed his activities against the Government in 1886, Governor Griffith ordered the King's arrest by the officer implementing the Ordinance in Akyem Abuakwa. Towards the end of 1886, therefore, King Amoako Attah I was arrested and sent to Accra. The Governor kept Amoako Attah a prisoner until he died on 2 February 1887.

In view of the fact that Amoako Attah II, who had succeeded his brother, and Chief Okyere continued to disobey orders of the Government,[7] the British decided to draw their net round Akyem more tightly, with the view to crippling the recalcitrant states. They hoped to achieve this by imposing conditions contained in the Ordinance on the new king of Akyem Abuakwa. Governor Griffith sent Assistant Inspector Lethbridge to Akyem Abuakwa and he emphasised, on 6 November 1887, to the new King, the importance of obeying the instructions in the Ordinance.[8] The climax of the Government's efforts in this direction was reached at the close of 1888, with the arrest and deportation of Chief Okyere to Lagos.[9] It was clear that in Akyem, as in the other regions, it was African politics which determined the mode in which the Ordinance was implemented.

1 C.4477, encl. 1 in Rowe to Derby, 22 January 1884

2 C.O. 96/137, no. 16, Rowe to Kimberley, 24 January 1882   3 See p. 108

4 Kirby was sent in 1882 as a Travelling Commissioner to proceed from Saltpond to Essicumah. He was to go from there to Akyem Akwapem and back to Accra. He was to impart to headmen and villages bordering on his track the wishes of His Excellency towards the opening up of the country to British influence and the cooperation and help expected from them towards such an end. C.O. 96/137, no. 24, encls. 1, 2, 6 and 7 in Rowe to Kimberley, 24 January 1882

5 See pp. 108 ff.   6 C.O. 96/164, no. 155, encls. 1 and 3 in Griffith to Derby, 12 May 1885

7 See p. 112

8 C.O. 96/189, no. 10, encl. in Griffith to Holland, 16 January 1880   9 See p. 110

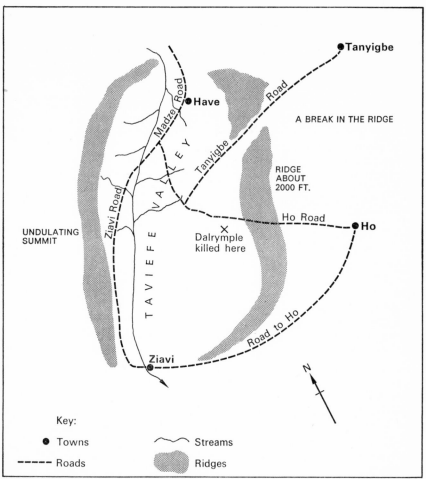

Tanyigbe

Have

A BREAK IN THE RIDGE

RIDGE
ABOUT
2000 FT.

Ho Road

Ho

UNDULATING
SUMMIT

X
Dalrymple
killed here

Ziavi

Road to Ho

N

Key:

● Towns

Streams

----- Roads

Ridges

The setting of the Taviefe rebellion 1888

It must be noted at this point that an added reason for the rigorous execution of the Ordinance in Akyem was that the activities of people like Okyere affected not only officers of the Government, but also the missionaries. The determination of the Government to reduce the power of the Amoako Attahs was thus partly due to the fact they were opposed to the missionaries, who were acting as agents of imperial advance into the interior.

In Kwahu, in particular, it was the opposition of King Yaw Donkor and his supporters to the missionaries that caused the Government to start implementing the Ordinance. Then followed a systematic attempt to reduce the power of Yaw Donkor, Chiefs Boama and Abankwa, all of whom were sworn enemies of the Basel Mission headed by Ramseyer, stationed in Abetifi. When the activities of the chiefs continued in spite of its attempts to halt them, the Government invoked clauses 3 and 29 of the Ordinance, which empowered the Governor to dismiss kings and appoint new ones. So on 29 March 1889 the Government elected to the Kwahu throne, a new king, Kwadjo Akuamoa, at Christiansborg Castle. Simultaneously, Yaw Donkor was deposed, arrested and imprisoned in Accra.[1] We can see, therefore, that the Ordinance was also employed to defend the missionaries against the local populations.

To sum up, events which occurred in the Protectorate between 1875 and 1890 fell into two major groups. Those in the first group worked directly against the British, while those in the second group arose largely because of local issues. Some of these activities were well organised, others were spontaneous acts of revolt. The strength of local politics was such that the British had to pass a Native Jurisdiction Ordinance to deal with them. But African political activity did not just affect the formulation of British policy in this way, it also affected its implementation. Thus we find that the aspects of the Ordinance which were stressed varied from region to region, depending on the nature of politics in each region. It was a testimony to its usefulness that the British succeeded in establishing control in the various parts of the Protectorate, with the exception of Wassa, where they were compelled to restore Ennemil Quow. Through the application of the Native Jurisdiction Ordinance to Akyem, Akwapem, Kwahu and Krepi, British influence was extended into all these regions.

1 C.O. 96/209, no. 74, Griffith to Knutsford, 13 March 1890

CHAPTER SIX

Post-confederation protests in the maritime states of the Protectorate

While the inland states and peoples of the Protectorate were so concerned about British activities, the maritime states of the Protectorate, too, in spite of the collapse of the Fante Confederacy, continued to protest against the Government. In the 1880s these protests were about taxation, representation, labour and land.

The protests about taxation aimed to prevent the imposition of obnoxious taxes on the people, and were directed mainly against house taxes, which the Government proposed to impose in 1888 and 1894.[1] The protests about representation were meant to secure from a reluctant British Government adequate representation for the Coastal peoples on the Legislative Council of the Gold Coast. Labour and land protests were warnings against British interference in the rights of the people, who argued that they were the sole judges of how to deploy their own labour force, and undisputed owners of the lands of the country.

Although these protests did not, as did the Fante Confederacy, seek independence from British control, they were nevertheless national issues. No dissenting voice opposed the prevention of Government-imposed taxes, the achievement of adequate representation on the Legislative Council, or the preservation of full control of land and labour. Thus, the protests were directly against the Government and not indirectly as, for instance, in Asante and parts of the Protectorate.

These protests were accordingly popular and supported by several classes of people, including kings, chiefs and people, educated Africans, societies, organisations and the local press. With such unanimous support, it was not surprising that the organisers of the protests had the best talents on the job. The organisation of the protests was therefore carefully done, taking the form of protest marches, petitions, deputations, etc.

These features of the protest movement in the coastal states, the popularity of its aims, countrywide support and careful organisation were important, because they contributed to the movement's effectiveness in influencing British policy.

Representation, deputation scheme and town councils

In the 1880s the people of the Gold Coast were deeply concerned because only two unofficial members represented in the Legislative Council a population of

1 C.O. 96/190, no. 87, Griffith to Holland, 26 March 1888; also *The Gold Coast Chronicle,* 6 November 1896

1·5 million living in a country 350 miles long with an area of over 30,000 square miles. Even these two representatives were nominated by the Governor, not elected by the people, so that they could not speak their minds freely. They had to agree with official policy or they would lose their seats at the next 'election'.[1] That was why, the people argued, undesirable laws (like those on taxation) were being passed in the Legislative Council.[2] 'Several laws are now and again passed which seem unadapted in several respects to the conditions of the people. But where you have the natives in possession of their own representatives then changes for the better must sooner or later take place,' wrote *The Gold Coast Chronicle*.[3] So the people of the Gold Coast began to agitate for increased representation in the Legislative Council.

In Cape Coast the people maintained that since the two unofficial members were Government nominees, they considered themselves not represented at all in *The* Council. They resented the action of Colonel White in summoning F. C. Grant, John Sarbah (senior) and W. F. Hutchinson as extraordinary members of the Council in June, 1887, since there was a rumour that these might become unofficial members. They appealed to the Government for the right to elect their own representatives to the Legislative Council.[4]

A leading spirit in this protest was James Brew, editor of *The Western Echo*, the Fante nationalist paper, who had been giving expression to the views of the Fante in his paper. In July 1886 he had actually circulated a letter in Cape Coast and Accra, urging his fellow countrymen to intensify the struggle for representation in the Legislative Council. The result was that the Accras immediately held a meeting at which they decided to put forth specific requests for an increase in their representation in the Legislative Council to the Government.[5] In Accra, as in Cape Coast, the press supported the people's demands and we find *The Gold Coast Chronicle* in 1895 demanding an increase in representation in the strongest possible terms.[6]

But the local colonial officials paid no heed to the pleas of the people. The people therefore began to think out a new way of making themselves heard, even before they gave up trying to convince the local Government. They decided on what came to be called the deputation scheme. The people felt that the Governor must have been distorting events on the Coast to the Colonial Office, otherwise there would have been more sympathy for their cause. So, to get H.M. Government in London to appreciate their case, they must send a delegation to give their version of the events on the Coast to the Imperial authorities.

A large meeting took place in Accra on 24 July 1886 to raise funds for the deputation scheme. Edmund Bannerman, a solicitor in Accra, organised this meeting, which was attended by R. Bannerman, J. F. Bruce, A. Bruce, R. A. Bruce, P. Vander-Puye, I. Vander-Puye, C. A. Williams, Bright Davies, the Rev. Freeman, and nearly twenty other educated Africans. The chiefs present

1 *The Gold Coast Aborigines*, 18 August and 2 September 1899

2 *The Gold Coast Chronicle*, 16 January 1891

3 *Ibid.*, 9 March 1891   4 *The Western Echo*, 15–30 June 1887

5 C.O. 96/173, G.C. Conf., Griffith to Granville, 27 July 1886

6 *The Gold Coast Chronicle*, 14 September 1895

were led to the meeting by Amankra, representing the King of Accra and his chiefs. King Tackie sent his linguist and three other chiefs were also present. The guest speaker was Edmund Bannerman himself and he took his theme from the issue of *The Western Echo* of 14 July 1886, on the deputation scheme. He pointed out that Prince Brew of Dunquah, 'their noble friend', was anxious that they, the Accras, should join with the Fante in this deputation. Robert Bannerman read a letter from James Brew stating that messengers from Fante would soon come to Accra for a conclusive meeting. J. F. Bruce, the meeting's chairman, also exhorted the gathering to continue the protest movement because they had many grievances, including the abolition of domestic slaves, for which they must seek a just redress. Alexander Bruce also spoke, pointing out how they, the inhabitants of the Gold Coast, had no part to play in the running of the affairs of the country.[1] All this exhortation was meant to induce the people to contribute towards the fund.

After this meeting, the leaders of the deputation scheme in the Eastern Districts drew up a systematic plan for the collection of the necessary funds. Bannerman, aided by his friends and some of the traders, decided to open a sort of national trust fund, and to start the ball rolling by contributing to it themselves first. The inhabitants of the sea-board towns were expected to contribute. Arrangements were made to collect contributions from the kings and principal chiefs of the Protectorate. In the interior parts of the Protectorate it was obvious that collection would be more difficult, so the leaders of the movement made a careful study of local grievances so as to encourage each state by promising the appropriate redress from the British Government, should the deputation scheme succeed. In some of these states foreign interference had very largely undermined the kings' authority and in all the states the abolition of domestic slavery was still a burning grievance. So Edmund Bannerman and his supporters made promises to these interior states covering a wide range of subjects. To some, such as Akyem and Akwapem, they promised the restoration of their former rights; to others, such as the Anlos, they promised the disbanding of the Hausa force; and to all they held out the hope of renewal of domestic slavery. They also promised the reduction of duty on spirits to the sea-board towns, and other coastal communities.[2]

The man entrusted with the task of collecting monies from the interior kings and chiefs was King Tackie himself. In August and September he sent messengers to all the states which owed allegiance to him. He informed the Kings of Manya and Yilo Krobo that they had to pay £350 each towards the scheme. He sent messengers to Akyem Abuakwa and Akyem Kotoku, Akwapem, Ada, Akwamu with similar messages detailing how much each of these states was expected to contribute. He sent for the people of Ningo to see him on the same issue, and finally he also sent to Anlo, urging them to pay so that the deputation could get duties lowered on spirits and the hated Hausas disbanded from their shores.[3]

When the messengers arrived in Anlo with King Tackie's letter it would appear that in spite of their usual aloofness the people found the promises so inviting that they acted at once. Chiefs Acolatse and Tamakloe sent messengers to hear the King's message. On hearing the message from Accra, the Anlo

1 C.O. 96/173, G.C. Conf., encl. in Griffith to Granville, July 1886

2 C.O. 96/179, no. 24, Griffith to Granville, 20 January 1887   3 *Ibid.*, encl. 3

delegates, without referring the matter to their chiefs, and very much unlike Anlo, authorised the names of the two chiefs to be attached to a document which welcomed the scheme. The war general Aholu and Chief Anthony of Wey, the second chief of Anlo, also gave their consent. When King Tackie and the other chiefs of Accra wrote to the King of Akwapem in September, they stated that even the 'Awoonahs who have been our enemies for the past twenty years have now joined us and have agreed willingly and joyfully to join in our deputation movement and had commenced collecting the tax'.[1]

From Akyem, too, the deputation scheme received considerable support. King Attah himself was the leading figure in the movement in his state and in spite of threats by the Government he continued to be 'one of the foremost in the deputation scheme'[2] till his death on 2 February 1887.[3]

The only place where the leaders of the movement encountered some difficulty was in Akwapem. Even here it was clear that Kwame Fori's reluctance to order collection of monies in his kingdom was not due to any fundamental opposition to the scheme. Unfortunately the King was not at the time on good terms with one of his chiefs, Akrofie of Lartey. The King had long hoped to be able to iron out their differences and when King Tackie's message about the deputation scheme reached him he thought this was his chance. Here was a rising organisation which could help him by putting pressure on Chief Akrofie to return to his allegiance. The king therefore insisted on the rebellious chief appearing in Akropong before he could deal with the letter on the deputation. But the deputation movement did not have the time to go into such minute details. They wrote back to the King of Akwapem, urging him to lay aside personal quarrels with the chief and get on with the collection. Kwame Fori was naturally disappointed. In that mood he was not prepared to pay his contribution, the size of which he now used as the second reason for not undertaking the project. King Tackie and the chiefs of Accra, taking into account their target of £5450 and the population and the size of Akwapem, had fixed King Fori's contribution at £720. Kwame Fori now wrote back to complain that the size of his contribution was too big and out of proportion to the movement's target.[4] Although the sum of £720 was a good deal of money in those days, it was quite clear that Kwame Fori's refusal arose out of his failure to utilise the movement to his own advantage.

In the Western Districts, attempts to collect money for the deputation scheme were made with equal zeal. It was reported that as early as October 1886 the states from Axim to Winneba made a fund-raising plan.[5] In February 1887 the scheme received a fresh impetus when an assembly of Kings of 'Mankessim, Denkyirah, Northern Assin and Dominassi and some of their principal chiefs' in Cape Coast came to a definite understanding as to how it would be carried out. It was reported that they further undertook to pay a sum large enough to cover all expenses and promised to pay in the amount by the end of the following month.[6]

---

1 *Ibid.*, encls. 6 and 4   2 *The Western Echo*, 10–27 January 1887

3 C.O. 96/170, no. 55, Griffith to Stanhope, 2 February 1881

4 C.O. 96/179, no. 24, encls. 4 and 5, 20 January 1887

5 C.O. 96/179, no. 24, encl. 3 in Griffith to Stanhope, 20 January 1887

6 *The Western Echo*, 14–28 February 1887

Generally, therefore, the deputation scheme received great support from the people of the Gold Coast. But the British Government was determined to thwart their efforts and in April 1887 it was announced on the Coast that Sir Henry Holland, the Secretary of State, was not prepared to receive the deputation.[1]

On hearing this decision the people acted swiftly. They decided that in view of the refusal of all their previous requests by the colonial authorities, their only course was to start local representative institutions in their own town 'in a humble effort to train up the people in the art of self-government'.[2] In this way the people would learn to carry out their own development projects. It meant that the people must set up a town council.[3]

Protests over town councils occurred in two waves. The first wave of protests was against the Government's reluctance to allow the people to establish their own town councils. The second occurred when the Government changed its mind, and decided to set up town councils, but only councils suitable for its own purposes. It was then to specific features of the proposed town councils that the people objected.

When the people of Cape Coast first resolved to set up a town council, they realised that this involved installing a king, who in pre-European days had supervised such institutions.[4] Now, since 1867 the British authorities had set their face against the placing of a king on the stool. They had maintained that the successors of Aggrey were not kings but mere 'head chiefs'. What the people now wanted was a king with full powers on the stool and a municipal institution or a town council to help him.

It was for this reason that the chiefs convened a meeting of the seven companies[5] in May 1887. At this meeting the people decided to elect a representative institution and to place a king on the stool to run the institution. Seven chiefs were elected, each to be responsible for the due observance of law and order by his company. The seven companies elected one head chief, known as Master of Arms from time immemorial; then, from among the educated classes, they elected seven gentlemen as councillors to represent the town and be responsible for the preservation of order under a system similar to that which is obtained in municipalities. Later, when the Cape Coast people made their requests to the authorities in connection with municipal development, they made the placing of a king on the stool a *sine qua non* of the town council. Their request to the Government was that the king himself should preside over the entire municipal set-up.[6]

The people of Cape Coast then put forward a number of specific requests to the Government. First, they requested that Brew should be recognised as king

1 *Ibid.*

2 C.O. 96/181, no. 246, sub-encl. in encl. 1 in Griffith to Holland, 5 July 1887

3 *The Gold Coast Echo*, 22 October 1888   4 *Ibid.*

5 In Akan communities, the inhabitants of each town or village have been from the very early days divided into companies (usually seven). Each company has its own quarter of the town. The company system, originally a military device, has been turned into a political instrument in most coastal towns.

6 C.O. 96/181, no. 246, sub-encl. in encl. 1 in Griffith to Holland, 5 July 1887. The list of Councillors included Grand (Mayor) Sarbah, J. Sago, J. W. Sey, Pieterson, T. J. Jones and A. Q. Yarquah. The Master of Arms was H. Brew.

presiding over their town council,[1] and Coker, Registrar of the Supreme Court, Accra, as 'Head Chief commanding the native forces at Cape Coast'. When these requests were turned down, they elected Kodjo Mbrah and sought his recognition as king, but although they persevered to get the Government to see their point, colonial officials like Colonel White and the D.C. of Cape Coast at the time refused to be moved.[2] So in January 1889 the chiefs of Cape Coast once again presented their case for a king to Governor Griffith, during his tour of the Western Districts. The District Commissioner's Court, which was the place of meeting, was crowded. All the leading people were present including F. C. Grant, Brown and Harrison. The people's spokesman for the occasion was Chief Sackey who made out a clear case, stating that it was the people's desire to place a king upon the stool in the person of Kodjo Mbrah. But Governor Griffith, too, turned down their request.[3]

At this juncture the chiefs of Cape Coast prepared two memorials which they despatched to the Secretary of State in March and June respectively. They pointed out in the first that the Governor had persistently refused to recognise a king in Cape Coast, but that such a post was most important because there was a need to encourage traditional institutions. The greater portion of the country, they argued, was far from understanding the usages of English institutions. Conversely, Europeans did not understand their institutions and so justice in European courts had often miscarried. Until they had a king, these important problems could not be solved.[4]

The chiefs must have thought it necessary to say exactly what type of institution they were asking for, so in the second petition they described in detail the pre-European municipal institutions which had existed in their towns. They pointed out that in the past there were councils of elders with judicial and legislative powers. Apart from these, other persons were elected whose function it was to see to the sanitary condition of each community, to superintend the clearing of paths and roads in the neighbourhood, summoning before the council those who infringed sanitary regulations or committed a breach of the public peace. They then pointed out that male persons in each ward formed companies, drawing attention to the existence of Tufuhenes of the several towns, and that in these towns facilities had existed for the people to take part in deliberations over which the chiefs and caboceers presided. By this system, every freeborn man had an interest in the welfare of his country. These institutions, which alone could help them to express themselves best, had been interfered with and therefore no longer worked. All they wanted, when they asked for municipal institutions, was a restoration of these ancient institutions and usages.[5] To contemporaries the Gold Coast movement must have appeared at this point as directed towards self-government, with representative institutions as a means of getting there. But the colonial government refused to grant these requests.

The second wave of protests occurred after two Town Council Ordinances

1 *Ibid.*

2 C.O. 96/201, no. 141, Griffith to Knutsford, 23 May 1889, also *The Gold Coast Echo*, 3 December 1888

3 C.O. 96/201, no. 141, Griffith to Knutsford, 23 May 1889

4 *Ibid.*   5 C.O. 96/202, no. 180, encl. in Griffith to Knutsford, 18 June 1889

were passed in 1889 and 1894 respectively.[1] The protests against these ordinances took the form of deputations and petitions. On 23 January 1895, the spokesman of a 'deputation from Accra wrote the Governor seeking an appointment with him'.[2] On 23 February King Anfoo Otoo of Abura sent a petition against the Ordinance to the Secretary of State. On 29 March, the 'Chiefs and Headmen of Himan' sent their petition. Thereafter, in rapid succession, one after the other, petitions poured in to Government House from Accra, Cape Coast, Anomabu, Ayan, Adjumako, Kwaman, Elmina, Shama, Sekondi, Adjuah, Axim, Apollonia and the adjacent territories including Eastern and Western Wassa.[3]

The main arguments which emerged from these petitions against the Town Council Ordinances dealt with the objections to the composition of the proposed council. Section 4, subsection 1, of the Town Council Ordinance (1894) provided that one half of the members of the council should be official members and should include the District Commissioner who should be *ex officio* President and Treasurer of the Council. The other half should be unofficial members elected or nominated by the Governor. The petitioners thought the provisions of this section entirely inconsistent with the general principles of municipal government. The memorialists submitted that the people should be vested with full powers for the management of the council and that the official element should be altogether eliminated. As the composition stood in the draft the Government would have predominant influence in the council. The memorialists, especially those from Accra, Elmina and the Western Districts, found even more objectionable the fact that the Government reserved for itself the right of nominating the other half, if the people refused to elect them.[4] The result would be, the people felt, that the town councils would be entirely composed of Government nominees. So they appealed to the Government not to proceed with the Ordinance in its existing form.

It should also be noted that in Accra, apart from petitions and deputations, the kings and people physically tried to prevent the formation of the town council. King Tackie was the leading spirit of the movement. He warned his people against accepting office as member of the town council, and actually refused to nominate one of his chiefs for election to the council which the Government was proposing to set up under the Ordinance.[5]

These protests affected both the formulation and the execution of British policy. The original British policy had been to resist the demands of Africans for town councils. But because of African opposition, the colonial authorities in London advised a reversal of policy. The Colonial Office instructed the local Government that instead of discouraging them, the local officials should now make preparations for setting up town councils. In September 1887 Sir Henry

1 C.O. *96/254*, no. 35, encl. 2 in Griffith to Ripon, 25 January 1895

2 *Ibid.*, 30 January 1895, encl. 5

3 C.O. *96/256*, no. 196, encls. 3 and 4 in Maxwell to Ripon, 11 May 1895, and dispatch; Griffith to Ripon, no. 140, 6 April 1895; no. 219, Maxwell to Ripon, 28 May 1895

4 C.O. *96/246*, no. 140, encl. in Griffith, 6 April 1895; C.O. *96/256*, no. 196, Maxwell to Ripon, 11 May 1895

5 C.O. *96/316*, no. 282, encl. 1 in Hodgson to Chamberlain, 4 July 1898

Holland gave specific instructions to Colonel White, the Acting Administrator, to prepare a Town Council Ordinance.[1] Before the year 1887 was out the Queen's advocate on the Coast had drafted an Ordinance for the establishment of municipalities in the chief towns of the Colony,[2] and in 1889 it was passed in the Legislative Council. To make it even more suitable for its purposes, the Government later revised and passed it as Ordinance No. 17 of 1894.[3]

This clearly represented a change in British policy, due to pressure from the Africans. The decision to set up town councils was taken in 1887, but it was only in 1898 that the first council was actually set up in Accra.[4] The delay was due to the unceasing protests against specific features of the proposed councils. First, the 1889 Ordinance had to be revised and was finally passed in 1894, but as the protests continued, all attempts to implement the decisions contained in the Ordinance were frustrated till about the middle of 1898.

Another effect of these protests was that the British were compelled to employ doubtful and farcical methods in the execution of their policy. For instance, because of the refusal of King Tackie and the people of Accra to cooperate with the Government in the matter of electing members of the Accra Town Council, J. R. Holmes, who was in charge of the whole operation,[5] had to go through a farcical election programme. On 3 January 1898 Holmes, complying with section 2 of the Town Council Ordinance, posted up a copy of the 'Voters List' on the notice board outside the Court House. He then went through all sorts of formalities till on the 18th he held a public meeting as notified, but no one attended. As there were no appeals to the Judge against the 'Voters List' he finally settled and signed it on the 22nd. He next tackled the problem of trying to persuade candidates to allow themselves to be nominated for election to the Council under the Ordinance. Eventually he succeeded 'in prevailing upon' Headman Sasraku to nominate Cudjoe Ababio, Head Chief of James Town; Thomas Wulff Cochram (Head Native Official for Messrs F. and A. Swanzy) to nominate Charles Bannerman, barrister-at-law; and Edmund Bannerman to nominate William Quartey Papafio, an influential 'native'.[6] But all this could not have been achieved without considerable pressure from the Governor himself who confessed that 'I personally induced Mr Quartey Papafio to allow himself to be nominated and I did my best to effect chief Kudjo Ababio's election hoping thereby if there were opposition to the payment of the rate – to get James Town district of Accra to remain quiet and so to break the force of opposition'.[7] The three persons nominated were declared duly elected unopposed on 1 February.[8] So it was that in July 1898 the British succeeded in setting up the first town council.

Finally, the British were compelled to use force in the execution of their policy due to the difficulties over representation. At the height of this agitation,

1 D.S.C.O. 96/181, Holland to White, G.C. no. 227, 5 September 1887; C.O. 96/195, conf., Minute of 1 December 1888 by Hemming on Griffith to Knutsford, 5 November 1888

2 C.O. 96/190, no. 87, Griffith to Holland, 26 March 1888

3 C.O. 96/254, no. 39, encl. 1 in Griffith to Ripon, 30 January 1895

4 C.O. 96/316, no. 282, Hodgson to Chamberlain and encl., 4 July 1898

5 C.O. 96/316, no. 282, Hodgson to Chamberlain, 4 July 1898   6 *Ibid.*, encl. 1

7 C.O. 96/316, no. 282, Hodgson to Chamberlain, 4 July 1898   8 *Ibid.*, encl.

one of its leading figures, Alex Bruce, was arrested twice, for what we cannot tell. Towards the end of 1886, it was reported, Freeman, District Commissioner of Accra, ordered the Hausas to break into Bruce's house and arrest him, and this they did.[1] We have yet another report which refers to a second arrest of Bruce on 9 September, 1887. The report pointed out that Bruce sustained personal injuries through wilful destruction of his property on his premises by Hausas acting under Assistant Inspector Freeman. On another occasion the Government committed a further outrage on King Tackie, who was already enraged at the treatment given to Bruce. When the King appeared in Court in connection with Bruce's case, the District Commissioner insisted that he should lower his cloth from the left shoulder as a mark of respect to him as the presiding officer.[2]

It is clear, therefore, that because these protests over Town Councils and representation were popular and carefully organised, they were strong enough to affect British policy in several ways. Even though the British eventually set up town councils (suited to their own purposes only and preventing increased representation of the people in the Legislative Council until the twentieth century), yet British officials felt the pressure of African opposition. In the first place, it was African opposition which forced them to come round to the idea of setting up the town councils; and it was African opposition again which delayed the setting up of those very councils; and finally, it was African opposition which compelled British officials to resort to the use of force to carry out their policy.

Taxation

While protesting about town councils and representation, the people were at the same time organising protests to prevent the Government from taxing them. The coastal peoples had always been opposed to taxation in any form, since the days of the 1852 Poll Tax Ordinance. That was why in the 1880s, the people began to organise protests against the Government, even before the decision to levy house rates in the principal towns of the Coast was officially announced as part of the Town Councils Ordinance passed in 1894. Since it was the towns which were directly affected, the protests against house rates were concentrated in Cape Coast and Accra, where all sections of the public supported the movement. The various sections which protested against the house rates included the Cape Coast elite and public, the Gold Coast press, the Accra women's organisation, educated Africans in Accra and the kings and people of Accra.

The first organised body to protest against the tax came from Cape Coast. It was the Cape Coast Committee, elected about the middle of 1887 by the town's people to plan and execute development projects in the town. This Committee seriously criticised the house tax. In October 1888 it eventually communicated the views of the Cape Coast public to the local British officials, when it categorically stated that the Cape Coast people would not pay the tax.[3]

1 *The Western Echo*, 31 December 1886

2 C.O. 96/192, no. 203, Griffith to Knutsford, 18 January 1888

3 C.O. 96/195, G.C. Conf., Griffith to Knutsford, 5 November 1888; C.O. 96/200, no. 21, Griffith to Knutsford, 24 January 1889

The Gold Coast press also protested. Several newspapers in Accra came out against the idea of house rates, and indeed against any form of taxation. The views of two of these papers, *The Gold Coast Chronicle* and *The Aborigines*, were particularly important. On 6 November 1896, for instance, *The Gold Coast Chronicle* contained very critical articles and comments on the question of the house tax declaring it to be a completely new thing to the people of the Gold Coast. The Government, the paper contended, made elaborate plans to exact taxes from the people, but none to develop the country, and so social amenities such as drinking water and roads were lacking. This made it difficult for the African trader to make enough profit to pay such taxes. It added that the proposed house tax did not suit Gold Coast conditions, because most people built their own houses with cheap materials – coconut beams for wood, swish or mud and thatch – being too poor to pay another to build for them. How could the authorities expect such poor people to pay rates in respect of such houses, the paper asked.[1]

The Gold Coast Aborigines, which described the house tax as hanging over the people like the sword of Damocles, emphasised the point that it was not the legitimate needs of the Gold Coast people that made the tax necessary, but the execution of British colonial policy, and that it was the Asante expedition which had exhausted the treasury at Victoriaburg. The Protectorate was saddled, the paper concluded, with all the expenses incurred to satisfy the voracious avarice of imperialism and the poor inhabitants of the country were being made to suffer for what was done for the benefit of those rolling in wealth in 'Benevolent England'.[2]

On 1 December 1896 the women of Accra staged a demonstration against the house tax. They started towards Government House to ask for an interview with Governor Maxwell on the subject. At Christiansborg, they were joined by the women of that town. As the Government would not permit them to proceed to Government House, they remained in the vicinity of Christiansborg, as noisy as possible, for the greater part of the day.[3] Then they decided that since the Governor would not see them they had better send a petition embodying their wishes and protests against the Government to the Secretary of State. The petition, in which the women protested strongly against the house tax and prayed for its repeal, was sent on 31 May 1897. In presenting their case, they pointed out that they, in the social and economic conditions of the country, were responsible for the family, and they could not afford to pay such a tax.[4]

Educated Africans, too, did not hesitate to register their protest. At a meeting of the Legislative Council on 24 November 1896, an unofficial member, J. H. Cheetham, asked 'whether a petition signed by the King . . . of James Town, presented to this Council and dated 22 January 1895, had ever been replied to and if not what were the reasons?'[5] The petition in question was against the house tax. Cheetham, of course, knew that it had not been answered

1 *The Gold Coast Chronicle*, 6 November 1896

2 *The Gold Coast Aborigines*, 28 May and 18 June 1898

3 C.O. 96/288, no. 2, Maxwell to Chamberlain, 2 January 1897

4 C.O. 96/298, no. 386, Maxwell to Chamberlain and encl. 4 September 1897

5 *The Gold Coast Chronicle*, 16 May 1898; *The Gold Coast Aborigines*, 18 June 1898

and he asked the question merely to show his disapproval of the Governor's handling of the matter. On 16 May 1898 a deputation waited on Governor Hodgson, protesting against the tax. The members of this deputation included E. Bannerman, leader, the Honourable Chief John Vanderpuye, a member of the Legislative Council, and Hutton Mills, barrister-at-law, who was the spokesman. They disliked the tax, they told the Governor, and now that they heard that the Government was preparing to use force to collect it, they felt it their duty to register their protests.

The Kings of Accra and Christiansborg together with their people played an important part in this movement against the Government. King Tackie took the lead, first organising his people to oppose the tax. On 7 April 1898 he sent a messenger round the town, giving notice by gong-gong that he would not pay the rate, and advising the people to support him; on the 11th he told the Town Clerk that he would not pay.[1] Tackie led the Kings of Accra and Christiansborg to request a public interview with Governor Maxwell. At the meeting, the kings alleged very strongly that they could not pay the rates; and all the people at the meeting swore that they would follow the example of their kings.[2]

King Tackie's next step was to order the fishermen not to leave the towns and to be ready when called upon. He also sent messengers to the bush villages, summoning the people in them. On 4 May 1898 a mass meeting attended by 2000 people was held at King Tackie's house and there seemed to be a prospect of rioting. The Government had to use force to prevent it.[3]

These protests affected the execution of the British tax policy. To remove opposition to the house rates and implement their collection, the local British officials first decided to use stipends to silence the leaders of the opposition. Governor Hodgson, for instance, decided to win King Tackie over. The King had been awarded a stipend earlier for certain services he had performed for the Government, but this had been withdrawn in June 1897 by Governor Maxwell, because of Tackie's protests against the house tax. Governor Hodgson thought that if payment were resumed, the King would stop his agitation against the Government. 'To the King of Accra,' he wrote to the secretary of State, 'I held out the hope that if he kept his people quiet, and loyally followed my advice, I would recommend to you that the stipend which was taken from him in the earlier stage of the proceedings should be restored.'[4] But King Tackie took no notice.

When Hodgson realised that this method was not effective, he decided that firm action coupled with threats might be more useful. In line with this decision, he appointed a strong and capable officer, J. R. Holmes, to take charge of arrangements for levying the tax. Holmes at once arranged for demand notices to be served on house owners in Accra. The Governor then threatened that the houses of defaulters would be confiscated and sold.[5] And indeed when King Tackie refused to pay for his two houses, assessed at 10s 5d and 3s 6d respectively, Governor Hodgson ordered that they should be sold. The Finance

1 C.O. 96/316, G.C. no. 282, Hodgson to Chamberlain and encl., 4 July 1898, Accra

2 *The Gold Coast Chronicle*, 16 May 1898

3 C.O. 96/316, no. 282, Hodgson to Chamberlain, and encl. 4 July 1898

4 *Ibid.*   5 *The Gold Coast Chronicle*, 30 April 1898

Committee authorised the Town Clerk on 18 April to order proceedings against the King and the Sheriff fixed 6 May for the sale of the two houses, if the rates were not paid before. But the King took no notice of these proceedings, and the protests continued unabated.[1]

When he realised that threats were also failing Hodgson decided to use a third technique. The threats he had recently issued would now be fully backed by force. As early as 23 April 1898 the Governor, sensing defeat, had thought of force as the most effective means open to him to compel the people to pay the house tax. He later placed the Accra Municipal District under the provision of the Peace Preservation Ordinance. He caused the towns to be patrolled night and day by pickets of Hausas and police, the one under Inspector Armitage, and the other under Sub-Assistant Commissioner Donovan. On 25 April the force, using batons, dispersed a large meeting held in the house of the King of Accra. Then the Hausas were let loose. On 6 May King Tackie's linguist and war-captain, Charles Kwame, was arrested for using what the Government called seditious language. Kwame was compelled to pay his tax while still in captivity, and was also forced to send messengers to his followers to pay up. Sub-Assistant Commissioner Donovan threatened the Captain that, if he continued to resist, 'I would arrest him and King Tackie and put them on the first steamer which would come to Accra'.[2]

As a result of the British using force the people's resistance to the house tax was gradually broken down. Before the end of 1898 payment began in Accra, and early the following year Cape Coast, too, began to pay.[3] The effects on British policy of the protests over taxation were, therefore, to be seen in the way in which that policy was finally implemented. So strong were the protests that force ultimately proved the only effective means.

The Compulsory Labour Ordinance

Other protests on the Gold Coast concerned forced labour. The refusal of the Gold Coast people to permit alien interference in their affairs caused the British one particular difficulty, among others, that of obtaining labour, even paid labour, for public works. To overcome this, the Government passed a Public Labour Ordinance No. 2 of 1883, under which paid labour could be recruited. But this proved unworkable. For instance, when Governor Griffith went to Apollonia in 1889 he found that the people simply refused to act as carriers for his personal luggage. Attempts to introduce a system of compulsory service[4] were delayed until the Asante expedition of 1895, when it became absolutely essential for the recruitment of carriers. The Ordinance enacted that 'it shall be lawful for a chief or Captain or headman to call on for service as carriers such number of able-bodied male persons of the labouring class resident in the district as may be required by the Government as carriers for public purposes, and that those who refuse to serve shall be fined £10 or imprisoned for three

1 C.O. 96/316, no. 282, Hodgson to Chamberlain and encl., 4 July 1898

2 *Ibid.* and encl. 9

3 In 1900 the house tax was abolished when the U.K. delegation of the A.R.P.S. successfully appealed to the Secretary of State against its continuation. See p. 145

4 G.O. 96/200, no. 59, Griffith to Knutsford, 27 March 1889

months'.[1] The service was to be temporary, expiring on 13 December 1896. But when this date approached, the Gold Coast military authorities announced that to maintain the existing garrison in Asante in an efficient state they had to continue recruiting carriers, so the Ordinance was extended for another year.[2] Worse still, it was still in operation in 1898, a full year after the expiry date.[3]

Both the original ordinance and its continuation came under heavy fire. *The Gold Coast Chronicle*, for instance, maintained that the king and chiefs were forced under the system to do what was in the estimation of officials 'honourable work' of finding carriers for the Government, and if they left to avoid what other monarchs in England and Scotland would not do, 'they are seized and forced to carry against their wish'.[4] There are reports that the King of Cape Coast was fined £100 and was detained in gaol as a criminal for many hours.[5]

An even more serious criticism concerned the brutal methods employed by Government officials to enlist people for this service. In a protest against these methods, a special correspondent of *The Gold Coast Aborigines* wrote that in November 1898 the Government tried to recruit seventy carriers in Cape Coast to carry loads from that town to Kumasi. But no one would go. So the police and the soldiery were sent to catch people in the town. The account went on:

> The scene that followed baffled all description. The only comparison would be an Arab slave raid. The police and soldiers rushed into the streets, caught hold of men and women – both strangers and residents – and took them to the prison yard. Those who resisted were kicked and beaten. One woman outside our store had her clothes torn off, and was then kicked. Traders who just arrived from the far interior were dragged off to prison and marched off with loads, guarded by soldiers. All the native traders fled to the bush.[6]

The treatment of the carriers actually in the service also brought complaints. The carriers were poorly paid[7]; some from Cape Coast complained in 1898 that when they had carried loads to Kumasi the previous year they had been cheated of 4s, being paid 16s each instead of £1 as promised. Moreover, while carrying loads, the carriers were often given lashes by 'gallant officers'.[8] For these reasons, the local press referred to the system of forced labour as a revival of slavery on the Gold Coast, and pointed out that it contravened the Gold Coast Emancipation Ordinance of 1874, which stated that 'whosoever shall by any species of coercion or restraint, compel or attempt to compel the

---

1 *The Gold Coast Chronicle*, 16 October 1897

2 C.O. 96/280, no. 545, encl. 2 in Maxwell to Chamberlain, 10 December 1896

3 C.O. 96/280, no. 545, Maxwell to Chamberlain, 10 December 1896; *The Gold Coast Aborigines*, 3 September 1898

4 *The Gold Coast Chronicle*, 27 July 1897

5 *The Gold Coast Aborigines*, 3 September 1898   6 *Ibid.*, 19 February 1898

7 The carriers received a shilling a day normally.

8 C.O. 96/280, no. 545, encl. 2 in Maxwell to Chamberlain, 10 December 1896

service of any person shall be guilty of a punishable offence'.[1] The forced labour system was described as an instrument of tyranny, as something worse than a 'press gang', a law capable of being passed only by 'a palm oil ruffian' and not an enlightened English Governor. The people called for its immediate repeal.[2]

So far, the protests over the compulsory labour service were directly against the Government. But later the people had to object also to the activities of a Mr Coker, who was supporting the Government in the carrier issue. This distraction undoubtedly affected the strength of the protest movement against the compulsory labour service and it was partly because of this that the Africans failed to force the Government to change its policy. Nevertheless, their protests were strong enough to cause important modifications.

This man Coker, from all accounts, was exceedingly ambitious. He coveted the position of a chief and was angling for the stool of Tufuhin, basing his claims on ancestral rights.[3] The Government now more than ever needed carriers to Kumasi and Kintampo, as it was busy establishing its rule in Asante and the country to the north. This situation probably accounted for Coker's decision to support the Government over carriers,[4] and there can be no doubt that personal considerations greatly influenced his conduct.[5]

The people of Cape Coast had always been opposed to Coker becoming a chief, basing their objection partly on his disqualification as a citizen, but also on his being what they regarded as a 'yesman', supplying the Government with carriers. Now that he sought British support in return for this specific service the people found him even more objectionable. He tried several means to achieve his aim. First it appears that he cleverly caused the news to circulate that in spite of the people's opposition, he would soon be raised to the position of a chief, as a result of a communication he had received from England. At once 'a Patriot' wrote to *The Gold Coast Aborigines* to demand 'whether our chiefs (and kings) are now to be nominted for us by the British Government?'[6]

While the Cape Coast public was still fuming over the prospect of a stooge being imposed on it, Coker dropped a bombshell. Shamelessly he embarked on a self-laudatory project to lure the Cape Coast people willy-nilly into accepting him as their chief. He sent a letter to *The Gold Coast Aborigines* supposedly written by the Acting Colonial Secretary, Riby Williams, to the District Commissioner of Cape Coast, but which appeared in Coker's own handwriting. In the letter the Colonial Secretary said that he had been directed by the Acting Governor to give the District Commissioner the following message: 'In view of the good service which Chief Coker has rendered on several occasions in connection with the provision of carriers' the Government would support him to assert his position as a chief in Cape Coast. The letter went on: 'His Excellency desires you to inform him that carriers would constantly be required to proceed from Cape Coast to Kumasi and Kintampo and that he hopes Chief Coker will be prepared to provide them at short notice.'[7] Below this was published a full text of another letter on the Coker Affair, but the editorial staff

---

1 *The Gold Coast Chronicle*, 16 October 1897

2 *Ibid.*, 1 March 1896; *The Gold Coast Aborigines*, 19 February 1898

3 *The Gold Coast Aborigines*, 11 June 1898   4 *Ibid.*, 2 and 9 April 1898

5 *Ibid.*, 16 April 1898   6 *Ibid.*, 2 April 1898   7 *Ibid.*, 9 April 1898

of the paper revealed that this second letter, which congratulated Coker was, like the first, written by Coker himself.

The public reacted swiftly. One correspondent wished to know who had made Coker chief and of what place.[1] The embarrassed Coker tried to deny that the documents were meant for publication. He said Mr Brown just came to Rev. Sackey 'on the Ecclesiastical Court up at Dawson Hill' and ran into print with the document against Sackey's wishes. This convinced nobody and a correspondent challenged Coker to come out with a full and detailed denial of the accusation of deceiving the public by publishing self-laudatory documents in the name of the Editorial Board.[2] Coker could not of course do this.

Attempts of District Commissioner Cummings to have Coker installed chief were fiercely resisted. The people decided to prevent Coker's procession through the streets of Cape Coast which, for the public, was the most essential part of the installation ceremony. The editorial staff of the *Aborigines* voiced the people's feeling: 'Be it known to all whom it may or may not concern that we will not have this man to reign over us', even if he were supported by the Gordon Highlanders and Royal Irish Fusiliers instead of Hausas and Police Constables.[3] Commissioner Cummings dared not proceed with his installation plans. And although several years later, Coker became Tufuhin (field marshal), he never became chief of Cape Coast which alone would have given him and the Government the power they wanted. Thus, because of the protests, the British failed to make their nominee a puppet chief of Cape Coast.

The proposed enstoolment of Coker was the means by which the British hoped to implement their policy of forced labour. In preventing the enstoolment, therefore, African protest caused a modification of British methods. True, the policy was carried out, but the British had to continue recruiting carriers by force, instead of receiving them peacefully from Coker, as they had hoped.

The land question

Of the post-Confederation protests that we have been considering here, that in respect of land was undoubtedly the best organised and the most effective. All sections of the coastal communities participated in the demonstrations and petitions against the Government's land policy. This was because of the sanctity of landed property which the people jealously guarded.

J. M. Sarbah in an appendix to his *Fanti Customary Laws* explains that there were three types of land-stool, family and private land. All land on the Gold Coast had owners. Except on rare occasions, he points out, land could not be alienated. Neither the stool-holder nor the family head, who was a trustee of the lands of these institutions, could dispose of them without the consent of all the members, who would rarely give it. Long-term leases of land occurred but this did not involve a transfer of ownership.[4] Clearly, then the sanctity of landed property was jealously guarded on the Gold Coast.

Since the protests over land were so strong, they affected the formulation of British land policy on the Gold Coast, compelling H.M. Government to modify its land policy several times and eventually to abandon it altogether. To bring out clearly how these protests affected the formulation of British policy, we

1 *Ibid.*, 16 April 1898   2 *Ibid.*, 30 April 1898   3 *Ibid.*, 11 June 1898

4 H. Sarbah, *Fanti Customary Laws*, London 1904, pp. 271–7

must first discover what that policy was originally and then consider the waves of protests and the changes they made necessary.

The Gold Coast Government needed to control land so as to be able to extract its wealth in the form of timber, minerals, etc. Secondly, the Government believed that the supreme power in the land should be the one to determine its ownership. The *published* reasons were different, namely, to protect land owners from unscrupulous speculators, and to check ruthless exploitation of minerals, forests etc.[1]

This policy of controlling the land was first formulated between 1891 and 1894. In 1891 the Government made a draft bill to regulate mining and timber industries.[2] But the local officials wanted to be sure that the proposed bill was in the best interest of the Government and discussions dragged on till 1894 when a new bill entitled Crown Lands Ordinance was drawn up. The terms of the new bill, published in 1895, can be summarised as follows:

1. Waste and forest lands and minerals were vested in the Queen for the use of the Government of the Colony.
2. Future grants of waste land, minerals and timber to non-natives were to be only with the concurrence of the Governor.
3. Native rights in land, i.e. grants of land by one 'native' to another were to continue as before.[3]

The Gold Coast Government claimed that by their bill it was only seeking to safeguard the interests of landowners. But the 1895 Lands Bill implied that there was Crown Land on the Gold Coast.[4] It was this idea which the people vehemently refuted.

The people argued that there was no waste or public land which the Crown could take over and that, if the Government did take over what appeared to be waste land, it would mean great hardship for them. This argument was contained in a petition sent to the Secretary of State by the kings and people of Cape Coast, Himan, Abura, Anomabu, Ayan, Adjumako and Kwaman about the middle of 1895. They argued that the peoples of the colony practised shifting cultivation and returned from time to time to lands long left fallow. Under the Ordinance the Government would take such lands under the title of 'waste lands'. The bill would therefore 'deprive them of the means of sustenance' wherever the Governor made a grant of such lands to Europeans.[5] These complaints were very bitter, especially those of the Himans and Aburas who confessed themselves totally unable to say what they had done to merit the forfeiture of their lands, 'their natural rights in their native soil'.

1 J. Casely-Hayford, *Gold Coast Native Institutions*, London 1903, p. 152

2 C.O. 96/247, G.C. Conf., Griffith to Ripon, 29 August 1894   3 *Ibid.*, encls. 4 and 5

4 C.O. 96/290, no. 92, Minute of 8 April 1897 by Mercer on Maxwell to Chamberlain, 11 March 1897

5 C.O. 96/256, no. 219, encl. in Maxwell to Ripon, 28 May 1895. It was King Amonoo IV of Anomabu whose name headed the list of signatories. Sarbah was later, in June 1897, to defend the view in the Legislative Council that all lands in the Gold Coast had owners. He quoted extensively authorities and District Commissioners like Adams, Williams and Bruce Hindle, etc. all of whom agreed that every piece of land belonged to either a tribe, country, town, company, family or an individual. *The Gold Coast Chronicle*, 2 February 1898; and C.O. 96/256, no. 196, encls. 3 and 4 in Maxwell to Ripon, 11 May 1895

Apart from protesting against the economic implications of the Lands Bill, the people also criticised the Government on the grounds that the Lands Ordinance of 1895 would abrogate their ownership of the lands of the country. These protests came from the local press, from memorialists in Accra and the Western Districts.

In April 1895 the king and chiefs of Accra got up a petition to Her Majesty the Queen, stating that the Gold Coast under British protection had been repeatedly told that she, the Queen, 'never claimed any right, title or interest in any lands whatever outside the walls of Her Majesty's Forts and Castles'.[1] A similar point emerged in the petition from the people in the western districts which shows that not only did the Colonial Government say this, but it actually recognised the land rights of the inhabitants by paying money in the past for lands purchased for public works. The same petition quoted the courts and the judges as upholding the fact that the people of the Gold Coast had 'inherent legal rights as posessors of their own soil'.[2]

After giving proof of their ownership of the lands in the country before the Lands Bill, these protests and petitions generally went on to show that the great events of the midnineteenth century did not destroy their titles to these lands, as the British sometimes claimed. The petitioners of the Western Districts, for instance, stated that the British could not lay claims to the lands of the Western Districts on the grounds that Dutch possessions were transferred to England in 1872,[3] for the simple reason that the Dutch had never claimed anything except the castle and forts. And Article III of the Convention for the transfer clearly stated that only what the Dutch Government possessed was to be transferred.[4]

Having shown that the lands had belonged to the people in the past and that nothing had happened to destroy their title to these lands, the petitioners, particularly those from Accra, as a climax to their arguments, asked why the Government was now trying to deprive them 'of their lands, their gold mines, their gum trees, their rubber trees, their kola trees, and everything of theirs that is worth having and which descended to them from their remote ancestors'. For these reasons they were compelled to label the Government's action confiscation, and prayed that the Queen 'will decline to accept property acquired by the spoliation of her own helpless but loyal subjects!'[5]

Because of the unceasing opposition to the Crown Lands Ordinance of 1895 the British were compelled to change their lands policy. In 1896 Governor Maxwell decided that, since the strongest objection to the first Ordinance concerned the question of ownership, he would have to formulate a new land policy which would avoid this difficult question. The result of the Governor's efforts

---

1 C.O. 96/256, no. 140, encl. in Griffith to Ripon, 6 April 1895

2 C.O. 96/256, no. 187, Maxwell to Ripon, 9 May 1895

3 On the question of ownership, another argument of the people later effectively disputed Maxwell's claim that the Queen owned the soil of the Protectorate, just as did the Asantehene, whom she succeeded. The people pointed out that neither the Asantehene nor any other ruler on the Gold Coast had ever owned the soil of the country. Even in Asante, the Asantehene had never had the free enjoyment of their landed estates. *The Gold Coast Aborigines*, 5 February 1898

4 C.O. 96/256, no. 196, encl. 1 in Maxwell to Ripon, 11 May 1895

5 C.O. 96/256, no. 140, encl. in Griffith to Ripon, 6 April 1895

was the Concessions Bill, passed in 1897. Maxwell called it 'a simpler measure' which would merely regulate the transfer of land,[1] whether from one African to another, or from an African to a European. The terms of the Concessions Ordinance were:

1. No native landowner could grant land exceeding 20 acres without the consent of the Governor.
2. Only the Governor could grant exclusive rights in land to companies, etc.
3. Annual payments in respect of land granted to companies, etc. may be paid in whole or in part to any chief who had consented to the granting of such land.[2]

Although it was Governor Maxwell's aim to remove the objections to the Government's land policy, by changing the original ordinance, the new Concessions Ordinance met with even greater opposition. The first feature that was bitterly criticised was the one bearing on paramountcy. It was clear to the people that the Government was claiming, through the ordinance, the right to exercise paramount power in the country. In fact, in the Government Gazette Extraordinary No. 8, 1897, the Governor himself explained that: 'It is necessary that the paramount power should exercise, concurrently with local chiefs where necessary, the power of allotting land and interests in land to applicants.' The people rejected this claim. They denied that the Government had the right to exercise paramount power, which belonged to the chiefs and people alone.[3]

Secondly, the criticism of the people was directed against the claims of the Government that, by the Concessions Bill, the Gold Coast people would be socially better off than they had been. Governor Maxwell's speech on the Concessions Bill in April 1897 expressed the idea that the people were, by the Bill, secured in all lands which they possessed then. Maxwell further pointed out that the Supreme Court would enforce the people's interests; and he told the chiefs that the exercise of powers hitherto exercised by them would not be injurious to them and that the Government would secure better terms for them in land transactions.[4]

But these claims were the very ones denied by critics of the Government's land policy. Through the *Chronicle* the opponents of the Concessions Bill pointed out that they were not convinced by the promises that Africans would fare well under the scheme. Beginning with the chiefs, they pointed out that, if they were to be better off under the new system, why did Part III of the Bill re Concessions Court carry such headlines as 'Powers of Chiefs to be subject to adjudication' and 'Jurisdiction of Supreme Court ousted as to matters within jurisdiction of Concessions Court'? As for the people, the *Chronicle* maintained that it was absurd for the Government to try to give them what they already had. Indeed, the editorial staff explained to an enraged people that the new system was for the convenience of Europeans, not Africans. They claimed that the Government's motives could be understood in Governor Maxwell's address to the African trade section of the Liverpool Chamber of Commerce (1897), in which His Excellency stated that the land laws under which the public land at

1 C.O. 96/272, no. 115, Maxwell to Chamberlain, 9 April 1896

2 C.O. 96/272, G.C. Conf., encl. in Maxwell to Chamberlain, 17 April 1896

3 *The Gold Coast Chronicle*, 29 March 1897   4 *Ibid.*, 9 April 1897

the colony had been left 'at the exclusive disposal of the native authorities, enabled the native to run up his mud hovel with its grass roof in immediate congruity to the stone house of the British trader importing thus the danger of contamination of every kind'.[1]

At this juncture the local press began to make a thorough search into the motives of the Government's land policy and concluded that the welfare of the European staff and traders was their primary concern. The people's rage increased when these facts came to light.[2]

Other facts which the *Aborigines* published were that Maxwell's ideas were based on the Indian Land law, by which the British Government in India had power to distribute the rights in the soil and rental as it thought fit, and also had the right to dispose of waste lands.[3] These considerations caused the people to express their fears very strongly that the Government, far from improving their social status, was about to reduce them to the condition of mere squatters and to cause their ancestral rights to be abrogated.[4]

The peak period of protests against the Concessions Ordinance began around May 1897 and ended about a year later. In May 1897, it was recorded that 'a noisy crowd' of women and boys paraded the streets of Cape Coast displaying a banner bearing words of protest. At the same time clerks and brokers in Axim organised themselves into groups, going about explaining to the chiefs that the Europeans would take away their lands if the Concessions Bill was passed.[5] Voluntary organisations sprang up in other towns, launching a countrywide campaign to explain the contents and implications of the new Lands Bill to the chiefs and people. One result of this campaign, apparently, was that the King, chiefs and people of Axim sent a petition to the Secretary of State through the Governor on 18 May 1897. They objected to a Concessions Court, suggesting in its place a Concessions Board, to which people versed in the knowledge of land tenure, including at least two chiefs, should be appointed. The Board would examine claims of landowners desirous of disposing of their lands to foreigners and others.[6] It was on similar lines that Mr Sarbah was to argue soon after this petition in the Legislative Council in defence of the people's stand. This argument in its fullest development was that, since the Supreme Court had in the past dealt so satisfactorily with land cases, the people

---

1 *Ibid.*

2 The 15 October 1898 issue of *The Gold Coast Aborigines* published the following information: 'We have before us extracts from a despatch from the Governor of the Gold Coast to Mr Chamberlain, written sometime in 1896, from which we have an inkling as to some of the underlying motives which urged the late Sir William Maxwell on to introduce the now famous Lands Bill of 1897. His Excellency was discussing the question whether anything could be done to improve the conditions of life on the Gold Coast in obedience to a request contained in a despatch No. 58 of the 11th March 1896, addressed to the Secretary of State for the Colonies. After dealing with various suggestions for the improvement of the health of the European residents, in the course of which he freely gives his opinion of the medical officers of the colony and reprobates the tendency in them of pressing into their service facts of doubtful application in their medical reports, he makes the important announcement that improvement in the law relating to tenure of land will soon enable him to allot sites for country houses to Merchants and other private residents.'

3 *Ibid.*, 5 February 1898   4 *Ibid.*, 28 May 1898

5 C.O. 96/294, G.C. Conf., Maxwell to Chamberlain, 1 July 1897

6 *Ibid.*, no. 306, 15 July 1897

could not see the need for a new and a separate court, which might not be as independent of the administration as the Supreme Court.[1]

Apart from the petition, the people also sent a cablegram to Queen Victoria: 'The Native Kings Chiefs people of Axim and Appolonia Districts Western Province G.C. pray and beseech Her Majesty to uphold Section 40 of instructions to Hill 15 April 1851.' These instructions dealt with the subject of non-interference with the traditions, etc. of the people. The cablegram continues: 'Your Most loyal subjects dare not celebrate Sixtieth anniversary with sorrow of heart anguish of mind disappointment and despair. Implore most humbly for prevention of confiscation of lands of inheritance infringement of our indefensible rights and tempering of justice. Reply case Bissoe.' Yet another cablegram was sent to the Prince of Wales, London. This said that the kings, chiefs and aborigines of Axim, Apollonia, 'appeal most earnestly to your Royal Highness and Christian England save them from past and threatened legislation of local Government signalising Diamond Jubilee by oppressive and confiscation Bills and Ordinances. Reply case Bissoe.'[2]

The next important stage in the protests against the Concessions Bill included the formation of the Aborigines' Rights Protection Society, which successfully protested against the Bill. The origins of the A.R.P.S. can be traced to several factors. The cultural factor was chronologically the first, and constituted the desire of the people to unite to preserve their national institutions and customs, which were in danger of being destroyed by the British.[3] This explains why the Mfantsi Amanbuhu Fekuw, a cultural Society founded in 1889,[4] came to an end upon the formation of the A.R.P.S. Obviously the Fekuw's cultural objectives were expected to be fully catered for by the new Society.[5]

Another factor was political. Since the collapse of the Fante Confederacy, educated Africans had hoped that a carefully organised political association could help them resume the pursuit of their objectives, such as representation in the Legislative Council and the suppression of obnoxious ordinances. Now that they had been agitating to achieve these very objectives, so far without success, they naturally thought it was time they formed such a political association. Finally, the formation of the A.R.P.S. should be regarded as the climax of the protests against the Government's Concessions Bill.

The events leading to its formation included inspiration from the London Aborigines' Protection Society, whose secretary, Fox Bourne, wrote to *The Gold Coast Chronicle* in 1891, suggesting the formation of patriotic groups in the chief towns of the Coast. Bourne was hoping to visit the Gold Coast and to collect information from these local committees for his Society. Although he was unable to visit the Coast, the contents of his letter inspired the inhabitants to make a definite decision that the formation of a political association, with local branches in the towns, would be most useful to them.[6]

A series of meetings in Cape Coast, held to protest against the Concessions Bill, also contributed to the formation of the A.R.P.S. One of these mass meet-

1 *The Gold Coast Chronicle*, 16 October and 5 November 1897; also African (West) no. 531, 1 January 1898

2 C.O. 96/294, no. 306, sub-encls. 2 and 3 in encl. 1 in Maxwell to Chamberlain, 15 July 1897

3 *The Gold Coast Aborigines*, 11 June 1898

4 Kimble, p. 330   5 *Ibid.*, p. 341   6 *Ibid.*, pp. 330–1

ings was held in Chapel Square (Cape Coast), on 17 April 1897. The King of Cape Coast, his chiefs and captains invited the Rev. A. W. Parker, superintendent of the Gold Coast Methodist Church, to offer prayer, which was full of inspiration. Even the heathens joined in singing 'Mi sunsum sweri yi Yami aye' (My Spirit arise and praise God). Even more surprising, it is said that after the meeting, the cane bearers, though heathens, entered the Wesley Chapel and prayed thus:

> O Lord of heaven and earth we have come into thy house on this momentous occasion to invoke Thy blessing on, and Thy aid in, this struggle. Thou has given us our lands which we have inherited from our forefathers. We are very poor and only live by our lands. But the Government under whom it hath pleased Thee to place us, after depriving our native Rulers of most of their powers and authority, are now bent on despoiling us of our individual ancestral rights in our land. We are weak and helpless before this foreign power, but we are nevertheless pledged to oppose this measure and defend our rights. . . .[1]

The next meeting was held in May to complete discussion of decisions made in the April meeting. For instance, the idea of being represented by counsel on the land question before the bar of the Legislative Council had been put forward at the earlier meeting, and before a final decision could be made during this second meeting, the question of exactly whom counsel would represent came up. And it was at this point that the meeting of kings, chiefs and people in Cape Coast resolved themselves into the Aborigines' Rights Protection Society, with the avowed aim of preventing the spoliation of their lands by the Government.[2] It was the Society therefore that counsel would represent in the Legislative Council. The Society was also to deal with other matters relating to representation and taxation, with which the people had so far been concerned.

Membership of the Society was open to all, but a small inner Committee was elected, consisting of J. W. Sey as President, J. P. Brown as Vice-President, two other vice-presidents, a Treasurer, a Secretary and a spokesman or Kyiami.[3] The Society grew rapidly and before the end of the year there were branches in Axim, Elmina and other towns in the Western Districts. The Eastern Districts joined later, in the early years of the twentieth century, when we find the Ga chiefs and people as members of the Society striving to prevent the passing of the Forest Bill.[4]

The remaining protests were, from then on, directed by the A.R.P.S. The Society's first duty was to arrange for J. S. Cheetham, unofficial member, to present a petition to the Legislative Council at its meeting of 27 May 1897, stating that the people wished to be heard, on the land question, by counsel in the Legislature. The petition was acceded to, and on the 4 and 5 June, Sarbah and Renner were heard at the bar of the Legislative Council on behalf of the people.[5] Sarbah's main objections were against the creation of a Concessions Court, and the definition of a 'native' in the Lands Bill. He argued that the

1 *The Gold Coast Aborigines*, 22 October 1898   2 *Ibid.*, 12 March 1898

3 Kimble, p. 341   4 *Ibid.*, p. 364

5 C.O. 96/294, no. 235, encls. 5 and 6 in Maxwell to Chamberlain, 10 June 1897

word should embrace mulattoes as well as other inhabitants, which was what the bill sought to avoid.[1]

The next task that the A.R.P.S. carried out was to found *The Gold Coast Aborigines* to give full expression to their ideas. It was this paper which continuously explained to the people the implications of the various steps that the Government was taking in the matter of the land question. It covered fully the activities of the people to prevent the passing of the Concessions Ordinance and exhorted the country to even greater efforts.[2] The *Aborigines* came out in support of free speech, when the Gold Coast Government tried to vilify Prince Brew of Dunkwa for publicly criticising it on the land question.[3] At the same time, by giving wide publicity to activities in connection with the anniversary of the A.R.P.S., the paper helped to bring about such patriotic feeling as had never been experienced before. People reading the stirring articles in the *Aborigines* were encouraged to play the role of patriots. The *Aborigines* itself claimed that one such patriot was Henry Barnes, a leading figure in the Protest movement, whose character 'permits us to put into his mouth the words of the famous song:

> I yield to my country
> Affection sincere;
> It aye holds in my bosom,
> A place so fond and dear![4]

Yet another patriot was Mensah Sarbah, who refused a 400 guinea gift for his many services to the country including his defence in the Legislative Council against the Lands Bill, saying:

> I do not spurn or refuse the very handsome retainer of four hundred guineas, but in serving my country, the land of my birth, within her borders, I seek no reward nor expect any remuneration; and did I ever dream of any recognition for such humble services as I have performed, the fact that, at such a crisis my countrymen selected me to plead their cause, is in itself a solemn honour which will not be unremembered or unappreciated by me.[5]

Thus the role of the *Aborigines* was to excite the patriotic feeling of the people and bring about a united front which the A.R.P.S. found useful in its final assault on the Lands Bill.

This final assault was the deputation scheme. When unity was achieved, the A.R.P.S. found it easy to revive the scheme, which had been given up in 1887, but which the society now considered the best way to achieve its ends. Because of the new spirit of patriotism, there was no difficulty in raising funds, and the delegation was able to leave the Coast on 24 May 1898. It consisted of Jacob W. Sey, President of the A.R.P.S., J. P. E. Jones and George Hughes.[6]

1 *The Gold Coast Chronicle*, 16 October and 5 November 1897

2 *The Gold Coast Aborigines*, 8 January 1898. Until the establishment of the *Aborigines* it was *The Gold Coast Methodist Times*, under the editorship of Attoh Ahuma, which served as the main outlet for the political grievances of the people.

3 *Ibid.*, 26 February 1898   4 *Ibid.*, 19 March 1898

5 Quoted in Brown, *An Active History of Ghana*, Vol. II, p. 115

6 *The Gold Coast Aborigines*, 28 May 1898

The *Aborigines* thus outlined the aim of the delegation:

> The men who left last Wednesday for the U.K. are proceeding to London to ascertain on the spot, with the assistance of able and eminent counsel in the first rank of the English Bar, . . . the best ways, methods and means whereby we and our native rulers may secure in the proper quarters, a patent hearing and impartial consideration of the grounds of the public objections to the Lands Bill. . . .[1]

When the delegation arrived in London, they at once enlisted the services of eminent counsel, H. H. Asquith, Q.C., with whose assistance they put forth their views. When they met Chamberlain, they presented him with a draft of the Lands Bill amended on the lines they had been suggesting on the Coast. They also requested that eight elected unofficial members should sit on the Legislative Council and three of these should also sit on the Executive Council. The people then stressed the point that a hut or poll tax would never be acceptable to their people.[2]

The protests caused the British once more to change their policy and in fact compelled them to abandon altogether the policy of controlling land. The Secretary of State for the Colonies agreed that 'native' law should apply with regard to the devolution of land, and that the Court which would decide upon these matters should be a judicial court. Mr Chamberlain also waived the hut or poll tax. On the question of representation on the Legislative Council, however, Chamberlain told the delegation to try to get unofficial representation enlarged in the Council itself by means of counsel, and to appeal to the Colonial Office only if they failed.[3]

The change which the protests effected in British land policy could be seen in a new Lands Bill which was finally placed before the Legislative Council, and took a very short time to pass.[4] The Bill, which differed 'very materially' from the previous bills, provided:

1. That there was to be no interference with the right of landowners to make grants of land.
2. That a special tribunal of the Supreme Court was to be set up to investigate all concessions. Without the approval of the tribunal no concession could be valid.

The new Bill therefore made no fundamental alteration in the rights of the 'natives' in respect of land. The idea of vesting unoccupied land in the Governor as public land was abandoned. The landowner was left free to make his own bargains in respect of the transfer of land. The protests of the aborigines against the establishment of a separate Concessions Court were heeded and concessions work was instead assigned to the divisional courts as suggested by the people and the U.K. deputation. In short, the aborigines remained in absolute possession of their lands.[5]

1 *Ibid.* 2 *Ibid.*, 3 December 1898 3 *Ibid.*, 19 November 1898

4 The first reading of the new Lands Bill was on 1 February 1900, the second 26 February and by March it had received the sanction of Her Majesty the Queen.

5 *Ibid.*

Briefly, then, the protests against the successive Lands Bills were very effective. In particular, the protests by the A.R.P.S. were well organised. From about 1886 to 1900, therefore, there was a series of post-Confederacy protests, which, because they dealt with burning national issues, and because they were carefully organised, had important effects on British policy. In respect of representation, town councils and labour, these protests influenced the execution of British policy, while in respect of taxation and land, the British were compelled to abandon their policies altogether.

CHAPTER SEVEN

The final resistance in Asante 1890–1901

The final resistance of Asante to British interference was one of the most determined against European rule in Western Africa. The effects of these activities were important, but before describing Asante politics between 1890 and 1901 a misconception must be corrected.

The belief that it was French and German competition which caused the British to take over Asante[1] has obscured the truth that it was largely Asante political activity which caused the British to rush into the interior of the Gold Coast.

In 1875 the French, who had left Guinea in 1871 appeared eager to return to the Protectorate of Porto Novo.[2] Meade's comments, that this would not be in Britain's best interests, betray anxiety over French activities on this Coast.

But it was never a question of the French encroaching on the Slave Coast, for, until 1864, this had been their most popular resort in the Gulf of Guinea. Even after that date, French merchants like Regis still traded here. They had no misgivings about operating in this area where British interest was rapidly becoming predominant, so long as this did not affect their transactions. But very soon the French firms realised that the high duties which Britain imposed on trade in these regions would cripple them,[4] and so they sought to safeguard their trading interests in the Popo regions.[5] And this meant a Protectorate over Porto Novo.

Similarly, German action in the Gulf of Guinea in 1884 was partly to protect their trade. In 1884 Fairfield at the Colonial Office pointed out: 'It is plain that the Beh trade is in German hands, and that the German traders have brought about this annexation in order to protect themselves against our high Tariff. Our Tariff is at the bottom of all our troubles.'[6] The Tariff referred to was the customs duties imposed on twenty-four different items by the Gold Coast Government in 1876. These tariffs raised revenue which was used to protect

1 Ward, *A History of Ghana*, pp. 301, 315

2 C.O. 96/116, Minute by Hemming, 23 September 1875

3 *Ibid.*, Minute by Meade

4 Minute of 9 October 1881 by Hemming on African (West) no. 265

5 Minute of 12 October 1881 by Kimberley on African (West) no. 265

6 C.O. 96/158, no. 342, Minute of 19 August 1884 by Fairfield on Young to Derby, 8 July 1884. 'Beh' is now spelt Bey.

British merchants. Consequently, they did not complain as bitterly as the non-British merchants, who, though paying as much, enjoyed no such protection in return. These tariffs were eating into their profits without the corresponding advantages, which made it easier for their British counterparts to pay them. The entire future of non-British trade in the neighbourhood of the Gold Coast was therefore threatened. In the circumstances, the other European powers felt that, unless they established claims to territory in these places, it would mean the end of their trading interests there.

A second factor to consider at this point is that Britain, having excited the local French and German officials in the neighbourhood of the Gold Coast, fell into a strange attitude of inertia. The British failure to defend what clearly were their rights in these regions encouraged the French and Germans to rush in for territory.

The chief influence on Anglo–German relations in the vicinity of the Gold Coast was the British attitude of timidity towards Germany. As soon as Germany's intentions were known towards the territory to the east of the Gold Coast, the Secretary of State for the Colonies sent an urgent telegram on the importance of 'the cultivation of friendly relations between the officers of this Government and any German authorities with whom they may be brought into contact'. Governor Young replied that he would do his utmost to carry out this policy and would strictly enjoin upon those officers of his government who were likely to be brought into any communication with any German authorities, 'the necessity and propriety of following that policy'. On the whole Germany, too, reciprocated this friendship, especially since, in 1890, it was part of a general arrangement in Africa between the two countries. Minor considerations might have caused modifications to this policy but they were always localised and applicable only to particular situations.

In 1884, for instance, even though Britain had earlier been anxious to dominate Bey Beach and had developed a close association with that country, as already indicated in Chapter 3, the Colonial Office found it necessary to warn the Foreign Office not to press British protests against German action there too much 'as it has been decided to acquiesce in the German Protectorate'.[1] The result was that the territory went permanently to Germany although 'we had a prior arrangement with the Bey people' and although 'British inaction on the coast meant the abandonment of King Lawson, their protege'.[2] When German action was feared to be imminent at Little Popo, all that Hemming, of all people, said was that the 'provisional treaty of Protection concluded by Lieutenant Furlonger will be sufficient for the present to bar any German attempts on Little Popo'.[3]

Or course it was not. It did not matter what form of document Britain possessed relating to Little Popo. She could only have kept the state if she had clearly and forcefully stated her claims and been prepared to defend them. Even mere moral influence would have been sufficient when backed by force. But the use of force was far from the calculations of the British Government. When

1 C.O. 96/160, African (West) no. 283, Minute of 2 December 1884 by Fairfield on Young to Derby on Togo 472, 20 October 1884

2 C.O. 96/158, no. 342, Minute of 19 August 1884 by Fairfield on Young to Derby, 8 July 1884

3 C.O. 96/161, no. 505, Minute by Hemming on Young to Derby, 10 November 1884

Hemming, for instance, realised that British inaction was becoming too conspicuous, all that he suggested was that 'we needn't welcome them (the Germans) and hasten to assure them that we cannot and will not dispute their position.[1]

Thus, when it came to drawing up the Bey Beach boundary between Togo and the Gold Coast, even Hemming meekly agreed that the boundary line proposed by the German commissioner should be accepted, and that 'a friendly representation to the German Government' should be made in the sense of the remarks submitted by Young, the Administrator of the Gold Coast.[2]

The British carried this attitude into Krepi. When in November 1886 Governor Griffith informed the Colonial Office about a Treaty the Gold Coast Government had entered into with Krepi, Hemming suggested that H.M. Government 'are already satisfied that it already forms a part of the British Protectorate, and they desire that the Crepees should be so informed'.[3]

The treaty itself, as summarised in Griffith's telegram, indicates that the Krepi authorities ceded their country 'inclusive of Panto, to Great Britain. The whole of the left bank of the Volta River previously free has been taken over'.[4] The extent of Krepi may be slightly difficult to define. The power of Kwadjo Deh diminished in the 1869–71 period with the Asante conquest of the left bank of the River and with the increasing independence of Taviefe, Adaklu, etc. but at the height of Kwadjo Deh's power the greater part of the division between Ho and Buem had paid him homage. Even in 1890, when his power was greatly reduced, Kwadjo Deh still controlled Buem, Nkonya, Dzolo Likpe, Eliate, Achlo, Gleme, Wli, Kota, Kpime, Agadza, Atikpe, Kplolo, Avatime, Te, Savie, Akpafu, Logba, Tutu Eyikpa, Akepalokai, Votre, Gulave. Freeman of the Gold Coast Government testified in January 1890 that while he was in Krepi nearly 100 chiefs and captains, representing the entire territory reaching up to Buem, swore allegiance to Kwadjo Deh.[5] Britain therefore had a right to a considerable portion of territory on the left bank of the river before the Germans came in, and this they should have known from reports of such commissioners as Riby Williams and Freeman, who had already been in these regions.

But at the Berlin Conference in 1885, when Dr Krauel, one of the German delegates, enquired, in a friendly way, whether Britain had any claims 'to Protectorate of exclusive influence over any of the countries lying to the north of Crepee', Hemming simply stated no claims to Buem at all.[6] This encouraged

1 C.O. 96/159, no. 384, Minute of 17 September 1884, by Hemming on Young to Derby, 2 August 1884

2 C.O. 96/165, no. 109, Minute of 14 May 1885 on Young to Derby, 12 April 1885; also African (West) no. 296

3 C.O. 96/173, Minute of 18 November 1886 on Tel. of 18 November 1886; also in African (West) no. 333

4 C.O. 879/25, African (West) no. 333, Griffith to Stanhope, 18 November 1886, C.O. 879/25

5 C.O. 96/208, G.C. Conf., 30 January 1890, encl.

6 C.O. 96/190, no. 96, Minute of 1 May 1888 by Hemming, 28 March 1888. Indeed the Germans were so surprised that they began to suspect that Britain's lethargy about Togo must have been because the territory was worthless. Thus a movement began in Germany soon after the Berlin Conference to sell Togo. Several West African German officials in-

German officials both in Togo and in Europe to make a bid for Krepi. In Togo German merchants led by Herr Krause, the representative in West Africa of the Stuttgart firm of Chevalier & Co., urged the local German officials to request the German Government to initiate expansion of Togo into the interior. In Germany it was Krauel himself who responded favourably to the pressure from the Colony, and in 1888 proposed that Britain should cede to Germany 'our territories east of the Volta'.[1] Soon the Germans went one step further and actually began laying claims to a number of towns in Krepi.[2] Not long after this the British abandoned Taviefe, and then Agotime, lying to the south of Krepi and already under British moral influence.[3] Germany extended her influence gradually into Krepi until 1890 when, as a result of the Heligoland Treaty, the rest of Krepi (except Peki) was handed over to Germany.[4]

As with the Germans in the east, so with the French in the west. The British simply handed over to the French large portions of territory to which they themselves were perfectly entitled. The rich rubber district of Aowin, for instance, was handed over as though on a silver plate to France. *The Gold Coast Aborigines* expressed surprise at the behaviour of the Government in trying to do 'all they can to buy the favour of our neighbours the French'.[5] It must have been the general weakness of the British in defending their territories that encouraged French commercial agents like Bretigniere, the local agent of messrs Verdier, to stake new and totally unjustifiable claims to large portions of the Gold Coast and other territories under British influence. Bretigniere was indeed the chief architect of the agreement between France and Britain which recognised as French the territory to the north of the Tano Lagoon. This area was part of Apollonia and clearly under British influence, and apparently the only reason for giving it away in this manner was that the French should adopt and promulgate an agreed tariff. But the easy manner in which the British handed over territory in Apollonia and elsewhere to the French encouraged Bretigniere and the French authorities to put difficulties in Britain's way.[6] Atibendikru and the territory of the King of Aowin were also given away to the French.[7]

As we saw in Chapter 4[8] Asante had kept the British at bay in Gyaman until about 1880. But after this, and especially in 1884, the British renewed their

---

cluding Baron von Soden, Governor of Cameroons and Togo, Fischer, the German consul residing in Accra and Schroder, the German agent on the Volta of Messrs Chevalier & Co. of Stuttgart testified to the strong feeling among a section of the German public to get rid of Togo. But at the same time German merchants resident in Togo itself knew better and pressed the home government to expand their Togo territory. Griffith to Holland and encl., 21 March 1888

1 C.O. 96/191, G.C. Conf., Griffith to Knutsford, 28 April 1888

2 C.O. 96/192, no. 184, 9 June 1888

3 See Minutes of 14 August 1888 by Antrobus on G.C. Conf., 13 July 1888

4 *The Gold Coast Chronicle*, 22 December 1890 and 21 September 1891

5 *The Gold Coast Aborigines*, C.C.C., 28 January 1899

6 C.O. 96/205, no. 337, Minute of 22 December 1889 by Hemming on Hodgson to Knutsford, 23 November 1889

7 C.O. 96/235, G.C. Conf., Hodgson to Ripon, 25 August 1895   8 See p. 91

efforts to increase their influence over that country, so that by 1886 they had
achieved some success in establishing control. But thereafter they became very
lethargic. The Gyamanhene, Agyeman, went all out to obtain active assistance
from them, but he failed, and in 1888, he was compelled to sign a treaty with
the French. Thus the British failed to defend their rights in Gyaman and, as a
result, they lost the greater part of it, including Bonduku, the commercial
capital, to the French.[1]

The result of British inaction was that a great deal of territory to which
Britain could have laid valid claim was abandoned to Germany and France.
The loss of Krepi, for instance, was so great that, when Governor Griffith
realised at the last moment how serious the situation was, he tried fruitlessly
to warn the Colonial Office against such a complete surrender.[2] He was too
late. So disgusted and so irritated was he by the surrender of Krepi to the
Germans, that in a spirit of revenge, he suddenly developed an affection for the
Taviefe political prisoners, whom he had so long detained when Taviefe was
under British influence, in spite of their acquittal by the Supreme Court. As
soon as he heard of the completion of the Anglo–German agreement, he released them and had the satisfaction of seeing the 'unbridled and troublesome'
Bella disappear into German territory.[3]

In the northern states of Salaga, Grunshie, Mamprussi and Gambaga, there
certainly was some competition. First a neutral zone was established, but in
1894 Griffith violated the agreement when he sent Ferguson to sign a treaty
with Salaga. It was this action which forced Von Puttkamer, the Togo Administrator, to send Klose to Salaga.[4] Klose left Salaga with Ferguson's treaty
in his pocket, but although Ferguson's account of this incident presented Klose
as having taken the treaty by force,[5] the German Imperial Government insisted that the King of Salaga gave the Treaty to Klose of his own accord.[6]
In the states of Gambaga, Mamprussi and Grunshie, too, there was some keen
competition between the French and the British. We have reports of African
kings who entered into treaty relations with both French and British.

After 1890 there were rumours that the French were preparing to take Asante
under their protection. Even though most of these rumours proved false, there
were at least a few occasions when it was absolutely certain that communication
passed between Asante and the French. There was the time when Owusu
Ansah went to Assinie to negotiate for arms to equip the Asante army.[7] About
this time (1894) Asante actually received large supplies of arms from the
French. On a second occasion, the Asante embassy in London tried to get help
from the French Government so as to thwart British aggression in Asante.[8]
But when Griffith, because of the news of a possible French collusion with

1 Ward, p. 301

2 C.O. 96/204, Tel. of 24 June 1890; C.O. 96/210, Tel. of 11 July 1890

3 C.O. 96/210, no. 186, Griffith to Knutsford, 15 August 1890

4 C.O. African (West) no. 479 in SAL/56/1 collected by Marion Johnson

5 C.O. African (West) no. 479 in SAL/43/1

6 C.O. African (West) no. 470 in SAL/52/1

7 This was just before the Asante embassy left for London   8 See p. 159

Asante earlier on, requested Asante in 1891 to submit to British rule, without first getting the consent of the Secretary of State for the Colonies, Lord Knutsford withheld his approval.[1] Meade, the Under-Secretary, pointed out that even though Asante refused British protection, the arrangement they had made with France would prevent their interfering there.[2] Apparently the Colonial Office at least did not consider the French threat all that serious, in spite of the excitement it had caused on the Coast. The agreements that Meade referred to were the Anglo–French border arrangements between 1880 and 1890,[3] and these indeed reserved Asante for the British, even though the Asante themselves would most assuredly have rejected any such inferences, had they been told of the contents of these treaties.

These examples clearly show that European competition in the Gold Coast was mild. Nor can it be said that the British gained more territory as a result of competition with other European powers on the Gold Coast. On the contrary, Britain lost a great deal of territory to which she could have laid valid claim but refrained from doing so, in pursuit of a policy of friendship with the other European powers. Although there is some truth in Ward's assertion that the British Government 'was now feeling . . . that if Ashanti did not become British it might soon become French or German',[4] this was not the only, nor indeed the main, cause of British penetration into Asante and the interior.

If European rivalry affected British penetration of Asante and the north on a much smaller scale than has hitherto been alleged, then a re-examination of the subject is necessary. We have already described, in Chapter 4, Asante activities from 1875 to 1890 and how these affected British policy towards the interior. The new wave of political activity from 1890 to 1901, which we must now consider, was certainly more effective. During the earlier events, Asante had been divided. Kokofu, Mampon and Nsutah had opposed the Central Government of Asante. But during these latter occurrences, Nsutah was restored to Asante allegiance, and Kokofu and Mampon were both on the point of returning to Asante when the British stopped them. What was more important, there was no dispute in Asante at this time, a development which enabled Prempeh to concentrate his energies on his dispute with the British, instead of dissipating them on internal strife as on the first occasion. Furthermore, his installation in 1894 did not merely strengthen his position *vis-à-vis* the British, but also generated Asante nationalism and created a united front against the British.

The aims of the later activities were also different from those of the earlier Asante exertions in Juaben, Salaga and Gyaman, in that they were definitely more serious, touching on the very independence of Asante. The Asantehene, like the Anlo, was seeking to preserve the independence of his kingdom. The various methods he adopted were all directed to one end: to secure international recognition for an independent kingdom of Asante.

For these reasons, these later activities were more countrywide and better organised. Because the methods employed were so effective, the British feared that if they did not act quickly, Asante would permanently shut them off from

1 C.O. 96/217, no. 179, Minute of 22 August 1891 by Knutsford on Griffith to Knutsford, 3 June 1891

2 Minute of 16 July 1891 by Meade on above

3 See W. Tordoff, *Ashanti under the Prempehs*, London 1965, p. 65   4 Ward, p. 301

the interior. This was largely why the British rushed into Asante and the interior between 1893 and 1900.

On this occasion, Prempeh's methods were twofold: political and economic. The political activities were designed to enable the king to re-establish effective control over the kingdom and forestall British efforts to take over. The economic methods were designed to make Asante economically independent of the Gold Coast Government and thus prevent British attempts to replace Asante control of interior trade with their own.

The political activities consisted of (*a*) restoring permanent Amantoo Unity, (*b*) restoring the provinces to Asante allegiance, (*c*) sending a deputation to U.K., and (*d*) forming an alliance with Samory.

To achieve a permanent Amantoo unity, Prempeh would have to bring back to Asante the secessionist states of Mampon, Nsutah and Kokofu. To achieve this, the King resorted to the traditional diplomatic machinery. For instance, since 1888, when the Kings of Mampon and Nsutah had fled northwards to Atebubu, Asante spies in that town had been trying to get the royal fugitives and their followers to return to Asante. The spies started a rumour that Governor Griffith had received £8000 from the Asantehene to hand over to him Atebubu,[1] which had come under the British since 1890. This had a great effect on Atebubu–Mampon relations. Right from the start the Mamponhene, Sekyere, although welcomed to Atebubu by Kwabena Asante, the King, found it extremely difficult to get any assistance from Atebubu military authorities. Then, one after another, the adherents whom Sekyere had brought with him to Atebubu deserted him and returned to Mampon in Asante, and the fact that they went so far as to install Sekyere's younger brother, Osunche, as King in his place,[2] showed that Asante success in this direction was most impressive. The Mamponhene found the situation so desperate that he was actually preparing to go back to Kumasi himself by mid-1892, when Ferguson arrived in Atebubu to stop him.[3] Even after this, some six months later, Sekyere was still anxious to win Prempeh's pardon, and, from all accounts, he succeeded in doing so.[4]

The King of Nsutah met even greater difficulties than the Mamponhene. No doubt, due to pressure from Asante agents, Edu Tre, the Nsutahene, never whole-heartedly pursued his own application to join the 'Bruno' Confederation with his followers. Edu Tre and his Nsutah fugitive supporters took the oath of the fetish priest, Dente, the initiation ceremony, as a matter of course, but he never had much enthusiasm for it. He never even forwarded the dues collected on the occasion to the Atebubuhene, Kwabena Asante, for onward transmission to Krachi, as custom demanded. Because of this, the fetish priest seized sixty Nsutahs at Krachi and threatened to seize more in Atebubu. He was obviously not used to people taking his oath in vain. Edu Tre's application for the membership of the 'Dente' Confederation was finally rejected by 1890.

1 C.O. 96/224, G.C. Secret, encl. 2 in Griffith to Knutsford, 4 July 1892

2 C.O. 96/238, G.C. Conf. Ferguson's Memo, 24 November 1889, Hodgson to Ripon, encl. 1, 18 November 1893

3 C.O. 96/224, G.C. Secret, encl. 2 in Griffith to Knutsford, 4 July 1892

4 Ferguson's Memo, 24 November 1889

At once he began to treat for peace with Prempeh, and this at the height of British influence in Atebubu. Two years later, he was ready with his people to depart for Asante, and even Ferguson's arrival in Atebubu with Hausas, with instructions to prevent him from returning to Asante, could not persuade him to change his mind.[1] Nsutah's restoration into the Asante fold was complete.

The Asantehene next set out to restore the Kokofus who had fled across the Prah. The restoration of Asibe and his Kokofus was the responsibility of the southern network of the Asante spy system. So vast was this system that all over the Protectorate emissaries of the King of Asante watched every movement of the Government. Late in 1893 Asante messengers with secret instructions arrived at Saltpond, ostensibly to look into the acts of an Asante man named Adu Twum who had sworn the King of Asante's oath at Quarman, thirty-six hours from Saltpond. When they were requested by the Governor to go to Accra and see him, they quickly withdrew into Asante. Adu Twum then openly swore the Asantehene's 'Great Oath' in Assin, and this meant much intercourse between the King of Assin and Asante, and the performance of many 'native' customs, before the affair could be settled. Obviously Adu Twum swore the Great Oath on purpose, and the Gold Coast authorities, realising this, had to order him out of the Protectorate.

There was yet another example of Asante messengers arriving at Prahsu, alleging that they were sent to inform the King of Assin that the Asantehene had punished those who had plundered Assin traders at Ferrar in Asante.[2] The third batch of messengers in the southern network of the Asante spy system appears to have achieved a great deal. This group was in fact the first to arrive in the Protectorate. Their destination was Kibi, the Akyem Abuakwa capital, where some important assignment awaited them. The first and most important task was to persuade Asibe and his candidate, Achereboanda, who had taken refuge at Atchichesu, in Akyem Kotoku, since their defeat by Asante forces, to return home.

Asibe, the Kokofuhene, was reported to be the keeper of the key to the room of the Golden Stool,[3] and if it was actually in his possession in Akyem, his return was essential for the full assumption of royal authority by Prempeh. The plan of getting him to return was again well thought out. It was reported that an Akyem Abuakwa man had violated the oath of King Amoako Attah II while staying in Asante. In accordance with tradition, he had to be repatriated. On this occasion, Asante messengers accompanied the 'culprit' into Akyem, and stayed for some time. Suddenly, late in 1893, a subject of the King of Asante residing in Akyem Abuakwa violated the oath of the great monarch and Amoako Attah also had to carry out the repatriation assignment. As a result of this, King Prempeh now sent to Kibi a full embassy, 'his son', three chiefs and many a man besides to thank Amoako Attah for what he had done.[4] They stayed in Kibi for at least a fortnight.[5] The reason for this communication

1 C.O. 96/224, Griffith to Knutsford (Secret) and encls., 4 July 1892

2 C.O. 96/236, G.C. Conf., Hodgson to Ripon, 23 September 1893; also C.7917, African (West) no. 458, February 1896

3 Asante oral tradition, informant Nana Kwaku Owusu

4 C.O. 96/236, G.C. Conf., encl. 3 in Hodgson to Ripon, 23 September 1893

5 C.7917, African (West) no. 458, February 1896

between Asante and Akyem was clearly to get the Kokofu refugees in Akyem Kotoku to return, and this had to be done through Amoako Attah. Secret messages must have been passed on from Kibi to Atchichesu in Akyem Kotoku, some twenty-eight miles to the south of the Akyem Abuakwa capital.

The results of these communications and secret activities of Asante messengers were spectacular. Early in September 1893 King Asibe of the Kokofus was won over, and he made plans to return to Asante with all the Kokofus with him as well as those in Denkyira. Achereboanda was also preparing to go with him. To win the Governor's approbation Asibe, who had secretly accumulated a large stock of gunpowder and guns, in preparation for linking up with the King of Asante,[1] intimated that he would welcome a Basel Mission School back in Kokofu, but the Governor was not deceived.[2] He acted quickly to prevent the Kokofus from returning into Asante, by detaining Asibe and Achereboanda.

About the same time that the Asantehene was trying to win over Kokofu, Yaw Sarpong's Juabens from Konongo and 1500 Bekwais, Kumawus and Agogos were said to be awaiting orders to form a junction with the main body of the Kumasi fighting forces.[3] This reference to the other Amantoo states as being one with Kumasi is significant and says much for Prempeh's efforts to keep the empire united.

The people of Juaben in particular (that is post-Asafu Agyei Juaben restored by the Asantehene while the ex-king was still an exile in the Protectorate) had remained steadily loyal to the Asantehene. It was only their king, Yaw Sarpong, who wavered a little.[4] But Prempeh sent messengers to him and the King of Agogo, warning them against disloyalty.[5] Again the people of Agogo, as distinct from their chief, were reported to be loyal to Asante.[6] As late as 1895, when British influence was advancing into these regions, Yaw Sarpong was not to be trusted by them. He would not openly side with the British.[7] Even more significant is the fact that the previous year he himself had repaired to Kumasi on a state visit.[8]

As for Bekwai, rumours spread late in 1893 that Asante had taken severe methods to check the tendency of the King to apostatise. In fact King Kwaku

---

1 C.O. 96/242, G.C. Conf., Hodgson to Ripon, 9 January 1894

2 C.O. 96/236, G.C. Conf., Hodgson to Ripon, 23 September 1893; also in C.7917, African (West) no. 458, February 1896

3 *Ibid.*, encl. 2

4 C.O. 96/238, African (West) no. 458, G.C. Conf., encl. 1 in Hodgson to Ripon, 18 November 1893, Accra; C.7917, February 1896. Hodgson categorically stated towards the end of 1893 that Juaben was an integral part of Asante. C.O. 96/238, G.C. Conf., encl. 7 in Hodgson to Ripon, 13 November 1893

5 C.O. 96/238, African (West) no. 458, G.C. Conf., Hodgson to Ripon, 22 November 1893, Accra, C.7917, February 1896

6 C.O. 96/238, African (West) no. 458, G.C. Conf., encl. 9 in Hodgson to Ripon, 18 November 1893, Accra

7 C.O. 96/262, G.C. Conf., Tel. of 13 November 1895

8 C.O. 96/248, G.C. Conf., Griffith to Ripon, 14 September 1894

Sei and Attobra, his linguist, were both reported to have been murdered.[1] Though this turned out to be false, what actually happened was just as important to Asante–British relations. For, on the information of Yami, another linguist of the King of Bekwai, Kwaku Sei was publicly rebuked and requested to 'eat fetish' with Prempeh with the hope that he would never again express the wish to go under British protection.[2] For the time being, therefore, Bekwai too had to conform.

The political advantage to Prempeh in uniting the different states of the empire under his undisputed control did not lie merely in the strength that this would give him against his opponents, it was also the only means of consolidating his position as king. Although elected to the Golden Stool since 1888, Prempeh had not as yet been formally installed. This could only take place with the cooperation of the Amantoo states. After his nomination by the Gyaasewahene, the Queen Mother and the 'family', the King-elect had to seek approval from the entire Kotoko Council at a public meeting at which Juaben, Kokofu, Nsutah, Bekwai and Mampon must *all* be represented. The emphasis was on all, for procedure was by unanimous agreement and not by majority vote. This was why it was so vital for Prempeh to bring them all back to Asante.[3] By mid-1894 he had almost achieved this. Mampon, Nsutah, Bekwai and Juaben were now once again one with Kumasi; only the Kokofuhene was still away with a number of his subjects. With affairs reaching a critical turn, therefore, Prempeh considered that he could not wait any longer, especially since five out of the six great Amantoo states were there to give him their allegiance. No mention is made of Sei being present at the enstoolment on 4 June 1894, when Prempeh at last formally became the occupant of the ancient Golden Stool of his ancestors, but Bekwai was represented by Etsia Yaw Buakyi, one of the most influential chiefs of that state. Asafu Boakye, Bantuma Ewua and Yaw Sarpong of Juaben all turned up in state making Kumasi 'look like on some memorable days gone by'.[4]

However, the fact that the whole of Asante was not then represented in Kumasi detracted somewhat from the occasion. All the same, the coronation did increase national feeling among all those present. Soon afterwards, deliberations were held about restoring peace and order throughout the entire empire and bringing back refugees to Asante. Forty pereguins (£324) were announced at the meeting of the great chiefs as the target to be realised for the state to be able to repatriate these refugees. Each district was requested to raise its quota. No sooner were the festivities over than two chiefs, Foku and Boaten, were dispatched to the coast with money to redeem Asibe and the Kokofus. Suddenly a palaver developed in Asante and the envoys had to halt at Edjuarbin. Apparently the coronation had reminded the great chiefs, still assembled in Kumasi, of 'the good old days' so much that they were not now satisfied with

---

1 C.O. 96/236, G.C. Conf., encl. in Hodgson to Ripon, 23 September 1893. Kwaku Sei, who succeeded Abbrebrsseh on the Bekwai Stool, was not anti-British like his predecessor. See p. 179

2 C.O. 96/238, G.C. Conf., Hodgson to Ripon, 22 November 1893; also in C.7917, African (West) no. 458, February 1896

3 Asante oral tradition; informant, Mr C. K. Dente. See also Mr Agyeman-Dauah's work on the installation of the Asantehene, I.A.S., Legon.

4 C.O. 96/248, G.C. Conf., encl. 2 in Griffith to Ripon, 14 September 1894

the prospect of restoring only Kokofu. The whole empire of former days, including Adansi, should be restored, they argued, and quickly ordered more money to be collected for the repatriation of the Adansis, too.[1] Prempeh must have felt that with this new spirit of unity generated in Asante, thanks to his diplomatic efforts, he would soon remove every obstacle from his path to lasting success.

Briefly, Prempeh's attempts to re-unite the Amantoo states were largely successful. Apart from Kokofu, all the seceded Amantoo states had been physically reconciled with Kumasi. And even Kokofu was in principle reconciled with Prempeh. An even more important result of Prempeh's work was the rise of a strong nationalist feeling which threatened the Gold Coast Government's hopes of resuming its 'divide and rule' policy in Asante.

The second aspect of Asante political activity was the restoration of the provinces. The attempt to restore the provinces to Asante allegiance and to gain the cooperation of neighbouring states had gone on since 1893. This was in fact the other reason for the spy system, and just as Prempeh and his great chiefs nearly succeeded in permanently re-uniting the Amantoo, so did he nearly restore the entire Amansin and consolidate friendly relations with neighbouring states.

Of these, Akyem was the most important, both from the point of view of its strategic position between Asante and the coast and of its military strength. King Amoako Attah II of Akyem Abuakwa was looked upon by the Asantehene as a powerful ally. Akyem was one of the main gateways through which British influence was rapidly advancing into the interior, and for this reason the Akyem monarch held a vital position. To win his friendship would not only be useful, as already indicated, in the restoration of Asibe and the Kokofus, but would also help to create a strong Asante barrier against the British advance.

Kwahu was the other state that Asante needed to recover, or at least bring under Kumasi influence, especially since the British were using this state, too, as a stepping stone into the interior. To achieve his aims in Kwahu, all Prempeh needed in September 1893 was a *casus belli*, because he had in readiness and within easy distance of Atebubu an army flushed with victory over Nkoranza.[2] Prempeh could find the *casus belli* in a difficult boundary dispute between Akyem and Kwahu. The Akyem Abuakwa chiefs involved in this dispute were those of Muso and Anyanam and the Kwahu chief was the one of Mpraeso. The Chief of Muso urged a Juaben chief to build a village on the disputed land, and this increased the animosity between Akyem and Kwahu. The Asantehene requested the latter to submit the dispute to his Court as a sign of loyalty, and was preparing to move his army into Kwahu if they refused. Amoako Attah was also ready to support him.[3]

The results of Asante efforts in Akyem and Kwahu were not as encouraging as Prempeh would have liked. His ally Amoako Attah succeeded in bringing Kofi Ahinkora of Akyem Swedru, Western Akyem, into the Akyem–Asante alliance as a counterpoise to the British, who, through Atafuah's conduct, had established themselves on the Insuaim Ferry in Akyem Kotoku.[4] Thus, as a

---

1 *Ibid.*, encl. 1   2 C.O. 96/236, G.C. Conf., Hodgson to Ripon, 23 September 1893

3 C.O. 96/237, G.C. Conf., Hodgson to Ripon, 6 October 1893; also African (West) 458, C.7912, February 1896

4 C.O. 96/237, G.C. Conf., Hodgson to Ripon, 19 October 1893

gateway into the interior for the British, the Insuaim Ferry lost some of its usefulness. To achieve a similar success in Kwahu, Prempeh should have attacked the state, but the Government forestalled the Asante forces and prevented the attack. However, even in the provinces, Asante efforts to resist British penetration were important enough to cause alarm among Gold Coast Government officials.

The third method of political activity was an Asante delegation to the U.K. The Asantehene and his chiefs, thinking that it was only the local government which refused to recognise the Asante claim to independence, decided to send a delegation to explain their point of view in London. The chief assignment of the delegation could be seen in the events immediately preceding its dispatch. From 1891 onwards, Asante was more than ever concerned about preserving her independence in the face of British challenge. In that year, Prempeh wrote to Governor Griffith with reference to the suggestion that Asante 'in its present State' should come and enjoy the protection of Her Majesty the Queen:

> I may say this is a serious matter of a very serious consideration and which I am happy to say we have arrived at this conclusion, that my Kingdom of Ashanti will never commit itself to any such policy; Ashanti must remain independent as of old, at the same time be friendly with all white men.[1]

On another occasion, the Kotoku Council stated that the questions raised by the Government's request were so grave and sweeping, touching as they did the constitution and construction of the King of Asante's independent kingdom, that considering the unfriendly attitude already assumed by Her Majesty's Government on the Coast to the kingdom of Asante it was impossible that mutual sympathy and understanding could be looked for in the Colony. The King and his council therefore decided to send a special embassy to England to lay before Her Majesty this and other matters of importance connected with the peace and progress of the Asante Kingdom, and its cooperation with the settlement of Her Majesty the Queen on the Coast.[2]

So at the beginning of January 1895, an Asante delegation left the Gold Coast for London. The members of the delegation were John and Albert Owusu Ansah and two chiefs, Foku and Boaten. When they reached London, Downing Street would not see them.[3] But they pressed on with their efforts to get a hearing. They engaged a counsel, and in no uncertain terms, put their view to him. At Lennox Gardens, London, S.W., the Asante embassy explained that the Asantehene would not object to a British Resident provided his powers were limited, i.e. there should be no interference with the laws and customs of the land, and that the tenure and succession of lands, property and stools should continue in accordance with 'native' laws and customs. Even more important, the embassy stressed that the Resident's powers should not clash with the powers and authority of the King.[4] But the counsel could not secure them a meeting with officials of the Colonial Office.

1 C.O. 879/35, African (West) no. 415, Griffith to Knutsford, 3 June 1891

2 C.O. 96/244, Tels. of 11 and 25 April 1894

3 *The Gold Coast Chronicle*, 19 June 1895

4 C.O. 96/271, G.C. Conf., Maxwell to Chamberlain, 19 March 1896

Finding no happy reception in London, the Asante embassy must have tried to explore other possibilities, including communication with French agents in the hope of enlisting French help.[1] Even though there was not much hope in this line of action, the Ansahs must have thought of using it as a threat to get the British Government to compromise. The embassy also considered the possibility of getting a British trading company to establish itself in Asante, probably because they saw in this their last hope of preventing the Gold Coast Government from seizing political power. A company would be run on specific terms of agreement to which the Asantehene would be a party. The Gold Coast Government, on the other hand, would use force to get what it wanted. The embassy worked very hard and actually got a British company ready to take over the development of Asante. To inform British colonial authorities of this arrangement, the embassy engaged the services of Jonathan E. Harris, of 95 Leadenhall Street (London), who wrote on their behalf to Lord Selborne, the Under-Secretary of State for the Colonies, on 26 October 1895. He pointed out that the Asantehene, by his representatives in London, had agreed to grant a British company a charter for the opening up of Asante to British enterprise and skill. So the British Government should not resort to force yet, since a British company in Asante might prove to be the solution to the problem as far as the local government was concerned.[2] It is significant that the Gold Coast Government took strong exception to these proceedings.

Some months before Harris wrote his letter, the Asante embassy must have completed their arrangements with the firm in question, a Liverpool firm — Radcliffe and Durant. For, soon after that, two Englishmen, Cade and his assistant, representing the firm, which all along had supported the Asante embassy in London, arrived in the colony and were about to proceed into Asante. But Governor Maxwell detained them on the Coast for fear of the consequences of their getting in touch with the King of Asante. Maxwell was definite that this would work against the interest of the Gold Coast Government. He telephoned the Colonial Office about it, thus preparing them against the embassy's request before they could make it. So when Harris's letter reached Whitehall, R. H. Meade of the Colonial Office simply wrote in reply that Her Majesty's Government could not take cognisance of the one who presented the said documents (meaning the trade agreement between the embassy and the Liverpool firm) styling himself as he did 'Ambassador Extraordinary and Minister Plenipotentiary to the King of Ashanti'.[3] Meade's argument was that Prempeh was only King of Kumasi and not King of Asante, so he could not act on behalf of Asante.[4] The British Government thus thwarted the Asante embassy, and towards the end of 1895 the mission returned without achieving its goal.

Because of this failure, Asante embarked on yet another method of resistance: an alliance with Samory Toure. This Mohammedan chief was for many years the greatest adversary of the French in West Africa. His influence on British relations with the Gold Coast is a vast subject in itself, still awaiting con-

1 C.O. 96/271, G.C. Secret, encl. 4 in Maxwell to Chamberlain, 19 March 1896

2 *The Gold Coast Independent*, 21 December 1895   3 *Ibid.*

4 It must be pointed out that the British were not consistent here, for if Prempeh was not King of Asante but only of Kumasi then they should not have requested him to pay the indemnity under the Fomena Treaty.

siderable research. It cannot, therefore, be discussed in great detail here, though I suggest that research would yield great dividends. The following outline indicates briefly how Asante planned to ally with Samory.

As early as mid-1894, persistent rumours began to reach the Coast that a warm friendship was developing between Prempeh and Samory. At first the Gold Coast Government did not understand why, and as late as 1895, an absurd notion persisted in British colonial circles that Samory was a tool in a French intrigue to get Asante. That there may have been some communication between Kumasi and the French is not in doubt, but the initiative must have come from Prempeh and not the French. On 2 October *The Gold Coast Chronicle* reported Samory's activities. 'One of Africa's most powerful Mohammedan chiefs', commanding a well equipped army, consisting of infantry and cavalry, intended to visit Kumasi, and many people were inclined to connect his presence in Kumasi at this time with French intrigue. Although people were not sure what the motives of Prempeh and Samory were, they were certain that the latter was visiting Asante to foster resistance to the attempt of the Gold Coast Government to establish a Resident in Kumasi.[1] On the 11th Captain Stewart, on a mission to Asante, reported from Echeabon to Governor Maxwell that he had heard that Samory's message to Prempeh was that he had been compelled to attack and capture Bonduku as the Gyamans had refused to let him open up a trade route through their country, and that the King of Asante thanked him for this. Stewart suspected that there was a private message, but could not guess what it was.[2]

On 27 November, *The Gold Coast Chronicle* stated with some authority that Prempeh had invited Samory to Kumasi and entered an offensive-defensive alliance with him, making him a present of slaves and gold dust.[3] The details of this alliance have come down to us from an eye witness, a Hausa officer sent to Bonduku by Governor Maxwell. Danburnu, the officer, claimed to have seen the Asante mission of 300 arrive in Bonduku with presents for Samory. They delivered a message from Prempeh asking the Mohammedan warrior to help him recover his lost states and to open a trade route through French territory to the coast. He said that Prempeh's messengers definitely stated that their master would not have anything to do with the British. Danburnu did not hear Samory's reply.[4]

It is clear that Prempeh was at this time turning to Samory for military assistance and the establishment of a trade route through Gyaman, which Samory had conquered.

At this point our story gets a little obscure. It is, of course, now assumed that because Samory was a Muslim he could not place his army at the service of an infidel court. Secondly, it has been suggested that since Samory was an inveterate foe of the French, he could not accede to Prempeh's request of creating a trade route to the Coast, through French territory. Although we cannot now

1 *The Gold Coast Chronicle*, 2 October 1895

2 C.O. 96/261, G.C. Conf., encl. 1 in Maxwell to Chamberlain, 25 October 1895

3 *The Gold Coast Chronicle*, 27 November 1895

4 C.O. 96/263, G.C. Conf., Tel. of 13 December 1895, Maxwell to Chamberlain, and encl. 1, 17 December 1895. Danburnu said that the 300 Asante he saw carried 30 loads of spirits, 30 kegs of powder, 30 loads of salt, 40 of kola nuts and 30 of cloth as presents to Samory.

prove them, we cannot ignore two relevant facts about this second theory. The first is the persistent rumour reaching the coast about this time, that a French officer suddenly appeared in Kumasi[1] (no doubt at Prempeh's solicitations). The second is that as Samory himself conquered Gyaman to establish a trade route through it, there is every reason to believe that he would want to see this route extended to the sea coast.

The facts do not seem to indicate that Samory declined to give Prempeh military assistance on religious grounds. On the contrary, there is every indication that Samory was preparing to assist the Asante when the British stepped in.

That Asante was expecting help from Samory is indicated by the self-possessed and confident manner in which the Asante court, in spite of the failure of the London embassy, received Governor Maxwell's messenger, Stewart, in October 1895. Stewart was requested to ask Prempeh to meet Governor Maxwell at Prahsu. Now, it was against Asante custom for the Asantehene to leave his country except for war. Stewart was struck by the confidence of the court in spite of its difficulties. He wrote to the Governor: 'There is not the slightest chance of the King coming to meet you, as when we made the offer, they all laughed at the idea of the King of Heaven and Earth going to meet anyone.'[2]

Prempeh's attempts to ally with Samory were important in his bid to check the growing influence of the Government in the interior.

Economic activities

Apart from political measures, Prempeh and his chiefs were involved in economic activities in their dealings with the British. Efforts were made by the King and his people to increase their economic control of the former provinces of Asante in order to meet the British challenge. This meant that Asante must establish an independent trade route[3] to the sea coast outside the Gold Coast, at either the French port Assinie, or the German port Lome. Of the two, Lome was definitely the more attractive, and this was the one the Asantehene chose. The Acting Governor, Hodgson, vividly described the Asante plan in January 1894: 'Kontempo would cease to exist as a market town, and the greater part of the trade which now finds its way to the Gold Coast would be diverted to the left bank of the Volta, and would probably pass down the trade road through Kpanto to Lome.'[4] To create contact with Lome, the Asante had to capture and

---

1 *The Gold Coast Chronicle*, 23 October 1895

2 C.O. 96/261, G.C. Conf., encl. 1 in Maxwell to Chamberlain, 25 October 1895

3 The Asantehene even tried to establish trade free from the Government's control by reaching a trade agreement with Dr John William Herivel of the Wesleyan Mission. According to an indenture made between him and Dr Herivel on 26 April 1892, a Trading Company to be called 'The Asantee and Prah Mining and Trading Company Limited' was to be formed to work the resources of Asante. The Company was to raise the capital, build railways, factories etc. and the King of Asante was to give land, timber for building, etc. The Company was to carry away timber, minerals, etc., levy custom dues and pay back to the Asantehene £200 per annum to be increased to £500 later. It was the Asante Government that was to authorise the Company to apply for a Charter from the Queen of Great Britain. See C.O. 96/244, G.C. Conf., sub-encl. in encl. 1 in Griffith to Ripon, 6 April 1894. But the Governor foiled these attempts of the Asantehene to preserve his economic independence of the Government.

4 C.O. 96/242, G.C. Conf., Hodgson to Ripon, 9 January 1894

restore their former market of Salaga in the neutral zone, from which Asante traders could travel to Lome without having to pass through British territory, since the neutral zone ran directly into German territory on the east. But to reach Salaga itself, Asante traders had to pass through territory under the Brong Confederation, now opposed to Asante. What then was this Brong Confederation?

The Brong Confederation of Krachi Dente began at an early date with the rise of Dente in Krachi. Agogo tradition maintains that Dente played an important part in the process of state formation in the area between Asante and Krachi.[1] Ferguson's reports indicate that there were fetish priests in the countries of the Krachi–Atebubu–Juaben districts with a common sympathy, and it would seem that all these fetish priests learnt their art at Krachi. This religious bond, the main cause of the Brong Confederation of states, was thus a potent political factor as well.[2] The Brong states finally engulfed in this Confederation were Nkoranza, Atebubu, Gwan, Basa, Yegi and Prang, and over all these Dente exercised some sort of control, mainly spiritual.

During the reign of Opoku Ware, Asante conquered the Brong peoples as well as Krachi itself, so as to capture the caravan trade of the Mohammedan states of the north-east, 'which send forth annually their caravans with cattle and slaves etc., to be exchanged for kolanuts'.[3] It was then that the Asante set up their huge Salaga market as the southern terminus of the caravan trade. They continued to hold Salaga as well as the intermediary Brong states until about 1880.[4] By this time, the Brong states, no doubt encouraged by British interference, rose against Asante. The priest Dente had envied Asante control of the Atebubu–Salaga trade route which yielded large profits. So in 1884 he decided to take over control of the north-eastern trade, and issued orders forbidding the use of the Atebubu–Salaga road to kola traders, who must now go through Krachi.[5] So began Kete–Krachi's prosperity at the expense of Salaga.[6]

To this economic power Dente soon added the political. But since political power involved military duties, Dente, whose religious preoccupations precluded a military ascendancy, had to work through Atebubu, whose King was the most powerful militarily in the Confederation. For instance, although it was Dente who gave the orders, the stopping of the kola trade to the north through Atebubu had to be physically effected by Atebubuhene, not only because it was more convenient for him than anyone else to do so, but also because he was entrusted with the task. Atebubu thus became the political headquarters of the Brong Confederation. In time the Confederation, due to its economic and political power, came to be used as an instrument against Asante. We have seen how states like Mampon and Nsutah applied for membership of the Confedera-

---

1 Agogo tradition by aunt of Queen Mother of Agogo 1928, Kumasi D.R.B.

2 C.O. 96/239, G.C. Conf., sub-encl. in encl. 1, 7 December 1893   3 *Ibid.*

4 Adm. 1/644, SAL/59/1, no. 264 of 17 October 1881. See also F. Ramseyer, *Eine Reise im Norden von Asante und im Osten von Volta*, Geographische Gesellschaft (fur Thuringen) Zu Jena, Mitteilungen Bd. IV, 1886, SAL/48/1.

5 Ramseyer, *Eine Reise im Norden von Asante*

6 Binger, *From the Niger to the Gulf of Guinea*, January 1892

tion,[1] so as to be able to stand against Asante.[2] It was this obstacle that Asante had to overcome before she could re-establish contact with Salaga.

To remove the Brong Confederation from their way to Salaga, the Asante planned a three-pronged attack, first on Nkoranza, on Atebubu and finally on Salaga.

In Nkoranza, as elsewhere in the Brong Confederation, the British succeeded, in the decade after 1880, in diverting trade through Atebubu, Kwahu and Akwapem to Accra. Gold Coast official reports describing this diversion of trade referred to Nkoranza as having helped to close the trade road to Asante,[3] although Nkoranza tradition modified this view, blaming the closure of the road on one particular incident of Asante traders having shown disrespect to Nkoranzahene's wife in Kintampo, and declaring the duration of closure to be very temporary.[4] However, the long Asante–Nkoranza friendship stretching back to Bafo Pim appeared to be strained during Prempeh's regime.[5] At a great meeting in Kumasi about the middle of 1892 the Antuahene, heading a party of young men, urged war against Nkoranza. And so it was that in 1892 Asante declared war.[6] Although there were these other reasons, the fact that Nkoranza had to be subdued as part of the Dente Confederation weighted the balance in favour of war.

Kofi Fah, the Nkoranzahene, began to look for allies. Messengers with gifts were sent to the coast to enlist British support, and others with more gifts left for Krachi Dente.[7] In sending gold and elephant tusks to the British, the Queen Mother of Nkoranza hoped to enlist their support against Asante,[8] but the British hesitated, just as disappointingly as the Brong Confederation. Asante, on the other hand, closed the net, first by reorganising Nkoranza's opponents and secondly by putting an army in the field against her.

Asante exploited existing differences between Banda and Nkoranza. Nana Kwame Baffo asserted, however, that it was Asante which had caused the difference. According to him, when the Asante saw that Nkoranza was becoming powerful, and decided to reduce her by force, they conceived the clever idea of urging Nkoranza on to a conflict with Banda so that the Banda war might reduce the number of Nkoranza troops that would eventually face Asante when war was declared. Nkoranza did pick a quarrel with Banda and, while they were

---

1 Applications for membership and assistance were made directly to the Fetish himself in Krachi. The Fetish then gave orders to Kwabena Asante of Atebubu first to conduct the ceremony and then send over to Krachi the membership fees of the applicants.

2 See Ferguson's Memo, 24 November 1889

3 C.O. 96/242, G.C. Conf., Hodgson to Ripon, 9 January 1894

4 Nkoranza tradition; informant, Nana Kwame Baffo

5 Signs of deterioration in this long friendship appear to have started during Mensah Bonsu's reign when Nkoranza stopped the Asante army marching to Gyaman under Omane and agreed to pay 8 pereguins (£96) tax imposed by the Asantehene. This first official tax was regarded later with disfavour as having set a dangerous precedent. Secondly, during Prempeh's time Asante felt Nkoranzahene was becoming too powerful and decided to humble him. Nkoranza tradition.

6 *Ibid.*   7 Ferguson's Memo on Abruno Revolt, 24 November 1889

8 Nkoranza tradition; informant, Nana Ankamako and others.

trying to press home a victory over Banda, the Asante army treacherously fell on them and a large number of Nkoranzas were killed.[1]

But the Banda affair appears to be more complicated than Nana Kwame Baffo's version of it. It is known that the Bandas had been for a long time fighting against Mo. Banda sought help from Bole to crush the Mos, who were allies of Nkoranza. Now, Banda and Bole were both friendly to Asante who entered an alliance with Banda preparatory to destroying Mo. At a later stage, Asante tried to get Bole to join Banda, an act which would hasten the destruction of Mo.[2] Mo was not completely destroyed before Nkoranza faced Banda, but the Mos were so weakened by the activities of their opponents that they could not help their allies in the Banda hills. This contributed to Nkoranza's defeat.

Nkoranza tradition refers to an oath, the Boakye oath, which commemorates the defeat in the Banda hills as a complete disaster. The Asante army captured a large number of Nkoranzas, mainly women and children.[3] By March 1893 sources close to the Gold Coast Government revealed that Nkoranza was completely restored to Asante.[4] But the same sources reported that Nkoranza once again had applied to the Brong Confederation for assistance.[5] But again Kofi Fah, Nkoranzahene, was disappointed. The Brong Confederation did not really work at this point. Although Dente ordered King Kwabena Asante of Atebubu to march to the support of Kofi Fah, he did not move. The Nkoranzas were so disappointed that they even thought of returning to Asante allegiance by defeating and bringing the weak Brong peoples to the north back to Asante allegiance. This would have enabled Kofi Fah to return with his people to his country without further molestation from Asante. To implement his decision he moved out of Atebubu to Wiase. This frightened the priest Dente, who hurriedly gathered together 1200 riffraffs and marched from Krachi to Wiase in the hope of giving Kofi Fah the military assistance he had asked for and which Atebubu had declined to give.[6]

These frantic efforts by Dente did not change the fortunes of Nkoranza. His forces were no use to Kofi Fah. Asante on the other hand arranged an impressive alliance of Boles and Bandas against Mos and Nkoranzas[7] and, according to Hani and Nsawkaw tradition, got both Nsawkaw and Badu to join Banda preparatory to matching their strength with that of Nkoranza.[8]

This was the situation when Prempeh embarked on the other aspects of his plan to clear the way to Salaga. His chance to get into contact with Salaga came with the Salaga civil war (1892).[9] According to H. Klose, the German traveller,

1 *Ibid.*, informant, Nana Kwame Baffo.

2 C.O. 96/242, G.C. Conf., see Hodgson to Ripon, 9 January 1894

3 Nkoranza tradition: informant, Nana Kwame Baffo. It would appear that the entire Nkoranza population moved into the Banda hills, probably for safety.

4 C.O. 96/232, no. 69, Griffith to Ripon, 6 March 1893

5 C.O. 96/235, no. 265, Hodgson to Ripon, 14 August 1893

6 C.O. 96/239, G.C. Conf., sub-encl. in encl. 1, 7 December 1893

7 C.O. 96/242, G.C. Conf., encl. 2 in Hodgson to Ripon, 9 January 1894

8 Hani and Nsawkaw tradition, I.A.S. 1966

9 For the wider background of the Salaga Civil War of 1892 see Mrs M. Johnson's account in *Research Review*, Vol. 2, 2, 1966, p. 36. See also her *Salaga Papers*.

this civil war was the rising of Kabachi, supported by the Dagomba King of Yendi, against old King Mama of Salaga. Another German traveller, G. A. Krause, who was in Salaga when the rebel forces entered it, says that the arrival of the Dagomba army was so sudden that nobody thought of defending themselves. Many just managed to save their skins but King Mama fell,[1] and the victorious Kabachi crowned himself King of Salaga. It was Kabachi, therefore, whom Prempeh had to approach in 1893. He decided to do this through the Boles, whom Ferguson described as strongly sympathetic with Salaga.[2] This must mean that Bole was an ally of Salaga under Kabachi, and therefore regarded by Prempeh as a useful intermediary. Apparently Asante's plans worked out on this, and the Salaga forces went over to the Asante side.

The final step to clear the way to Salaga was the subjugation of Atebubu. About November 1893 an Asante force marched into Atebubu and burnt down Abease and two other towns in the north-west. Then the Asante army began preparations to subdue the small Brong states between Atebubu and the Volta, including Gwan and Basa.[3] It was clear that, after overrunning the Brong states, the Asante forces were hoping to effect the long awaited junction with the Salaga forces. There was a clear connection between Asante operations and those of Salaga. Hodgson, basing his facts on the information of the Inspector General then in the interior, stated that Kabachi Wula was by the close of 1893 moving on Yegi. He expressed great fear that, if the allied forces (Asante–Banda–Salaga) should succeed in their various operations, then Nkoranza would be absorbed by Asante and Salaga, and the greater portion of trade then passing through Kintampo to the Gold Coast would be diverted.[4]

Briefly, therefore, Asante had achieved a strategy that was at the point of succeeding – the Bandas in the West, Asante forces in the east and centre and Salaga forces in the north, all striving to crush the enemy and re-establish Asante–Salaga trade. This was how Ferguson put it; he said that the victory of the allies would mean the absorption of the Brong people, including Atebubu itself, into Asante: 'The Brong people would be subdued and Salaga would do direct trade with Ashanti.'[5] Clearly, between 1892 and 1894 Asante was on the way to restoring imperial control of the Salaga trade route.

Before considering the ultimate result of this conflict, let us note briefly the other efforts of Asante to establish an independent trade route to the sea and prevent British interference in the interior. Apart from Asante's attempt to reach the coast through German territory, we also have a reference to Prempeh dealing with the French in the present Ivory Coast. It was said to be the Asantehene's wish 'to open a direct road from Kumasi to Kinjarbo'.[6] Since about the same time other reports confirmed that Asante was able to acquire

1 N. Klose, *Togo unter Deutscher Flagge: Reisebilder und Betrachtungen*, Berlin 1899, p. 362. Krause says that the rebels numbered 800 soldiers of whom 200 were horsemen, and that the possessions of the Salagas fell to those plundering Dagomba hordes.

2 C.O. 96/242, G.C. Conf., sub-encl. to encl. 2 in Hodgson to Ripon, 9 January 1894

3 C.O. 96/238, G.C. Conf., encl. 1 in Hodgson to Ripon, 18 November 1893

4 C.O. 96/242, Tel. of 13 January 1894, Hodgson to Ripon

5 C.O. 96/242, G.C. Conf., sub-encl. in encl. 1 in Hogdson to Ripon, 9 January 1894

6 C.O. 96/247, G.C. Conf., encl. 2 in Griffith to Ripon, 11 July 1894

large supplies of gunpowder from the French,[1] this Franco–Asante contact must have been confined to an attempt by Prempeh to secure, temporarily, ammunition supplies which the British would not permit him to buy from the Gold Coast ports.

These Asante measures were indeed very strong. It is true that there were some loopholes in Asante political activity since 1875. Kumasi authorities, before the 1890s were mainly concerned with local issues in Nkoranza, Atebubu, Juaben, Salaga, Kwahu, etc., although they were also trying to prevent British penetration of these areas. These local disputes weakened Asante resistance to British demands, but from 1894 the increasing nationalist feeling and the determination of Asante to preserve her independence strengthened the resistance of the entire movement. No wonder, therefore, that it had important effects on British policy.

Effects of Asante activities on British policy

Asante activities hampered the British policy of penetrating the interior of the Gold Coast. Before this time, in the 1880s, Britain had adopted the 'divide and rule' method. This had been slow because it had been indirect, involving intrigues to effect secession in Asante. But because of the Asante activities of the 1890s Britain had to change this indirect and slow method of penetrating the interior and embark on an open and rapid method of acquiring territory in the hinterland.

These activities affected British policy in three main ways. The first was the hasty British occupation of Asante's former provinces, which Prempeh was trying to recover. It was, for instance, the desire of the British to penetrate Akyem and Kwahu quickly that caused Hodgson to break up the alliance between Amoako Attah II and Prempeh, which the Asantehene had effected to prevent British occupation. When Hull mentioned in his letters to the Acting Governor the exchange of courtesies between the two monarchs, Hodgson hastily instructed Hull to proceed to Kibi, ostensibly to obtain the signatures of the King and chiefs to the bond which they had to sign in connection with the return of Chief Kwabena Okyere to his town of Wankyi, 'but really for the purpose of watching the movements of the King and ascertaining what his disposition is towards this Government'.[2] The information the Government collected caused it to act quickly, sending a force which forestalled further Asante success in both Akyem and Kwahu, preventing Prempeh from attacking the latter (1893).

Another area into which the British rushed was the Brong Confederation. To achieve this they employed the services of a keen observer, George Ekem Ferguson, born in 1864 of Fante parents in Anomabu, and educated in Cape Coast, Freetown and later at the Royal School of Mines in the U.K.[3] Like other educated Africans, Ferguson found an outlet for his vast talents in Government service, and it was through him that Britain acquired the Northern Territories so quickly.

Ferguson helped Britain in a number of ways. First, he understood what was happening in the 1890s in the Krachi area. He learnt of the religious, economic

1 *Ibid.*, encl. 1   2 C.O. 96/237, G.C. Conf., Hodgson to Ripon, 6 October 1893

3 Brown, *An Active History of Ghana*, p. 50

and political influence of the Brong Confederation and his explanations on its nature were extremely useful to the British. For instance, although the Government had earlier heard of its existence through Kwaku Panyin, linguist of Kwabena Asante of Atebubu,[1] it was only when Governor Griffith sent Ferguson to Atebubu that the Government learned from his reports that Atebubu itself was the military headquarters of the Confederation and that it would pay to hold on to it.[2]

In consequence, all the confederate states came to attach themselves to the Government which now controlled their military capital. On learning that Prempeh, with a victorious army, was preparing to effect a junction with Salaga forces,[3] Hodgson at once sent Ferguson on 22 September 1893 to Atebubu, with instructions to organise a system of espionage for obtaining intelligence about Asante affairs generally and the movements of their army in particular. At the same time Hodgson suggested to the Secretary of State that he thought a demonstration of force in Atebubu was necessary. If his proposal was approved, he would send all available Hausas, about 580, to Atebubu with machine-guns and seven-pounders. He envisaged some difficulties, suggesting that the military resources of the colony might have to be strengthened from imperial sources. Hodgson pointed out that he had requested the Inspector General himself, though absent from headquarters, to return at once to command the army.[4]

When five days later Kodjo Afful, linguist of the King of Atebubu, arrived in Accra with the news that the Asante army was actually moving into Atebubu, Hodgson could wait no longer for Colonial Office approval, but at once instructed Sir Francis Scott to march in force to Atebubu. At the same time he wrote to the Asantehene, threatening that if he attacked Atebubu he would have to reckon with the British Government.[5] Since Prempeh was having difficulties in acquiring firearms and ammunition, he could not afford to face a force with precision guns.

The presence of the British army in Atebubu, the political capital of the Dente Confederation, provided military and moral support for all member states and affiliated peoples. One by one they revolted against Asante and began to petition the Gold Coast Government for protection. Reports from the Inspector General of the Gold Coast Constabulary indicated that the presence of the British force in the north-east portion of the Protectorate 'has altered the complexion of political affairs and requests to join the Protectorate are about to be made by many of the towns under Ashanti rule lying to the West and North West of Abetifi'. It was Yao Sarpong of Juaben, now completely estranged from his people, who started the ball rolling by asking for British protection on 30 October 1893.[6] He was followed early in November by Nkoranza and Agogo.[7] Then in quick succession a host of other states began

1 C.O. 96/208, no. 23, Hodgson to Knutsford, 14 January 1890

2 C.O. 96/215, no. 75, Griffith to Knutsford and encl. 1, 9 March 1891

3 C.O. 96/236, G.C. Conf., Hodgson to Ripon, 23 September 1893

4 *Ibid.*, encl. 9   5 *Ibid.*, 29 September 1893

6 C.O. 96/238, G.C. Conf., Hodgson to Ripon, 13 November 1893 and encls. 4 and 3

7 C.O. 96/238, Tel. of 14 November 1893 and encl. 7 in G.C. Conf. 14 November 1893

to send in requests for protection, thus encouraging the British to sign Protectorate treaties with them all.

On 15 November Acting Governor Hodgson instructed Ferguson to proceed into the interior and sign treaties with countries between Kwahu and Atebubu, including all the states bordering on the Volta.[1] So all the states under Krachi Dente came under British protection, when one after the other Ferguson signed treaties with them. By 27 December, he was further instructed to sign treaties with Bona, Wa, Lobi and Walembele and Yariba,[2] no doubt with a view to isolating Bole, whose contemplated junction with Banda and Asante would promote the Asante plan of coalescing with Salaga and diverting trade to German Togo.[3] The whole region north and west of the neutral zone around Salaga quickly came under British protection; the Brong states including Nkoranza not excepted.[4]

At the height of the treaty-making the British decided to break up the Asante military alliance since this would speed up the colonisation process. So Scott sent Ferguson with Hausas to stop the Boles from joining the Bandas.[5] As Ferguson approached the Bole forces fled.[6]

This enormous British effort to penetrate the interior resulted in the defeat of Asante. Asante's failure to turn the Dente Confederation to good advantage and the success of Britain in doing this, by seizing its political capital, Atebubu, was an important factor in the final collapse of Asante power in the north. The failure of Asante to win over the hostile Dente Confederation was of course primarily a diplomatic failure, but Asante hoped to substitute force for diplomacy. And yet even here the strains to which the Asante army, chiefly armed with flintlock guns (only between 300–700 were armed with Sniders), had recently been put weakened it. In spite of their earlier victory over Nkoranza, in their third encounter with them, Asante arms proved ineffective, only five Nkoranzas being reported killed. And this was at a time when Asante's opponent, Nkoranza, had no better ally than the militarily weak Dente with his squad of 1200, all armed with old flintlocks.[7] The military decline of Asante

1 *Ibid.*, 18 November 1893, encl. 2

2 C.O. 96/239, Tel. of 27 December 1893, Hodgson to Ripon

3 C.O. 96/242, G.C. Conf., Hodgson to Ripon, 9 January 1894

4 Encls. 1 and 2 in Hodgson to Ripon, G.C. Secret, 11 January 1894, C.O. 96/242. The Treaty-signing at this time was carried out as follows: From December 1893 Capt. Lang, R.E. signed treaties with Kings of Wiase, Basa, Nkanaku and Enynowofi, all under the sway of Dente. (Griffith to Ripon, G.C. Conf. 6 April 1894 and encls. 2, 3, 4, 7, 8, 9, 10.) Ferguson, too, signed treaties with Kings of Amanting, Nkoranza and Abeasi, encls. 2, 3, 4 in Griffith to Ripon, G.C. Conf., 7 April 1894, C.O. 96/244. In April and May, Ferguson signed treaties with Bona, Dagarti and Mamprusi. Also in April and May he signed treaties with Gambaga, Bona and Wa. C.O. 96/247, G.C. Secret, encls. 1, 2, 3 in Griffith to Ripon, 12 July and 8 August 1894. On 2 July Ferguson completed a treaty with Mossi, 8 August with Chakosi, encls. 1 and 2 in G.C. Secret, 28 September 1894, C.O. 96/248. Finally he signed treaties with Gambaga to Salaga in the Neutral Zone, G.C. Secret, 11 October 1894. C.O. 96/248. Article 11 of these treaties was to the effect that the people concerned would grant commercial and political privileges to British subjects but would not extend the same to other people. Article 111 says that the people would not accept protection etc. from any other power. See C.O. 96/244, G.C. Conf., 6 April 1894.

5 C.O. 96/242, G.C. Conf., encl. 2 in Hodgson to Ripon, 11 January 1894

6 *Ibid.*, 29 January 1894, encl. 1

7 C.O. 96/238, G.C. Conf., sub-encl. in encl. 2 in Hodgson to Ripon, 14 November 1893

continued with the defeat of Banda. Probably because of the flight of the Boles at the approach of Ferguson, the Bandas, assisted by Asante, were defeated by the Mos, allies of Nkoranza.[1] Even the victory of Kabachi Wula, the Asante protege of Salaga, over his opponents and the flight of the panic-stricken Yegis before the savage fury of the conqueror[2] did not change the declining fortunes of Asante forces. So it was that Asante military efforts in the north were defeated.

Thus in a matter of a few months, driven by Asante activities, the British extended their influence to Akyem, Kwahu, the Brong Confederation and a host of other northern states, with which they entered treaty relations.

The third area into which the British suddenly moved was Asante itself. It was in 1888 that Cape Coast merchants first asked the Government to station a Resident in Kumasi to promote their commercial interests. Although they made out a strong case for this request,[3] Lord Knutsford, the Secretary of State, and Governor Griffith, still pursuing the slow 'divide and rule' method, ignored it.[4] But as soon as the later Asante activities began, the British changed their method of penetrating Asante, and decided to move in quickly and occupy the kingdom.

It was because of this change that in 1891 Governor Griffith sent Hull to Kumasi to invite Prempeh to come under British protection. The King refused.[5] In April 1894 the Gold Coast Government again requested Asante to accept a British Resident in Kumasi and sent Mr Vroom, as Secretary for Native Affairs. The impatient way in which he conducted this mission revealed the British desire to enter Asante as quickly as possible. Vroom even threatened to leave Kumasi when it was taking him too long to win the Asante round. The threat was obviously only meant to quicken the process of taking over Asante, for when it failed Vroom later changed his mind and stayed for further negotiations. He eventually left Kumasi, with the Asante problem still unsolved.[6]

Since the Asante intensified their pressure by sending an embassy to England, the British sent yet another mission to Kumasi in January 1895, only a few months after the previous one, this time comprising Vroom and Captain Stewart.[7] This mission also failed. But the British were now determined to occupy Asante as quickly as possible, and made feverish preparations. When, towards the end of 1895, the British heard that Asante was about to secure Samory's assistance to strengthen her resistance movement, they literally

1 C.O. 96/242, Tel. of 13 January 1894, Hodgson to Ripon

2 C.O. 96/243, G.C. Conf., sub-encl. 2 in encl. 1 in Hodgson to Ripon, 21 February 1894

3 C.5352, Griffith to Knutsford, 6 April 1888. The traders pointed out that great financial advantages would accrue to the Government as a result of establishing a Resident at Kumasi. 'We would point out,' they wrote, 'that any expense that may be incurred will be amply recouped to the Government by the increase in revenue to be derived from the increased import of British goods and the benefit to British manufacturers and traders.'

4 C.5352, C.O. to Chamber of Commerce, 12 July, 18 September 1888

5 C.O. 879/35, African (West) no. 415, Griffith to Knutsford, 3 June 1891

6 C.O. 96/245, G.C. Conf., Griffith to Ripon and encls. 8 and 9, May 1894

7 Claridge, p. 392

rushed into Asante with troops to effect the occupation of the Kingdom. On 14 November, Governor Maxwell heard through an Akyem trader, Yaw Baikun, coming from Asante, that Samory was already on his way to Kumasi's aid[1]; by the 18th Maxwell's preparations for an expedition were nearly completed.[2] By 20 January he had already arrested Prempeh.

The pretext for the arrest and removal of the Asantehene deceived no one. That Prempeh was unable to pay more than £2000 of the 1874 indemnity,[3] which the British themselves had stopped demanding, was surely no reason for removing him; the real reason was to make it impossible for him to coalesce with Samory.

From these examples we can conclude that Asante activities constituted the chief hindrance to the development of British political influence in that area, and caused the British Government to change from a policy of slow infiltration to the hurried acquisition of territories in the hinterland of the Gold Coast.

Asante made one more attempt to resist British demands. The aim of this rebellion, the Yaa Asantewa War, was to drive the British out of Asante. It was a continuation of, and as widespread as, the pre-occupation measures. Clearly it was a popular movement. Asante as a nation was never more opposed to British influence than in the last years of the century. The frequent references in Asante oral tradition[4] to their hatred of schools was no more than their hatred of the British, the spread of whose influence was, in the Asante mind, synonymous with the establishment of schools. The ease with which the revolt caught on was a proof of its popularity. In July 1899 the chiefs had begun to plan for the rebellion.[5] By the close of the year, Kumasi was ready. When on 28 March 1900 Governor Hodgson delivered his fatal message about Prempeh not returning and seizing the Golden Stool, at a public palaver of kings and chiefs at Kumasi,[6] the people began their rising within a week. The fact that some states refrained from fighting signifies little. Only Bekwai really opposed Kumasi; the other states would have fought against the British, had they not been prevented by circumstances beyond their control.[7] Those who fought against the British included Ejisu, Offinsu, Adansi, Nsutah and Kokofu.

Detailed accounts of the Yaa Asantewa War have been given by Biss,

---

1 C.O. 96/262 and encl., Maxwell to Chamberlain, G.C. Secret, 14 November 1895

2 *Ibid.*, 18 November 1895. At the same time, Maxwell wrote to Samory, asking him not to help Kumasi, in such a tone as would remind 'my friend the Almany Samory' of the religious differences between him, a Muslim, and the pagan court of Prempeh. *Ibid.*, 23 November 1895

3 C.O. 96/270, Tel. of 20 January 1896, Maxwell to Chamberlain

4 Asante oral tradition; informant, Nana Domfekyere. Asante oral tradition from such different sources as Ejisu, Kumasi and Juaben cites the Asante hatred of schools as one of the causes of the 1900 rebellion. Nana Domfekyere and Kwaku Owusu emphasised that the rebellion was in part an attempt by Asante to prevent the British building schools in Asante. By this they meant that they wanted to stop the spread of British influence in Asante.

5 *The Gold Coast Chronicle*, 29 July 1899

6 C.O. 96/359, G.C. Conf., encl. 1 in Hodgson to Chamberlain, 7 April 1900

7 These circumstances are explained below on p. 177.

Armitage and Montanaro, Lady Hodgson and Claridge,[1] on whom the following account is largely based. Only a brief outline of the campaign is given here, to show the determined stand of the Asante, even at this last moment.

When the Ejisus and the Kumasis attacked the Governor and the garrison in the Kumasi fort, the first problem of the British was to clear the villages around Kumasi of the enemy, so as to sustain food supplies from the plantations for those taking refuge in the fort. For this purpose Captain Middlemast arranged on 23 April that a force should proceed from the fort under Captain Marshall, Special Service Officer, to attack the villages. The rebels attacked the force, which lost five killed and fifty wounded and had to return to the fort. The rebels pressed on, and the British had to withdraw outposts they had placed at Bantama; subsequently the Hausa cantonments between the fort and Bantama had to be evacuated. The rebels on the Bantama side of the fort were so aggressive that only the Maxim gun kept them in check. About 2500 people rushed to seek shelter in the fort. There were then 6000 rebels besieging the fort, which was being defended by 200 Hausas. Soon the Hausa cantonments were destroyed by fire. The Kumasis had a strong stockade, and in an attempt by Captain Aplin to get the Hausas to storm this, he lost 2 killed and 133 wounded, including officers. By the end of April the fort was already suffering from shortage of food, which became acute in May. Large numbers died of hunger and the hygienic conditions degenerated. Early in June, the Kumasis built a new stockade one mile from Kumasi on the Cape Coast road, and their activities now harassed the garrison, which had been reduced to such straits that starvation seemed imminent.

A column including the Governor was compelled to leave the fort for the coast on 23 June to hazard death from rebel bullets in preference to death by starvation.[2] They reached Cape Coast on 14 July, helped by people like Kwesi Mensah, chief of Manso Nkwanta. Before they reached Nkwanta, the column had to fight its way through territory disputed by rebel forces. They had a rough time of it, particularly at Patasi and Terrabom. The detachment which was clearing the way for the column did not find it easy. First Captain Leggett who was in charge of the detachment fell, and his place was taken by Captain Marshall, who was also killed almost immediately.[3] Had not the column reached Nkwanta in time, complete disaster seemed certain. From Nkwanta the Governor and his party reached safety, for the entire division under Bekwai would not fight the British for reasons we shall soon discuss.[4]

The relief of Kumasi was not easy. While the Governor and his party were still in the fort, news of the rising spread far and wide, and this led to vigorous reaction on the part of the states all over the country. The right of passage between Kumasi and the coast, always important to Asante and the coastal

1 C. J. Biss, *The Relief of Kumasi*, London 1900; Armitage and Montanaro, *Ashanti Campaign, 1900*, London 1900; Lady Hodgson, *Siege of Kumasi*, London 1901

2 C.O. 96/360, G.C. Conf., Hodgson to Chamberlain, 14 July 1900

3 C.O. 96/361, G.C. Conf., Hodgson to Chamberlain, 24 July 1900

4 The route of the column led through Patasi and Manso Nkwanta where they entered friendly country. The chiefs and other individuals whom the Governor took with him from the garrison included the Kings of Mampon, Juaben, Aguna, Nkwanta, Nsutah; and those from Kumasi were Kobina Kokofu, Kwame Tua, Kofi Sencheri, Yaw Betekum and Yaw Awuah.

peoples, suddenly became even more so. It was the northern half of this route which now became the object of immediate contest, since whichever side controlled it would ultimately win the war. Bekwai occupied a key position on the route, and it was, therefore, unfortunate for the Asante that this state had defected.[1] The Bekwaihene himself was busy organising his division as well as sending information to the advancing British forces. In spite of this serious drawback, the Asante side did not despair. Adansi and Kokofu effected an alliance, and were determined to prevent the passage of British troops to Kumasi. The allies in general, and Adansi in particular, nursed grievances against Bekwai at this time, and this was bound to strengthen King Nkansa's resolution to oppose Bekwai and her British allies. It will be remembered that in 1886 Bekwai had defeated Adansi and had driven its inhabitants across the Prah. In time, the King and people of Adansi returned to their homes but their defeat had deprived them of the rich gold mines of Obuasi, which went to the conqueror. Adansi's defeat had been due to her disinclination to support the Asante side. But now that Bekwai, her conqueror, was ranged on the side of Asante's enemies, Adansi was automatically swept into the Asante camp by her determination to revenge the 1886 defeat. That it was the loss of the gold mines that worried King Nkansa and his people there could be no doubt.

When the news of the rising reached Bekwai and neighbourhood, the King of Bekwai was expected by the neighbouring states to provide protection for them all. Bekwai's responsibilities were even weightier on this occasion because she controlled all the gold mines in the entire region. As soon as the news of the rising was received in Ahuren, the gold miners there fled to the King of Bekwai for protection. It was significant, also, that two miners called Jones and Cookson were known to be in Bekwai at this time, and the fact that they were anxiously looking for British help from the coast is probably an indication that they realised that the Adansi–Kokofu alliance was against Bekwai, their patron, and against themselves. Adansi made her hostility against the Obuasi miners so apparent that they fled to the coast without orders.

On 20 May 1900, Captain Hall, in an attempt to break through to Kumasi, advanced with British troops from the Prah to Fomena and managed to get Kwaku Nkansah, King of Adanis, to make several promises, none of which he could, of course, carry out. At this point, Jones and Cookson, the two miners, came to Fomena from Bekwai with the news of the defection of the Kokofus. Although the British did not know it, this news was welcome to the Adansis, for it showed them that their agreements with the Kokofus were to be carried out.

The King of Bekwai did everything he could to overcome the Adansi–Kokofu alliance. He invited Captain Hall to advance north and occupy Esumeja between Bekwai and Kokofu so as to keep Kokofu's movements under surveillance. On the 23rd the Bekwais themselves drove a small detachment of Asante from Abodum and burned it. But all these efforts on the part of the British and the Bekwais did not prevent the Asante side from inflicting some serious defeats on the British troops. The two miners, Jones and Cookson, whom Captain Hall had left in Fomena to await the arrival of Captain Slater and some Hausas, were returning to Bekwai on the 24th, when they were attacked suddenly. With great difficulty the two Europeans managed to get to

1 For a discussion of the defection of Bekwai, see pp. 179-80

Kwisa to report to Captain Slater what had happened. Captain Slater set out for Fomena to find out why the attack had been made, and when two hours from Kwisa was heavily attacked from all sides. Slater and several men fell at the first volley, and some of the Hausas fled to the coast. In Esumeja Captain Hall did not know of the defection of the Adansis and sent two different parties of carriers to Prahsu to bring up stores and ammunition from there. These, too, were attacked near Dompoasi, with heavy casualties. By the stiff resistance of Kokofu and Adansi, therefore, the British troops found Kumasi completely cut off, and it was not even certain whether they would be able to relieve the fort before its resistance collapsed.[1]

The British were by now expecting reinforcements from different parts of Africa, and Colonel Willocks, the Commandant of the war, also landed at Cape Coast. The Government troops therefore gathered fresh morale and decided to break through the Adansi–Kokofu cordon, which had for so long prevented them from reaching Kumasi. But it was not so easy.

On 2 June Colonel Carter was trying to reach Captain Hall at Bekwai and Esumeja, but he was attacked and lost four men killed and seven wounded. Four days later, when he again tried to advance and was leaving Kwisa for Bekwai, Colonel Carter was again ambushed and forced to retire with even heavier losses. Before the action began, the Adansi were so well hidden that not until heavy fire pounded into the British column near Dompoasi did they realise the nearness of the Adansi. Apart from its suddenness, the Adansi attack was so well organised and persistent that the British fire from the seven-pounder and Maxim was completely without effect. The Adansi covered a long stretch of the path, thus making it an effective trap, for the deeper the British column tried to go to escape punishment the greater that punishment became, and by the time they realised this, they had already gone deep enough into the trap to make retreat even more disastrous. Adansi fire thus brought down officers and men all along the line. The gun's crew were nearly all shot down, so that only Lieutenant Edwards was left to work it until he himself fell. Lieutenant O'Malley, working the Maxim, was shot through the side, and soon afterwards, the gun itself was put out of action by a bullet destroying the water-jacket. Captain Roupell was shot through both wrists, and Colonel Carter over the left eye; he ordered a retreat, but before this could be carried out and the column return to Kwisa, further damage was done. The guns of the British were now out of action, their ammunition was running out, their dead and wounded were strewn along the path. Colonels Carter and Wilkinson, Captain Roupell, Lieutenants Edwards and O'Malley, Surgeon-Captain Fletcher, Colour-Sergeant Mackenzie and eighty-six men had been wounded, many fatally, and others were killed; 40,000 rounds of ammunition had been expended. It was a terrible disaster for the British.[2]

When Colonel Willocks, still on the coast, heard the news he telegraphed the Secretary of State for 800 more troops and Special Service officers and sent urgent messages, to Colonel Carter to remain at Kwisa, and to Captain Hall in Bekwai asking him to send down a force to meet Carter and assist him north. This gave the Asante side another opportunity to inflict a severe defeat on the British. When on 16 June Captain Wilson, Royal Irish Fusiliers, with 112 men

1 Claridge, *A History of the Gold Coast and Ashanti*, Vol. II, pp. 509–19

2 *Ibid.*, pp. 513–19

of the Nupe Company, going down from Bekwai to Kwisa, reached the fateful stretch near Dompoasi, the Adansi opened fire once more. As before, the Adansi occupied the bush for a long distance along the road; as before, the marchers fell dead or mortally wounded, all along the road. Captain Wilson himself was one of them, and it was with great difficulty that his men secured his body. Others had to be abandoned, and these included six killed and others fatally wounded. When they reached Kwisa, Colonel Carter had abandoned it, contrary to orders, and the difficulties of the column therefore increased until they reached Fumsu. The whole affair must now be considered as an ignominious retreat, and it can be seen that, had Bekwai supported the Asante side, the bravery and fighting acumen of that side would have changed the ultimate course of events.

Disconcerted by the firm stand of the Adansis, the British decided that their only hope of effectively dealing with the village of Dompoasi, the scene of unbeaten Adansi resistance, was to attack at night and in a downpour, so as to take their opponents by surprise. It was only when Colonel Burroughs resorted to this method that he was able to take the village.[1]

But having done that, he realised that only half the work was accomplished. For it was not only the Adansis but also the Kokofus who were determined to prevent the British from relieving Kumasi. The Kokofu had all this time been very busy, threatening the flank of any force advancing by the main road. Colonel Burroughs therefore decided to take Kokofu, and with 650 men, one 75-millimetre gun and five Maxims and reserves, he advanced to the attack. Half a mile to Kokofu, the Asante opened a tremendous fire on the British troops, and in spite of the guns they held their ground. Even in retiring under a storm of lead from the Maxims, the Kokofu Asante employed admirable skill and effected a most orderly retreat. Any other but an Asante army would have fled in the wildest terror in face of such tremendous fire from the huge guns. The British realised that their opponents were not strangers to warfare. The admirable thing about the Asante on this occasion was that while they were retiring they were still fighting with full strength; as one company was at the point of withdrawing, another quickly engaged the enemy. British efforts to storm the place failed, and worse still the British companies, on account of the thick forest, fired into each other. All the Asante army was then enveloping the Government troops, who were by now falling very fast. By the time Colonel Burroughs ordered the retreat, the third British disaster in two months was inflicted with a heavy casualty list.[2]

This success of the Asante side had several causes. The time-tested methods of forest warfare which Asante had evolved since the eighteenth century now stood them in good stead. The orderly retreat, which avoided a break in action against the enemy, was a well-tried response to Maxims etc. which the Asante knew they could never possess. Skill was the Asante answer to the better equipment of the enemy. Now and again it was the right answer. During the Kokofu action, for instance, Asante skill overshadowed British better equipment. Determination, too, was a quality of Asante forces, as the series of victories won by the Adansi–Kokofu allies over British forces demonstrated.

These victories also testified to another quality of the Asante. Adaptation and reforms, as we have seen in the Introduction, were important in the

1 *Ibid.*, p. 521   2 *Ibid.*, pp. 522–3

development of Asante. Asante and, for that matter, other African institutions were so capable of adaptations that one cannot help admiring the genius of their founders.

Numerous reforms had already been effected in the Asante army since the time of Osei Tutu, and some of these we have already enumerated. In 1900 there was another innovation. This was the stockade. The idea seems to have occurred to the Asante military authorities when, during the 1895 expedition into their country, the British troops built Laagers at their stopping places. The stockade served almost the same purpose. To build it, the Asante troops first cut a path to the spot which must be hidden from the view of the enemy, but within gun-range of its position. This means that, in the majority of cases, the stockades had to be built near a path and parallel to it. The tree trunks which had been cut down in the clearing of the path were tied together in two rows six feet high and six apart. The space between the two rows was then filled up with timber, stones, earth, etc. leaving numerous loopholes. Stockades were known to be over one-quarter mile long. As the enemy passed, the Asante soldiers kept up continuous fire through the loopholes, without being seen or hit when the fire was returned. A trench immediately behind the stockade served as a use-shelter to which the soldiers could retire before loading.[1] The Adansi and Kokofu successes, already described, were largely due to the use of stockades, which were yet another example of modernisation in the Asante fighting forces. Later the use of stockades again caused great discomfiture to the British troops, and it was quite clear that but for extenuating circumstances, to which we shall soon refer, ultimate success would have smiled on the Asante army.

Meanwhile, by the end of June, the British side felt that unless they could break through quickly the garrison would certainly fall, hence the decision now to make a dash for Kumasi whatever the danger. So Colonel Willocks and headquarters staff left Prasu on 1 July for Bekwai. On the way they heard of the escape of Governor Hodgson, who was then making for the coast with his party. Willocks and his troops were able to prepare for the breakthrough in friendly Bekwai, and it was from here that, still harassed by Asante troops but helped by Peki, another Bekwai directed state, the relief force reached Kumasi on 15 July, the very day that the garrison's ration was completely exhausted.

After the relief of Kumasi, the second part of the campaign began, and it was Colonel Willock's plan to clear the country to the south of Kumasi so as to establish easy communication with the coast for supplies and reinforcement. The first move was an attack on the hitherto unbeaten Kokofu with 75-milli-metre guns and seven-pounders and Maxims, and eventually Kokofu resistance collapsed. In spite of their past several engagements with the enemy, the Adansi still had enough resources and energy left to threaten the British who therefore had to attack once more. As usual the Adansi put up a powerful resistance. They often made inroads into the ranks of the enemy and but for the volley of lead from the Maxims coupled with the fact that they had by now over-strained their resources, the Adansi would have won the day. But this time they had to give in.

Meanwhile the Asante forces around Kumasi had built numerous stockades behind which they were firmly entrenched, awaiting the enemy should they

1 *Ibid.*, pp. 516–17

venture out of Kumasi. Thus the Asante stockade on the Intimide road made a bold stand against a column of three companies of the West African Frontier Force under Major Melliss with a 75-millimetre gun. A fierce hand-to-hand fight ensued, when Asante troops defied the gunfire. Only when they were outnumbered did the Asante flee. Another stockade on the Kintampo road resisted the enemy with similar bravery. Other stockades were also preparing to dispute their position when Colonel Burroughs, who was in charge of the operations around Kumasi, suddenly changed his tactics and began taking stockades by night, a measure he considered the only possible means of clearing the southern road sufficiently to return to Bekwai as ordered by Colonel Willocks. The friendship of Peki towards the Government helped their operations; without it they would have found it more difficult to establish communication between Bekwai and Kumasi.

There were yet other strongholds of the Asante army, and it became clear to the British that unless they could destroy these strongholds the Asante would march to take Kumasi. The Ejisu stronghold appeared to be impregnable and, as the British troops advanced on it, the Ejisus put up a gallant defence. Although they retreated finally before the superior fire of the British, they completely crushed, at Bomkra, the next British column led by Captain Benson. This victory of the Ejisus occurred in circumstances which need some explanation. One of the British officers, Captain Benson, had succeeded by the middle of August in collecting some 3000 Akyem levies; with these he advanced later on Ejisu. Claridge describes these levies as a disorderly and indisciplined crowd.[1] Even more serious was the accusation that the Akyem were 'as arrant cowards now as they had been when serving under Captain Butler in 1874'. We have seen in Chapter 2 that there was a reason for Akyem behaviour in 1874, namely a non-aggression pact with Juaben; and although they allowed themselves to be recruited for the war merely because of the remuneration, they knew that they would never fight. Captain Butler and other officers who did not know this called them cowards. A similar process occurred in 1900.

We have also seen earlier in this chapter,[2] that Prempeh had, through the diplomatic branch of his government, established communication with King Amoako Attah II of Kibi, Eastern Akyem. We have seen that when communication was thus established in 1893 between Asante and Akyem, secret negotiations were carried out between the two parties. These touched upon many things, including the cooperation of Amoako Attah, or at least his neutrality in Anglo–Asante conflicts. So when in 1900 Captain Benson recruited these Akyem as levies to fight against Asante, he was merely restaging the 1874 drama in circumstances which could not have failed to lead to the disaster of Ejisu. It must have been the plan of the Akyem to remain in service for as long as there was no conflict with Asante troops, and by this means collect as much as possible of the promised pay. At the first sign of any engagement they would all disappear, to avoid having to fight the Asante who were their allies. King Amoako Attah was among them, and he and his chief war Captain were among the first to go. This was probably to be the signal for a mass retreat. The Ejisu force pressed on at this point and the British officers found that they had only a few of their supporters left at this critical moment. They had lost a great deal of ammunition when the Akyem carriers threw down their loads before disap-

1 Claridge, p. 550   2 See p. 154

pearing from the field. Captain Benson was therefore forced to retire to avoid further punishment from the Ejisu force. As soon as he reached Odumase he committed suicide, so heavy was the defeat and so great his despair.

The Ejisu resistance had been one of the most determined in the entire military history of Asante. The Queen Mother, Yaa Asantewa herself, was, of course, the leading spirit in the rising and she contributed a great deal to the victory. Because of the firm resistance of Asante forces, Colonel Burroughs suddenly changed his tactics and began taking stockades by night. The Asante realised that their only answer to the precision guns of the British was now rendered ineffective. Without stockades Asante would be at a terrible disadvantage. Yaa Asantewa therefore called all the chiefs taking part in the campaign together in a council of war to consider what should be done. No effective answer was found. Two months later, in September, in spite of their difficulties, the Asante were still determined to pursue the war. Yaa Asantewa was still in the field supported by Kofi Kofia, now the Captain-General of the war, Nkansa, Nantwi, Kwesi Bedu and Kobina Cherri. Asante stockades and strongholds still existed in the direction of Kintampo, Offinsu, and Berekum. Indeed the force under Kofi Kofia on the Berekum road, consisting of the hitherto unbeaten Achimas, was so formidable that Sir James Willocks decided to lead a column there himself. Again in spite of the huge guns and Maxims of the enemy, the Asante gave in only after a grim hand-to-hand struggle.[1]

By October Asante ammunition was giving out and it became impossible for them to make any further stand against the enemy. The British now had many advantages. They had reinforcements and supplies from the coast. They had recruited men and officers from all over the continent – including the Central African Regiment, Sikhs, local levies, Lagos troops, Sierra Leone troops and the W.A.F.F. from Northern Nigeria. The leaders of the rebellion were compelled by these adverse circumstances to surrender to the enemy.

There were several reasons for the failure of the rebellion. These include the detention of Asante leaders by the British in the Kumasi fort during the rebellion, the lack of ammunition and the defection of Bekwai.

When the rebellion began the great chiefs were detained in Kumasi fort by Governor Hodgson. Those arrested and detained in the fort were the Kings of Juaben, Kumawu, Owusu Sekyere (later King of Mampon),[2] Asibe, King of Kokofu, Opoku Mensah, the Gyasehene.[3] There was some doubt whether these people were detained or whether they preferred to stay in the fort, but this doubt arose simply because Governor Hodgson tried to justify his action by saying that the detainees were loyal to the Government, implying that they remained in the fort at will.[4] Asante oral tradition rejects this view,[5] and Hodgson's own later statements on the subject contradict the earlier ones. He said that he had to keep them in the fort 'in order to prevent their arming their tribes which they would assuredly do if they returned'. He had to threaten

1 Claridge, pp. 555–6

2 C.O. 96/359, G.C. Conf., Hodgson to Chamberlain, 7 April 1900

3 Kumasi tradition; informant, Kwaku Owusu

4 C.O. 96/359, G.C. Conf., Hodgson to Chamberlain, 11 April 1900

5 Kumasi tradition; informant, Nana Kwaku Owusu

them that, if they disobeyed, they 'would be dealt with accordingly when the time came'.[1] Indeed it was said that it was Kwame Tuah, the Asante cook in the fort, who, because of his attachment to the British, advised the Governor not to allow the kings, who had come for discussions with His Excellency, to return, warning that if they did they would certainly fight the British.[2] Thus even though the detainees strove hard to leave, as evidence by their letter to the Governor – '. . . we beg to ask permission from His Excellency and go back to our countries',[3] – Hodgson paid no heed.

Normally the great kings and chiefs gave their people leadership during crises. In their absence the Asante decided to canvas for the war under Yaa Asantewa's name, because, so tradition says, they thought the British would not arrest her like the others.[4] It is further said that the actual organisation of the rebel forces was entrusted to Captain Boadu of the Ejisu division. He was supported by other captains within the Gyaase division, including Adu Kofi, Anantahene, Affrifah, Asaman Kwame.[5] All these were below the status of the great Amantoo kings who normally organised such wars, and although they did their best to resist the British, the Asante war effort did not measure up to its former standard. Some states did not fight because their leaders were away in the hands of the British. Definitely therefore the detention of Asante leaders in the fort was an important factor in the defeat of Asante.

The second reason for the defeat of Asante was the lack of firearms. The fighting forces, as we have seen in Chapter 4, had been reorganised.[6] There is nothing to suggest that Asante lost its fighting spirit. Of arms and munitions of war, however, it cannot be said that Asante had as much as was desirable in 1900. There have been suggestions that during the Anglo–Asante conflict the British placed restrictions on arms imports into Asante and that this was the way in which Britain weakened her opponent. There is no doubt that frequently Asante had to resort to Grand Bassam and Assinie in order to get arms. Before 1894, but especially around this date, Asante traders were frequently interfered with not only by turbulent civilians, but also by British forces, and the Asantehene frequently complained about this to the British authorities.[7] All this must mean that Asante found it increasingly difficult to get arms. In any case the Brussels Act of 1890, which charged European powers interested in African colonisation to place embargoes on the importation of firearms into the interior of Africa, must be presumed to have affected Asante and other interior districts.

Oral tradition is not definite on the subject. For, while Kona tradition refers to the fact that during the time of the rebellion some of the great chiefs declined

1 C.O. 96/359, G.C. Conf., Hodgson to Chamberlain, 11 April 1900

2 Juaben and Kumasi traditions

3 C.O. 96/359, G.C. Conf., encl. 1 in Hodgson to Chamberlain, 11 April 1900

4 Kumasi tradition; informant, Kwaku Owusu

5 Other captains included Asema, Captain of the Atwema Group and Amasie.

6 See p. 99

7 C.O. 96/234, G.C. Conf., Hodgson to Ripon, 12 February 1894; C.O. 96/244, G.C. Conf., Hodgson to Ripon, 5 March 1894

to fight because of the lack of sufficient firearms, Kumasi and Juaben traditions indicate that Asante had enough arms to fight.[1] But perhaps what really mattered in 1900 was not so much the quantity of weapons as the quality. In 1894 two keen observers of the interior, Ferguson and Scott, both remarked that Asante did not have effective arms.[2] It is true that a portion of the Asante army was by 1894 armed with Sniders,[3] but according to Scott's estimate it appears that the majority still had the old Dane Guns of 1874.[4] Ferguson reported that when he went over the Asante–Nkoranza battlefield in February 1894 he could not see any traces of Snider cartridge but only slugs.[5] Such weapons would be quite ineffective in 1900 in face of the precision guns of the British troops. We cannot therefore wholly dismiss the possibility of lack of effective weapons damping the spirits of the Asante, who were aware that the British possessed precision guns.

The third reason for the defeat of Asante was the surprising defection of Bekwai, which up to the reign of Abbebresseh had been extremely anti-British, and, as already discussed in Chapter 4, led Asante during the interregnum against the 'allies' of the Gold Coast Government. There were several reasons for this. In 1891 Prempeh was anxious to prevent treachery in face of the British challenge in Asante. But the King's efforts in this direction offended the Bekwaihene, Kwaku Sei, in 1891 and his displeasure came to influence official policy at the Bekwai court ever afterwards. It all began with a meeting at Kumasi in that year to which both the Amantoo and the Amansin were invited. The chief question discussed was the Gold Coast Government's proposal that the Asante should allow the opening of schools in their country. It was at this meeting that the Bekwaihene got up and spoke in favour of the proposal, to the great surprise of all. Says Bekwai tradition, 'Bekwai offended the Asantehene by saying this and he was asked to "drink fetish" to the effect that he would not mention the coming of schools to the country again'. At the same time Bantama took a sword and swore an oath that he would destroy the town of any chief who said he would serve the British Government. Asafu Boakye, the Asafuhene, took the same oath and all the others swore an oath to the same effect. This clearly amounted to a severe censure of Bekwai's conduct 'so that when Bekwai had to drink fetish he did so as though "he was taking salt" (that is as though it was very pleasant) although it was against his wish'. In effect, the whole meeting turned into an assembly critical of the Bekwaihene and he and his courtiers never forgot the bitter experience of being isolated and criticised at the Great Council of Asante. Bekwai defected. The Bekwais themselves said later that it was this incident that 'destroyed' Asante, and that Asante would have otherwise been independent.[6]

---

1 Kona and Kumasi traditions; informants, Kofi Mensah and Kwaku Owusu.

2 C.O. 96/245, G.C. Conf., Griffith to Ripon, 22 May 1894

3 As early as 1879 the arming of the Asante fighting forces with Sniders on a large scale was begun.

4 C.O. 96/245, G.C. Conf., Griffith to Ripon, 22 May 1894

5 C.O. 96/244, G.C. Conf., sub-encl. to encl. 1, 21 February 1894

6 L. W. Judd, D.C., 'Ancient History of Bekwai Division from narrative of Linguist Kobina Busumuru and Edu Kojo the blind ex-Krontihene in the presence of Omanhin Kofi Buakye and various Elders', 4 June 1928, Bekwai D.R.B.

We can better understand what the Bekwais meant if we consider their position in Asante. It must be noted that normally the defection of one town, in this case Bekwai, would not have made much difference to Asante resistance to British penetration. But as we have already seen, Bekwai had grown into an important state. This change took place as follows: During the Civil War, Bekwai fought for Prempeh against Achereboanda; after the war, Prempeh rewarded them by placing Ahuren and its dependencies under the Bekwaihene. From about 1890, therefore, Bekwai gained a vast territory made up of Ahuren, Asiase, Mpento, Anaaho, Kusiase, Ampeha, Mroto, Amanfrom, Bosoma, Beposo, Dompa, Wawase, Wiaso, Dagyaaso, Ataaso, Timiabo, Bogyaa, Tibensani, Duamen, Bisiase, Kyereso, Odumasi, Dumkura, Kotoyiem and Nsoamoa.[1] Thus Bekwai came to head the entire division known as Amansie (not to be confused with Amansin, the term for provincial Asante). The states in the Amansie division had in the past owed allegiance to Kokofu, Ahuren or Bekwai, but now they all looked to Bekwai for political direction. Consequently Bekwai now controlled the whole of the southern approach to Kumasi.

It was unfortunate for Asante, therefore, that Bekwai should at this juncture defect and, what was worse, go over to the British side.[2] When the Bekwais learnt that the Government was sending another expedition into Kumasi (1895), they sent messengers to meet the expedition, accepted the British flag and put themselves under the Government. When in 1900 the rebellion began, Bekwai being in control of the southern approach to Kumasi made it relatively easy for the British to break through the Kokofu–Adansi resistance and to relieve Kumasi. Bekwai remained throughout the campaign an important base from which the British operated, otherwise British forces could not have arrived in Kumasi in time to relieve the garrison, which would have surrendered to Asante. It was Bekwai's control of the Amansie division and her conduct in siding with the British which proved to be the downfall of Asante. Thus Asante, like other states in Africa, succumbed to the militarily superior might of Europe.

The failure of this final resistance of Asante led to the consolidation of British power over Asante, which became a colony under the direct supervision of a Chief Commissioner, who was responsible to the Governor of the Gold Coast.

Conclusion

It has been shown that there were two types of activities in the Gold Coast in the second half of the nineteenth century. The first consisted of attempts by the Gold Coast people to preserve their ancient traditions, liberties, laws, customs and institutions and gave rise to strong protests, as was testified by foreign observers who noted the existence of African ideas 'equally ancient

---

1 Ahuren tradition; informant, Ohene Ata Gyamfi

2 In 1895 Bekwai's alliance with the Government began in earnest, when the Governor requested H. Vroom, D.C. for Tarkwa Mines to send Wilson, who signed himself as manager of the Obuasi Mines, to get the Bekwais in line with British desires. The Bekwais agreed to give the Government mining concessions, so that they could set up the Obuasi Mining Company, for monetary compensation. Bekwai's acceptance of British overtures must have been partly due to the money, but more important was the fact that Bekwai had already defected from the Asante cause. So it was easier for the Bekwaihene to ally with the British.

and deep-rooted, which pervade the native mind '.[1] It was this determination of the people to preserve their institutions that caused Sir Arthur Kennedy, a man of unrivalled West Coast experience, to refer to the Gold Coast as 'a peculiar people'.[2]

Places where such protests occurred included Anlo, Fante, Wassa and Akwapem. In these places, three main causes of protest could be distinguished: questions of independence, the preservation of customs and institutions, and economic concerns.

In Anlo and Fante, questions of independence came to the fore. The Anlo (Somme) told the British not to meddle with their independence. The Fante Confederacy fought for internal self-government. In Wassa we have a good example of a state intent on preserving its ancient liberties and institutions. Here the people pointed out that the placing of a new king on the stool had been the right of the people from time immemorial, and so the British must stop trying to usurp this right from the people of Wassa. Protests over the land question were also directed against foreign interference in the customs and institutions based on land, the possession of which had become sacrosanct. Again in Anlo and other coastal states, we have examples of the refusal of the Gold Coast people to tolerate British attempts to direct their economic habits and impose taxes on them. In Anlo the people opposed customs dues. In Accra and Cape Coast, the inhabitants protested against the payment of direct taxes. Such activities, directed against the British, were caused by popular and national grievances, and protonationalist in outlook.

The second type occurred largely over local issues, such as dynastic and economic disputes, in which the British interfered on behalf of one side, hoping to exercise political influence in the state. One side, therefore, disliked the British, the other supported them. We have examples of this in Asante, Akyem and Krepi. In each case, we have noted the existence of two opposing sides during the fracas.

The organisation of both types of activities took several forms. Chiefs and their peoples, societies and associations sent petitions or delegations to the Gold Coast Government or to officials in the U.K. Protest marches, demonstrations, and very often armed attacks were among the methods of protest.

These activities were strong enough to affect British policy, sometimes in its formulation, sometimes in its execution.

Protests in Fante, in Wassa, and over the Lands Bills affected the formulation of British policy. The Fante Confederacy forced Britain to change her territorial policy, and instead of retrenchment, to embark on territorial acquisition. In Wassa Britain was forced to abandon the policy of installing and maintaining a new king, yielding to the arguments of the people that these ancient rights belonged to them. Because of the protests against the successive Lands Bills, Britain had to amend her policy several times till finally she abandoned altogether the policy of controlling land in the Gold Coast.

In Anlo the British were compelled by protests to execute their policy with haste, force and unusual cruelty. Force, subtlety and threats were also resorted to in the implementation of their policy in relation to taxation, labour and representation. British policy in Krepi and Akyem was similarly implemented.

1 Sarbah, *Fanti Customary Laws*, pp. 32–3

2 Adm. 1/462, no. 80, Kennedy to Kimberley, 3 August 1870

In Asante, its execution up to about 1890 was delayed by local politics, but thereafter, because Asante activities threatened to keep the British perpetually from the interior, they had the effect of quickening the pace of penetration into Asante and the interior.

In the second half of the nineteenth century, therefore, there was persistent political activity, including protest, on the Gold Coast, which today is Ghana. This political activity affected British policy in various ways. The old notion that the formulation and execution of British Gold Coast policy at this time depended only on Downing Street and the 'European scramble' respectively needs to be drastically modified. The activities of Africans constituted an important factor in both the formulation and execution of that policy.

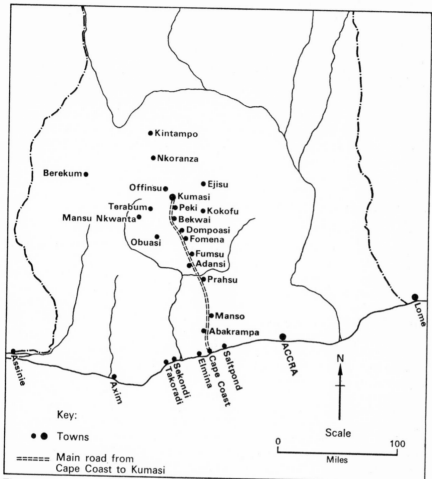

Key:

● ● Towns

====== Main road from
Cape Coast to Kumasi

Scale

0   100

Miles

N

The setting of the Asante rebellion 1900-1901

Extracts from *The Gold Coast Aborigines*

1. Vol. I, no. 24, C.C.C., 11 June 1898

The Gold Coast people

'. . . It is because we recognise and appreciate "the depth of the national feeling in matters affecting ancestral interest" which exists with the people of the Gold Coast and the deep-rooted race instincts and institutions which enable them to hold their native customs and institutions in honourable esteem and observance that induced us to advert to a manifestation which was so much out of accord with the traditions of the people. The Gold Coast native, notwithstanding the force of foreign influence which for centuries has been brought to bear upon him, has never exhibited the moral weakness to despise and discard his native customs and manners. On the contrary, he has upheld these and endeavoured to improve them where improvement was possible; and as a result there is to be found on the Gold Coast a stand of genuine native culture and refinement. . . . It was therefore with the feeling that the excellent ideal of improved native life furnished by the native of the Gold Coast stood the risk of being debased by a malicious proclivity engendered by foreign influence, which tempted us to raise a cry of warning. Overwhelmed by a force of foreign influence which would engulf and extinguish all that is natural with him, the African has need to be wary lest unwittingly he be made to share the fate of the New Zealanders and Maoris. And the Gold Coast people who have shown that they possess the strongest power both of resistance and discrimination should see to it that their prestige does not suffer from the exigency of the stress which is now being brought to bear. The African loses everything by becoming Europeanised while he gains everything by remaining African; it is to his interest then that he should not attempt to change his skin. . . .'

2. Vol. I, no. 36, C.C.C., 3 September 1898

The Gold Coast

'. . . Sir William Griffith in December 1890 caused a circular letter to be addressed to the Kings and Chiefs of the Protectorate in which he informed them . . . Her Majesty did not intend interfering with them or their country. Four years after this, this very Governor propsed to pass a Lands Bill, under which all the Lands in the colony were to be vested in the Queen, and certain of the Natives – the offspring of the black and white – were to be deprived of their rights in any such lands or of holding such property. This measure aroused the feelings of the people to the highest pitch, and protests from all quarters were sent in against it; and as a result that Bill was withdrawn.

'In 1896 the late Sir William Maxwell, then Governor, brought in a fresh Lands Bill, under which the Natives felt they would have been little more than settlers upon their own lands. The opposition was even fiercer than to the previous measure. Some of the chiefs obtained permission to be represented by counsel before the Legislative Council, to urge such objection as they had to the Bill, yet, in spite of all these, the late Governor had it in view to pass the Bill, and this determined the people to dispatch a deputation to the Colonial Office to put before Mr Chamberlain their reason for opposing the passing of the Bill in such a form. . . .'

Contemporary sources

1 GOVERNMENT RECORDS

Public Records Office, London
 (i) C.O. 96 Series: 1871   C.O. 96/89
                      1875–80   C.O. 96/115–33
                      1881–85   C.O. 96/134–67
                      1886–90   C.O. 96/172–213
                      1891–95   C.O. 96/215–63
                      1896–1901 C.O. 96/270–362
 (ii) C.O. 402/12
 (iii) F.O. 37/479 and F.O. 37/500

Confidential Prints
List of Papers printed for the use of C.O. African Series:
African (West) nos 75–8   C.O. 879/7–9
               nos 232–354   C.O. 879/18–28
               no. 384   C.O. 879/31
               nos 406–15   C.O. 879/34–5
               no. 531   C.O. 879/49
               no. 578   C.O. 879/57

Parliamentary Papers
Accounts, Bills, Papers, etc. printed by order of the House of Commons and Papers presented to both Houses of Parliament by command of Her Majesty
 (i) Further Correspondence respecting the Ashantee Invasion, London, March 1874:
    Vol. XLVI no. 1 (C.890) p. 1
               no. 2 (C.891) p. 254
               no. 3 (C.892) p. 483
               no. 4 (C.893) p. 755
               no. 5 (C.894) p. 831
 (ii) Dispatch from Sir G. Wolseley:
               no. 6 (C.907)   p. 905
               no. 7 (C.921)   p. 921
               no. 8 (C.922)   p. 943
               no. 9 (C.1006) p. 1045

(iii) Further Correspondence respecting the Affairs of the Gold Coast:

Vol. XLVIII	(C.3687)	July 1883	p. 453
Vol. LV	(C.4477)	July 1885	p. 579
Vol. XLVII	(C.4906)	September 1886	p. 233
Vol. LXXV	(C.5357)	April 1888	p. 109
Vol. LXXV	(C.5615)	December 1888	p. 203

Parliamentary Debates

The Parliamentary Debates of 18 March 1901: Vol. XCI, 1901 (15 March to 27 March 1901), p. 339

Ghana National Archives, Accra

  (i) Adm. 1/687, 1866–69, from the Gold Coast to Sierra Leone
 (ii) Adm. 1/461, 1866–69, from Sierra Leone to Colonial Office
(iii) Adm. 1/462, 1870–72, from Sierra Leone to Colonial Office

2 PRIVATE PAPERS (as classified in Ghana National Archives)

SC 5/9, 53, 55, 56, 59	Vroom Family Papers
SC 2/53, 45, 78	Bannerman Papers
SC 1/9, 13	Blankson Papers
SC 3/5, 10	Gold Coast Historical Society Papers
	Ghartey Papers

3 DISTRICT RECORD BOOKS

These were records kept by the early District Commissioners. Those cited here can still be found in the former District Offices, although other records in the series have now been removed to the Ghana National Archives in Accra. The years written against each District indicate the relevant Volume.

Obuasi District Record Book, 1928–51, kept in D.C.'s Office, Obuasi
Birim District Record Book, 1925–53, kept in D.C.'s Office, Oda
Bekwai District Record Book, 1925–53, kept in D.C.'s Office, Bekwai

4 FURLEY COLLECTIONS (University of Ghana, Balme Library)

 (i) K.V.G. 727, 1868–69
    K.V.G. 728⎫
    K.V.G. 729⎬ 1869–71
    K.V.G. 730⎭
(ii) BZ/3002, 1870
    BZ/B79, 1870–72

5 NEWSPAPERS AND JOURNALS

The Gold Coast Chronicle, Accra
The Gold Coast Independent, Accra
The Gold Coast Echo, Cape Coast
The Gold Coast Aborigines, Cape Coast

The West African Gazette, Accra
The Gold Coast Free Press, Accra
The Gold Coast Methodist Times, Cape Coast
The Gold Coast People, Cape Coast
The Gold Coast Times, Cape Coast
The African Times
The Western Echo
The Daily Telegraph
Journal of the African Society, Vol. III, 1908
L'Explorateur, Vol. III, Paris 1876
Blue Book 1883, (C.3687) no. 113
Salaga Papers, collected by Marian Johnson (formerly Librarian, I.A.S.) Legon 1965
Report on Mission to Atabubu by Ferguson, London 1891

6 BOOKS

ANAMAN, J. B. *The Gold Coast Guide*, London 1902
ARMITAGE, C. H. and MONTANARO, A. F. *Ashanti Campaign, 1900*, London 1901
BADEN-POWELL, R. S. S. *The Downfall of Prempeh*, London 1898
BEECHAM, J. *Ashantee and the Gold Coast*, London 1841
BINGER, L. G. *From the Niger to the Gulf of Guinea*, London 1892
BISS, C. J. *The Relief of Kumasi*, London 1901
BOSMAN, W. *A New and Accurate Description of the Coast of Guinea*, London 1705
BOWDICH, T. E. *A Mission from Cape Coast Castle to Ashantee*, London 1819
BOYLE, F. *Through Fanteeland to Coomassie*, London 1874
BRACKENBURY, H. *A Narrative of the Ashanti War*, 2 Vols, London 1874
BUTLER, W. F. *Akim-Foo*, London 1875
CASELY-HAYFORD, J. E. *Gold Coast Native Institutions*, London 1903
CRUICKSHANK, B. *Eighteen Years on the Gold Coast of Africa*, London 1853; references are to the 1966 edition
DUPUIS, J. *Journal of a Residence in Ashantee*, London 1824
ELLIS, A. B. *A History of the Gold Coast of West Africa*, London 1893
—— *The Ewe-Speaking People of the Gold Coast*, London 1881
—— *The Tshi-Speaking People of the Gold Coast*, London 1887
HAY, CAPTAIN J. D. *Ashanti and the Gold Coast*, London 1874
HODGSON, LADY *Siege of Kumasi*, London 1901
HORTON, J. A. B. *Letters on the Political Condition of the Gold Coast*, London 1870
—— *West African Countries and Peoples*, London 1868
HUTTON, W. *A Voyage to Africa*, London 1821
KEMP, D. *Nine Years on the Gold Coast*, London 1898
KLOSE, H. *Togo unter Deutscher Flagge: Reisebilder und Betrachtungen*, Berlin 1899
MACDONALD, G. *The Gold Coast, Past and Present*, London 1898
MEREDITH, H. *An Account of the Gold Coast of Africa*, London 1812
MOREL, B. D. *Affairs of West Africa*, London 1902

MULLER, G. *Geschiechte der Ewe Mission*, Bremen 1904

RAMSEYER, F. *Eine Reise im Norden von Asante und im Osten von Volta*, Gesellschaft für Thuringen zu Jena, Mitteilungen Bd. IV, 1886

RAMSEYER, F. and KUHNE, J. *Four Years in Ashantee*, London 1875

REINDORF, C. C. *The History of the Gold Coast and Asante*, Basel 1895; references are to the 1966 edition

SARBAH, M. *Fanti Customary Laws*, London 1904

—— *Fanti Law Report*, London 1906

—— *Fanti National Constitution*, London 1906

SHOEMAKER, J. P. *Lastste Bladzijde onzer Nederlandsch West-Afrikaansche Historie*, Hertogenbosch 1900

STANLEY, H. M. *Coomassie and Magdala*, London 1875

Later works

1 BOOKS

ACQUAH, G. A. *The Fante of Ghana*, London 1919

AJAYI, J. F. A. and ESPIE, I. (ed.) *A Thousand Years of West African History*, London 1966

APTER, D. E. *Ghana in Transition*, Princeton 1955

BALMER, W. J. *A History of the Akan Peoples*, London 1925

BAUER, P. T. *West African Trade*, Cambridge 1954

BOAHEN, A. A. *Juaben and Kumasi Relations in the Nineteenth Century*, I.A.S., Legon 1965

—— 'Asante, Fante and the British, 1800–1880' in Ajayi and Espie (ed.) *A Thousand Years of West African History*, London 1966

BROWN, C. N. *An Active History of Ghana*, London 1964, 2 Vols

BROWN, E. J. P. *Gold Coast and Ashanti Reader*, London 1929

CASELY-HAYFORD, J. E. *The Truth about the West African Land Question*, London 1913

CLARIDGE, W. W. *A History of the Gold Coast and Ashanti*, London 1915, 2 Vols; references are to the 1964 edition

COOMBS, D. *The Gold Coast, Britain and the Netherlands*, Oxford 1963

CROOKS, J. J. *Records relating to the Gold Coast settlement from 1750–1874*, Dublin 1923

DEBRUNNER, H. *A Church Between Colonial Powers*, London 1961

FIELD, M. J. *Akim-Kotoku*, London 1948

—— *Religion and Medicine of the Ga People*, London 1952

FULLER, F. C. *A Vanished Dynasty: Ashanti*, London 1921

HAILEY, LORD *Native Administration in African Territories*, London 1951

—— *An African Survey*, Oxford 1938

Hani and Nsawkaw Tradition, I.A.S., Legon 1966

HARGREAVES, J. D. *Prelude to the Partition of West Africa*, London 1963

HUTCHISON, C. P. *The Pen Pictures of Modern Africans and African Celebrities*, London 1928

JOHNSON, M. *Ashanti East of the Volta*, Legon 1965

KIMBLE, D. *A Political History of Ghana 1850–1928*, Oxford 1963

MCINTYRE, W. D. *The Imperial Frontier in the Tropics, 1865–75*, London 1967

MCPHEE, A. *The Economic Revolution in British West Africa*, London 1926

MANOUKIAN, M. *The Ewe-Speaking People of Togoland and the Gold Coast*, London 1952

MARTIN, E. C. *The British West African Settlements 1750–1821*, London 1927

METCALFE, G. E. *Great Britain and Ghana, Documents of Ghana History 1807–1957*, London 1964

MEYEROWITZ, E. L. R. *The Akan of Ghana*, London 1958

—— *The Sacred State of the Akan*, London 1951

MYATT, F. *The Golden Stool*, London 1966

NANA ANNOR-ADJAYE *Nzima Land*, London 1931

RATTRAY, R. S. *Ashanti*, Oxford 1923

—— *Religion and Art in Ashanti*, Oxford 1927

—— *Ashanti Law and Constitution*, Oxford 1929

REDMAYNE, P. *The Gold Coast Yesterday and Today*, London 1938

ROBINSON, R. and GALLAGHER, J. *Africa and the Victorians*, London 1961

SAMPSON, M. J. *Gold Coast Men of Affairs*, London 1937

TORDOFF, W. *Ashanti under the Prempehs*, Oxford 1965

WARD, W. E. F. *A History of Ghana*, London 1959

WELMAN, C. W. *The Native States of the Gold Coast, Peki*, London 1925

WILKS, I. *Ashanti Government in the Nineteenth Century*, Legon 1964

—— *The Northern Factor in Ashanti History*, I.A.S., Legon 1961

WOLFSON, F. *Pageant of Ghana*, London 1958

WOLTENG, J. (ed.) *Bescherden Betr. de Buitenlandse Politik van Nederland 1848–1919*, Vol. I, Hertogenbosch 1919

2 UNPUBLISHED THESES

AMENUMEY, D. E. K. *The Ewe People and the coming of European Rule*, M.A. thesis, University of London, 1964

WOLFSON, F. *British relations with the Gold Coast, 1843–1880*, Ph.D. thesis, University of London, 1950

3 JOURNALS

Research Review, Vol. II, 2, Legon 1966

Transactions of the Historical Society of Ghana (T.H.S.G.): Vol. II, pt. 1 (1957); Vol. III, pt. 3 (1958); Vol. VII (1964); Vol. IV, pt. 3 (1965)

West African Review, Vol. XXXI, 387, February 1960

1965 Report

Oral sources

I have found it necessary to use oral sources for several reasons. First, oral traditions serve as a useful check on such written sources as Colonial Office records in the P.R.O. or the Adm. series in the Ghana National Archives. These and other written sources grew out of letters by British officials on the Coast, though not always at the scene of the event. In some cases, the authors of these letters did not have an insight into the customs or traditions of the people. Their reports on the activities of the people consequently were deficient at times. For instance, British official reports of meetings with Anlo authorities before the 1880s were inaccurate; for while they thought all the time that they were negotiating with the King of Anlo, they were in fact dealing with his messengers, who had no right to confirm the decisions that the British said they did. The Awamefia himself could only have been consulted privately by the British and not in a public palaver.

At other times British official reports were prejudiced and unbalanced. To justify their anxiety to deprive the people of their independence and impose imperial demands on them, British officials painted black pictures of African society. At times, too, the difference between oral tradition and written sources is due to the fact that the European agents and the inhabitants naturally viewed the events in the country from entirely personal angles. It is therefore necessary to consider both points of view in order to get as close to the truth as possible. For instance, one needs to know from the Asante themselves why they rose up against the British in 1900 rather than accepting the report of Lady Hodgson only. She spent only a few weeks in Kumasi and was, in her book, concerned to explain the English point of view about the war to an English public.

In some cases, too, we have gaps in our knowledge due to the lack of written sources. An example is the relation between Nkoranza, Banda, Mo, Bole, etc. We need oral sources to make good these deficiencies. The oral research project I carried out in Anlo, Asante, Brong Ahafo, etc. was therefore meant to provide material which was used in making good these deficiencies in the written sources.

To find suitable informants, I first drew up a list of questions, and later a list of towns where such information could be collected. The basis for the choice of towns was their historical significance. Thus I chose Anloga, traditional capital of Anlo, Wuti, the home of the Right Wing Division Chief of Anlo; Kumasi, Capital of Asante, Nkoranza, situated on the Kumasi–Kintampo trade route, and so on and so forth. Upon reaching the town, I collected oral tradition from the 'court historian' and then from other informants, who gave the non-official version. To find the latter, I indicated the necessary qualifications to my guide; they were: a ripe old age, actual experience, if possible, of the events he would describe, and membership of an anti-official organisation, i.e. opposed to the ruling stool.

The use of oral tradition assumes its validity as a reliable source of information. But oral tradition has its deficiencies. To obtain a fairly accurate picture of the past by this method, therefore, I have had to cross-check information from several sources, taking into account the background of each informant.

Before finally incorporating it in a work like this, the end product of oral tradition should again be checked against written sources if there are any, and this I have done as well. Below are some examples of how, when and where I collected oral information, together with other relevant information to show the validity for this work of the material collected.

Anlo

Informants:

Amega Adoo, Amega Dzefi, at Anloga, and elders at the Court of Chief Gatey at Wuti, August 1963.

Amega Adoo (77 years old), is an elder of the Akladza family of the Like Clan in Anloga. Anloga is the seat of Anlo Government and the home of the paramount Chief (King) of the Anlo subdivision. An elder of the Like Clan of Anloga is a useful source of information on the attitude of the Anlo Government to Europeans, to the states west of the Volta like the Gas, Akwapem, etc. This is because the Like Clan played a leading role, both in the Anlo wars and in the subsequent negotiations with the enemy.

Amega Dzefi (72 years old) is the Clan head of the 'Wiweme' at Anloga. His information is necessarily a check on that of Amega Adoo. This is because the 'Wiweme' Clan is very much a 'strangers' clan which played no important part in the Anlo Wars (1860s). They therefore look at major issues in Anlo from a different point of view. When Amega Dzefi informed me about the Anlo Wars, for instance, he did not think they were as important as Amega Adoo would like us believe. He rather emphasised the part the commoners played in the political development of the state.

Elders at the Court of Chief Gatey at Wuti. There were five elders present when I collected information here. Wuti was the home of Chief Tamakloe, the Right Wing Division Chief. These elders were therefore conversant with matters affecting the wings as distinct from the centre-division of the Anlo community. Their views on the politics of Anlo reveal their uncompromising stand against European interference. These sources reveal that it was delegates from Wuti who urged that the white man's mistake in thinking that he was dealing with the King, when in fact it was only his messengers, should not be pointed out to him. This gave Anlo an advantage over the British.

Summary of relevant oral tradition in Anlo

Amega Dzefi: The social and political development of Anlo. During the Anlo Wars with the states west of the Volta, the King and his closest supporters hailing from the Adzovia and Bate clans, supported by other clans like the Like, Gave, etc. began to wield great power in the subdivision. They, the Wiwemeawo, thought the wars should be stopped to allow the energies of the subdivision to be re-directed into peaceful pursuits. For this reason, they formed youth associations known as *Soheawo*, i.e. commoners, devoted to relieving suffering. Various youth associations rendered useful social services to their members. Even more important was the fact that the Soheawo became important pressure groups within Anlo community. They very often forced the hand of the King and his supporters on important issues.

Nkoranza

Informants:

Nana Kwame Baffo III, Nana Kodjo Baffo, Nana Ankamako and others, at Nkoranza, 20 and 21 December 1965

Nana Kwame Baffo III (54 years old) and Nana Kodjo Baffo (62 years old) are Nkoranzahene and elder at the Nkoranza Court respectively. Nana Kodjo Baffo was the real informant, and he gave his information in front of the Chief. The information collected here deals with trade, taxation, Asante–Nkoranza War, and relations between Nkoranza, Bole, Mo, Banda, etc. On questions of trade, for instance, Nkoranza, lying on the important northern trade route to Kintampo is probably the best source of information.

Nana Kodjo Baffo, introduced by the Chief as the Nkoranza 'court historian', is therefore the best possible source of relevant information on this topic, on which British official reports are far from true. It was the British who were anxious to close the trade route so as to obtain its control from Asante, and yet they reported that it was Nkoranza which closed this route. Nana Baffo rejects this view. Again the view expressed in British official records about Asante levying oppressive taxes on the provinces is denied by Baffo who explains that taxation in Nkoranza at least was only on special occasions. He also explains the causes of the Asante–Nkoranza War and the relations between such peoples as Nkoranza, Bole, Mo, Banda, etc. These explanations are vital to a proper understanding of the Brong Confederation and its relations with Asante, discussed in Chapter 7.

Nana Ankamako. There are two divisions in Nkoranza. The first is the one led by the Chief and his elders; and its members are regarded as the ruling class. The second is the 'subject' class and the original inhabitants of Nkoranza. They are led by Nana Ankamako (66 years old), High Priest of Ntoa at Seseman, Nkoranza. He and his followers naturally view Nkoranza affairs from a different angle, and I collected information from them as a check on the official version. The topics were, therefore, the same as those dealt with at the Nkoranzahene's palace.

On taxation, Nana Ankamako and his elders differed from the Nkoranzahene. They felt that Asante taxation was heavy. On the question of war between Nkoranza and Asante, they mentioned events which the Nkoranzahene might not like to, namely, that the cause was an Asante stool-bearer having an affair with the Nkoranzahene's wife. On the question of closing the trade route, they agreed with the official version that it was not the Nkoranzahene who closed it, but they pointed out that it was Asante which closed it temporarily to create artificial shortages in Kintampo so as to push up kola prices.

Summary of relevant oral tradition of Nkoranza

Nana Kwame Baffo III and Nana Kodjo Baffo

(i) Nkoranza Wars. After the Techiman War, Asante and Nkoranza swore at Tafo never to fight each other. But Kumasi traders passing through Nkoranza to and from the north reported to the Asantehene that the Nkoranzahene was becoming very powerful. It was felt in Asante that this rising power should be subdued. Although the Nkoranzahene proved his loyalty by fighting against Mampon on the side of Asante, a message from Kumasi requested him to swear an oath of allegiance to the Asantehene and 'eat fetish' with Kumasi. The Nkoranzahene refused, arguing that he was independent of Asante. This message caused an uproar in Kumasi, and at a general meeting, it was decided that war should be declared on Nkoranza. The old men, led by a deposed chief, warned that they must not break the Tafo agreement, but the young men, led by the Atuahene, insisted on war. So Nkoranza allied with Mampon and Atebubu in preparation for the war which Asante declared on them.

There were other causes of tension between Nkoranza and Asante. They originated during the reign of Mensah Bonsu. On one occasion, Asante traders in Kintampo were discourteous towards the Nkoranzahene's wife. It was during Mensah Bonsu's reign that the first official taxation was paid to Asante, and the Nkoranzas never approved of this.

(ii) Trade and taxation. Nkoranza did not close the trade route to Kintampo. On the only occasion when they did this, it was a temporary position. The only permanent event in which Nkoranza played a part was the collection of trade tolls at Agyema and Nkwanta, where both Asante and Nkoranza officers were stationed as toll-collectors. There was no regular taxation. The only reason the first tax of £96 was imposed on Nkoranza was that Nkoranza stopped Asante troops from proceeding to Gyaman.

(iii) Banda Oath. This oath was the result of the war between Nkoranza and Banda. Asante wanted to reduce the number of Nkoranza troops before launching its own attack on Nkoranza, so it encouraged Nkoranza to attack Banda. During the Nkoranza–Banda conflict, Asante suddenly appeared in the rear of the Nkoranzas and defeated them.

Nana Ankamako and others

(i) Nkoranza Wars. The reasons for the outbreak of hostilities between Asante and Nkoranza included the affair between the stool-bearer of Asante and the Nkoranzahene's wife, and the refusal of the Nkoranzahene to take the oath of allegiance to the Asantehene.

(ii) Boakye Oath. This oath arose out of a war in which the Nkoranzas fought the Bandas. During this war, Nkoranzas lost many men; among them were the chief, Efa and a wing chief called Asadampa. It is believed that these men were trapped behind a rock and that they were killed on a Wednesday. So Wednesday (Wukuada) became part of the oath.

(iii) Trade and taxation. There was an important market at Kintampo and Nkoranza never closed the trade route permanently. It was the Asantehene who closed the routes temporarily to create artificial shortages of kola in Salaga or Kintampo to force prices up. During this embargo, only the Asantehene's kola would be allowed to go to these markets. The Nkoranzas resented paying taxes to Asante as they thought they were too heavy. They also resented having to fight for Asante.

Kona

Informant:

Nana Kofi Mensah, Kona, 21 and 22 December 1965.

Nana Kofi Mensah (96 years old) was an Asante trader, who traded both to the north and to the south. The route he took southwards was the Kumasi–Cape Coast route and it passed through Adansi, Kuissa, Atobiase, etc. Nana Mensah was, therefore, someone with first-hand knowledge, of trading conditions in the Asante Empire. Moreover, he said he had been a playmate of Prempeh I. His outlook on important issues in Asante was, therefore, bound to be coloured by official attitude, which I considered to be a useful check on the provincial attitude of Nkoranza. So I collected information from him on taxation and trade, so as to check Nkoranza tradition against it. Nana Kofi Mensah also agreed that taxation in Asante was levied only after a war, and that there was no regular direct taxation. He also referred to trade tolls collected by the Asantehene's agents. This confirmation of the fact that there never was regular direct taxation in Asante is important, because it shows that the allegation made in written sources that one of the causes of the Asante civil war was unnecessarily heavy taxation cannot be defended.

Summary of relevant Kona tradition

(i) Tolls. Nana Mensah traded in rubber, going to Cape Coast and coming back to Asante with spirits. The traders went in a convoy and at Kwisa they had to pay tolls, calculated on the amount of goods a trader had. He normally paid about £32 on the rubber he carried. These taxes were collected by the Asantehene's agents. The only other tax was the 'apia too', which was paid after a war to defray the cost of the war. Apart from private traders, there were state traders who paid no tolls.

(ii) The 1900 rising. The reason the Asante rising was put down was that there was a shortage of firearms in Asante, so some of the people decided not to fight.

Kumasi

Informants:

Nana Domfekyere, at Kumasi, 17 September 1966; Nana Kwaku Owusu, at Kumasi, 18 September 1966

Nana Domfekyere (95 years old), claims to have been involved in the events of the Yaa Asantewa War. Most of his answers to my questions were, therefore, first-hand information, and for that reason were valuable. However, he did not fight in the war, as he belonged to the group of people who felt that it was pointless fighting the white man. I consider his views useful, therefore, as representing, the feelings of one of the two Asante divisions, which existed throughout the civil war.

Nana Domfekyere's evidence is useful in other ways. His information on the availability of firearms during the 1900 rising corroborates that of Nana Mensah at Kona. Secondly, it serves as a useful check on written sources. With regard to the causes of the rising, for instance, Nana Domfekyere puts the British attempt to seize the Golden Stool at the top of a list of grievances of the Asante, and in this he is largely in agreement with the written sources.

Nana Kwaku Owusu (100 years old) is the elder brother of the late Sanahene, Nana Kojo Nyantakye of Kumasi. He claims to have fought in the 1900 rising on the Asante side. He is, therefore, a useful informant, first, because of his close association with the court of the Sanahene (the stool in charge of immigration). Secondly, I consider him a reliable source because like Nana Domfekyere, he has first-hand information on the Asante rising. Furthermore, he belonged to the Asante side which fought against the British. His views are therefore useful as a check on information collected from Nana Domfekyere.

In this way, I was introduced to the views of both sides in the Asante rebellion, and this enabled me to reach a more balanced view of the rebellion than would have otherwise been possible. It was against this view, then, that I checked the written sources on the subject. Nana Kwaku Owusu agreed with Nana Domfekyere and the written sources that the British attempt to seize the Golden Stool played an important part in the origins of the rising, but he disagreed with the view that some states remained neutral because of the lack of firearms.

195

In coming to a decision on this point, I took into consideration the fact that Nana Owusu fought in the war, while Nana Domfekyere did not. Nana Owusu also informed me about Yaa Asantewa, the chiefs detained in the Kumasi fort and the reasons for the defeat of Asante. I found all this information useful as a check on written sources.

Summary of relevant Kumasi oral tradition

Nana Domfekyere

(i) Piakyere (Yaa Asantewa) War. Causes. Supporters of the British were molesting the supporters of 'Abendwa' – Golden Stool. The British wanted to capture the Golden Stool and the people rose up because the Golden Stool was very precious to them. The people united under Yaa Asantewa and fired on Armitage. Ejisuhene played a leading role in the war.

(ii) Why some states supported the British. The Asante did not like the establishment of schools in their country, because they felt that through schools British influence would be established. The state of Bekwai, however, supported the idea of establishing schools, and later the Adansi also supported it. Kotiko was the Adansihene. He had fought with the Bekwaihene, Gyamfi, and had been defeated. At first there was no bad feeling between Bekwai and Adansi. The trouble started when Adansi was defeated in the Bekwai–Adansi duel. The defeated Adansi king brought the British to Obuasi to mine for gold. The Asantehene did not like this because, traditionally, hoes should not be used by the white man in digging Asante soil, according to the orders of Okomfo Anokye. The Asantehene was against the British coming to Asante. The Bekwaihene wanted the British to come because he was hoping to gain from the gold mines. So it was the desire for wealth which caused the defection of Bekwai. The support of some states for the British was due to the breakdown of tribal cohesion. Nkwantahene led the British into Asante.

Before Prempeh was removed, trade was prosperous, but afterwards, trade declined because Asante traders were molested on the way to the coast. This led to shortage of guns and because of this, Juaben, Mampon and Agona refused to fight the British, saying they had no guns to fight with.

Nana Kwaku Owusu

The Asante rising of 1900. Yaa Asantewa came from Boankara in Ejisu; she was the sister of the chief of Ejisu, Kwesi Afrani. The cause of the war was that the Governor came and called a meeting of the chiefs – Mamponhene, Juabenhene and Kokofuhene – and told them that he had come for the Golden Stool. The Mamponhene said he was the king of the orphans, and that in the absence of the king, he was ruling. The Kokofuhene denied knowledge of the whereabouts of the Golden Stool; Juabenhene, too, did the same. The people were infuriated by the British request.

The Governor appointed Armitage as captain of the troops and sent troops to Wawase, hoping to get the Golden Stool, but they could not find it. So the Governor sent Armitage and his troops to Bare. Armitage called a meeting of the Bare people, and when they refused to go, he fired on them. The Barekesi (Bare) people retaliated. War ensued. Armitage and his troops could not withstand the Barekesi people and took to their heels. The Governor, his wife and some troops were in the fort in Kumasi.

196

Before the rising, the Governor had released Kokofuhene and Mamponhene, on the understanding that they would support the British. But when trouble started over the Golden Stool, the two Kings, Owusu Sekyere and Asibe, went over to the Asante side and the Governor realised that he had been tricked. He therefore arrested and kept Asibe in the fort. Later the Gyasehene, Opoku Mensah, was also arrested.

At Dente (Dentesu) the Ejisus and others gathered and resolved that they would never surrender the Golden Stool. Boadu was made captain of the group and they used Yaa Asantewa's name in campaigning for more troops for the war. The great chiefs, such as the Juabenhene and the Mamponhene, were not present at this meeting because some of them were detained in the fort. That was why the young men decided to use Yaa Asantewa's name.

Later, some of the great chiefs, because they did not take part in the Dentesu decision, refused to fight and even supported the British. When the Governor wanted to leave Kumasi for the coast, one Kwakye Nketia, an Asante, also in the fort, led him to Pekwai, Manso and Nkwanta through certain villages. They passed first through Abrodea, then through Hiankose and Mosease to Nkwanta, Nketia's village. Asibe was taken to the coast. Agonahene supported the British as did Osei Mampon who later became Mamponhene.

Before the rising trade was prosperous and there was no shortage of guns, but the Asante were defeated by the British because they realised that they could no longer withstand the British.

OTHER SOURCES OF ORAL TRADITION

Elmina tradition
Informant:
S. Vroom (70 years old) July 1963 at Elmina

Oguaa tradition
Informants:
Dr J. W. C. de Graft Johnson (71 years old) February 1964 at Cape Coast and Mr Kwesi Johnson (76 years old) March 1964 at Cape Coast

Krobo tradition
Informant:
Nene Azu Mate Kole, Konor of Manya Krobo (52 years old) May 1964 at Odumase, Krobo

Asante tradition
Informant:
Mr K. C. Dente (55 years old) 3 January 1967, Legon

Index

In compiling this index, consistency in indexing African names, especially those of the earlier part of the period, has been regarded as of less importance than ease of reference. An attempt has been made to ensure that as far as possible an individual is to be found under the name, or part of name, by which he would be generally known: but the reader should also bear in mind that alternative spellings of names exist in many cases.